Also by Reverend Al Sharpton

Rise Up: Confronting a Country at the Crossroads

The Rejected Stone: Al Sharpton and the Path to American Leadership

Al on America

Go and Tell Pharaoh

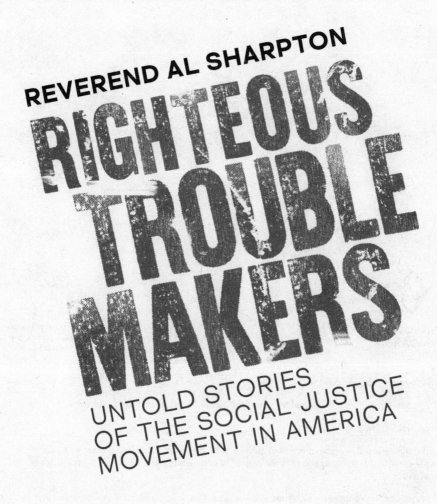

REVEREND AL SHARPTON

RIGHTEOUS TROUBLE MAKERS

UNTOLD STORIES
OF THE SOCIAL JUSTICE
MOVEMENT IN AMERICA

HANOVER
SQUARE
PRESS

HANOVER
SQUARE
PRESS™

Recycling programs
for this product may
not exist in your area.

ISBN-13: 978-1-335-63991-2

Righteous Troublemakers: Untold Stories of the Social Justice Movement in America

This edition published by arrangement with Harlequin Books S.A.

Hanover Square Press
22 Adelaide St. West, 41st Floor
Toronto, Ontario M5H 4E3, Canada
HanoverSqPress.com
BookClubbish.com

Printed in U.S.A.

I dedicate this book to the lesser-known soldiers for justice, many of whom have worked with me and National Action Network (NAN) over the past thirty years despite not having been formal staff members. Whether they were marching for Rodney King in 1991 (the year NAN was founded) or marching for George Floyd today, these individuals have been steadfast in their support. This list is by no means complete but represents those individuals who have helped advance the social justice movement over the last quarter of a century in the areas of voting rights, police reform, women's rights, LGBTQIA rights, and more.
Thank you for your work.

Beverly Alston

Acutha Bakar

Leonard Bentley

James Bligen

Ben Brown

Anthony Charles

Gene Collins

Fitzgerald Cox

Josh Cureton

Cynthia Davis

Christine Dudley

Nadirah El-Amin

Neal Faison

Sheldon Fisby

Marcia Fitzgerald

Theresa Freeman

Dottie Golson

Ben Gooding

Russell Graddy

Bill Griffin

Lawrence Harvey

Reverend Carolyn Haynes

Jamillah Hedgemond

Pat Henry

Mother Sarah Hunt

Henry Johnson

Nathaniel "Brother Monk" Jones

Reverend Magora Kennedy

Margaret Lamb

Maxine Lewis

JD Livingstone

Stan Mallory

Charles Matthews

Marcia McCoy

Helen McMillan

Lois Menyweather

Bishop Anthony Monk

Norman Nash

Katherine Nichson

George and Eloise Obagane

Louis Papa

Alishe Pascal

Paula Peebles

Anthony Phillips

Heru Plunkett

Tena Pondexter

Dr. Noretta Ray

Norman "Grandad" Reid

Brenda Ricketts

Sharon Smith

James Sneed

Rick Taylor

Marie Thompson

Ossie Thompson

Ms. Ivy Walton

Donald "Hasan" Washington

Dr. Ramona Whaley

Denise Wray

Dr. Camille Yarborough

CONTENTS

INTRODUCTION

THE MARCH AIN'T OVER

"What will be our legacy? Will future generations remember you for your complacency or your inaction? Or will they remember you for your empathy, your leadership, your passion for weeding out the injustice and evil in our world?"

—BRIDGETT FLOYD, George Floyd's sister

In August of 2020, National Action Network (NAN), with the support of the National Association for the Advancement of Colored People (NAACP), the National Urban League (NUL), and the Hispanic Federation along with several clergy groups, unions, and civil rights groups organized the Get Your Knee Off Our Necks Commitment March in Washington, DC. I announced the march while giving the final eulogy for George Floyd, who was murdered by former police officer Derek Chauvin in Minneapolis, Minnesota, on May 25, 2020, after Chauvin knelt on George's neck for nine minutes and twenty-nine seconds. I hadn't planned on organizing a nationwide march, but the moment and the people demanded it.

To say that George's murder launched an uprising would be

an understatement: between 15 million to 26 million people participated in demonstrations in America. The protests were at their peak on June 6, 2020, when half a million people raised their voices in nearly 550 places across the United States. According to scholars and crowd-counting experts, that kind of turnout made the protests the largest movement in the country's history. George's death was an inflection point. The Black Lives Matter movement, which had already taken root in several cities and communities around the country, forced Americans from coast to coast to say, "Enough is enough" to police brutality.

The march was planned for August 28, fifty-seven years to the day when, in 1963, Dr. Martin Luther King Jr. famously delivered his "I Have a Dream" speech. As I made my way to the podium on that hot summer day, an older Black man caught my eye. He wore an original button from the original 1963 march on the lapel of his lightweight jacket.

"Rev," he shouted, waving me over. I approached him. We talked a bit and he told me that he'd attended Dr. King's march and came to stand in solidarity with the new generation of changemakers. "The march ain't over," he said.

"No justice, no peace," I said.

He nodded, turned, and disappeared into an audience two hundred thousand strong. I didn't catch his name, but this man was on my mind as I took my place at the podium, literally standing on the same marble step where King had called out the infirmities that plagued Black Americans fifty-seven years ago, addressing the "unspeakable horrors of police brutality," voter suppression, and Jim Crow, among other indignities. It didn't go unnoticed by me nor others that only a few hours earlier and just one mile away, President Donald Trump had stood on the South Lawn of the White House to condemn us. In his mind, we were agitators bent on destroying "the American way of life." To my way of thinking, we didn't come to start trouble. I said as much in my speech, my voice echoing on the loudspeakers.

"We came to stop trouble," I said. "You act like it's no trouble to shoot us in the back. You act like it's no trouble to put a chokehold on us while we scream 'I can't breathe' eleven times. Mr. Trump, look right down the block from the White House. We've come to Washington by the thousands." The sound of the cheering crowd was like that of a roaring ocean, powerful. If we were troublemakers, then we were of the righteous sort, fighting the good fight and demanding a new national reckoning with hate, bigotry, systemic racism, and police brutality.

Despite our nonviolent show of force, I couldn't rid myself of the feeling that we were on shaky ground: a worrying presidential election loomed only three months away, the pandemic had upended life as we knew it, hate crimes were up, and Americans were coming to terms with the fact that our policing system was fundamentally flawed. In my previous book *Rise Up*, I wrote that our country was at a crossroads. Standing at the base of the Lincoln Memorial, it felt as if America was cleaved in two, Republicans and Democrats divided, the very soul of the country struggling to survive. When I raised my face and looked out among the thousands of masked attendees, something inside me shifted, however, and my frustration dissipated. Maybe it was the summer sun that warmed my face, making a promise of brighter days. Maybe it was seeing Martin Luther King III standing shoulder to shoulder with his twelve-year-old daughter, Dr. King's sole grandchild, their family legacy intact and stronger than ever. Then it dawned on me: I saw every race, gender, and background of people staring back at me from the crowd. It was easily the most diverse march I'd been to, and listen, I've been doing this work for a while.

There was a time, not so long ago, when I didn't see any white allies at our marches, especially not at those dealing with with police brutality. No longer. At Dr. King's original march, women and members of the LGBTQIA community were sidelined. Bayard Rustin, who many considered to be the lead architect of the original 1963 march, hid his homosexuality for fear that it would negatively impact the movement. Contrast that with David John, the executive director of the National Black Justice Coalition, a civil rights organization dedicated to Black LGBTQIA/SGL people, who spoke at the 2020 march, saying, "I stand here in the spirit of our brother Bayard Rustin.... If you care about Black people like I do, if you love Black people like I do, you've got to love and care about all of us." In the name of social justice, today's movement includes all kinds of people and addresses all kinds of inequities. It's intersectionality at its best. Today, people understand that my struggle is yours and vice versa. Our hardships and victories are entwined. It's one of the reasons I say that the fight today is for social justice and not any one silo—civil rights, LGBTQIA rights, women's rights, and so on. Today, it's all one fight.

As someone tutored in the King tradition, I was brought up to keep his dream alive. So, it was overwhelming to stand at the base of the Lincoln Memorial and witness the reality of his dream. I wondered if Dr. King had felt as I did while looking at the tapestry of humankind spread across the National Mall. I was inspired, hopeful, and renewed in both my spirit and my sense of determination. *This* is America the beautiful. I adjusted the microphone and said, "We come today, Black and white and all races and religions and sexual orientations to say that this dream—Dr. King's dream—is still alive. You may have killed the dreamer, but you can't kill the dream because truth crushed to earth shall rise again." Together, we would rise up to demand what Dr. King called the "riches of freedom and the security of justice" for all. Together, we would right the wrongs of our great country, and forge a new path forward. Our collective action is the realization of Dr. King's dream.

A few days later, I found myself thinking about the older man who'd greeted me at the march. He knew my name, but I didn't know his. How many other marches had this man participated in during his life? How many homemade protest signs had he made, how many buttons had he collected? Had he, like me, raised his voice in call-and-response chants until his throat was sore? If he'd attended the original march on DC, he'd been protesting for a long time and was probably a little older than myself. Here we were, he and I, the last of a generation who'd watched this country falter time and time again on issues of race and was stumbling still. Yet it was undeniable that in our lifetimes progress *had* happened. Positive change was still in the process of unfolding.

I found myself thinking of history's unknown and unsung heroes, the nameless and the forgotten, the courageous change-makers we've either overlooked or cast aside, preferring to shine a light on the actors who take the main stage. I thought of all the other people who had participated in the march, and I was humbled, amazed, and grateful to be in *their* presence. It's these men and women who carry the true baton of the social justice movement, handing it off to the next generation of righteous troublemakers who pick up where they left off. Their contributions are real and all too often they're ignored. Without them, I'm just a guy in a suit with a microphone. But listen, I've been around long enough to have also been that guy on the ground linked arm in arm with those who may never make a rousing speech but who, instead, make their contributions known and felt in other ways: canvassing their neighborhoods to support a local politician, setting up group transportation to and from the voting booths, designing protest signs, or simply helping to keep morale high. These tireless individuals are the everyday heroes who do the grinding and unglamorous work of activism, who open the doors for the rest of us. They know that justice doesn't rest on one person but is, instead, carried forward by us all. Sea change requires an ocean.

This book grew out of my appreciation and awareness of some of the lesser-known rabble-rousers who came before me, those everyday activists who inspired change while waiting in the wings, people like Amelia Boynton Robinson—the so-called matriarch of the voting movement who inspired the later activism of Stacey Abrams and LaTosha Brown—and Pauli Murray, whom Eleanor Roosevelt respectfully nicknamed "the Firebrand," and whose early work informed the legal arguments of both Thurgood Marshall and Ruth Bader Ginsburg. It also shines a light on individuals who channeled personal tragedy into public activism: Mamie Till-Mobley, mother to Emmett Till, whose brutal murder sparked the civil rights movement; Gwen Carr, mother to Eric Garner, whose death by police chokehold foretold George Floyd's murder only six years later; and Philonise Floyd, George's brother, who, since his brother's death, I've watched come into his own as an activist, public speaker, and advocate for social change. The public may not have known about these American tragedies had it not been for the courage of Moses Wright, Ramsey Orta, and Darnella Frazier, witnesses to the respective crimes.

As I often say in church: we know the glory, but we don't know the story. Many of the changemakers in this book paid a price that few among us would pay, risking their own personal safety or happiness for the advancement of the greater good. Most of us know the story of Ruby Bridges, the young girl who desegregated the all-white William Frantz Elementary School in Louisiana in 1960. Lesser known, however, is how the Bridges family struggled to deal with the constant death threats nor how Ruby's father, Abon, lost his job over sending his daughter to school. Few know the inspiring story of Barbara Henry, Ruby's teacher, nor the kindness shown to the young student by child psychologist Dr. Robert Coles. Yet it's because of their combined actions—and the actions of countless others—that we enjoy the progress of the social justice movement. The world is full of brave people performing courageous acts of justice all the time, even when no one is watching. This book aims to rectify the record and celebrate the legacies of those who, for whatever reason, never got their moment in the sun.

Whole biographies can be written—and there have been some already—on any one of the individuals profiled herein, some of whom are well-known. That isn't the goal of this book. Instead, by shining a light on key moments and experiences within these individuals' lives or by seeing them in a new light, I hope that readers may find inspiration themselves to rise up, join a movement, and help advance the cause of social justice. If these everyday heroes managed to answer the call of activism, you can, too. That said, *Righteous Troublemakers* is also about the movement we're living through right now.

When George Floyd was murdered, his family had no way of knowing that his death would spark the largest demonstrations of public support in the history of the social justice movement. No one wakes up and says, "Today's the day I become a victim of police brutality or white supremacy." But when Derek Chauvin put his knee on George's neck, George became, like Emmett Till before him, a martyr, a symbol for the movement. God lifted up these sacrificial lambs so we could do His bidding in their names and in their honor. Here, I detail some of the behind-the-scenes work that went into building a movement that forced today's national reckoning on race, revealing both the personal—those emotional moments that impacted me most—and the professional, as reflected in the fight to secure the passage of the George Floyd Justice in Policing Act.

My work rests on the shoulders of the changemakers who came before me, many of whom I've included in this book. Most had no idea that their actions would help effect change and yet, at the behest of their better angels, they went ahead and did the work anyway. At different points in my life, they have inspired, sparked, and challenged my own sense of activism. It behooves me to turn a lens toward their accomplishments and acknowledge their contributions, big and small. Without a Fred

Gray, there wouldn't have been a Thurgood Marshall. Without a Thurgood Marshall, there wouldn't have been a Ben Crump. If Theodore Roosevelt Mason (T. R. M.) Howard and Moses Wright hadn't come forward on behalf of Emmett Till, would Darnella Frazier have gotten on the stand for George Floyd? Would she have pushed the recording button on her phone? Without them, I wouldn't have been able to rise up in the manner that I have. Without them, there's a chance that, in 2021, a jury in Minnesota would have let Derek Chauvin off the hook.

It's my hope that, in reading this book, you'll glean some new tactics, tools, and strategies that you can employ in your own journey toward becoming a righteous troublemaker. Everyone— even you, no matter who or where you are—can do something to make the world a better place, one that grants equality and justice for all. We need more righteous troublemakers in the fight for justice. By the time you finish reading, you should have no other choice but to become an agent of change because the march ain't over, and neither is the dream.

1

THE CORNERSTONES OF
A MOVEMENT

"Here's the truth about racial injustice. It is not just a Black America problem or a people of color problem. It's a problem for every American. It is keeping us from fulfilling the promise of liberty and justice for all, and it is holding our nation back from realizing our full potential."

—VICE PRESIDENT KAMALA HARRIS

By now, the world knows the story of George Floyd's murder and the subsequent trial and sentencing of former police officer Derek Chauvin: on May 25, 2020, in Minneapolis, Minnesota, George was murdered by Chauvin, one of four police officers who arrived on the scene after receiving a call from a local store clerk who suspected George may have paid for cigarettes using a counterfeit twenty-dollar bill. During the arrest, Chauvin knelt on George's neck for over nine minutes while George called out for his mama, who had recently passed, before dying himself. Chauvin's crime was videotaped by Darnella Frazier, a seventeen-year-old bystander, who released the videotaped footage the night of George's death.

Frazier's video drove much of the public's understanding about what transpired in front of the Cup Foods convenience store on that fateful day at the corner of Chicago Avenue and Thirty-Eighth Street in Minneapolis. Had her video footage not surfaced, the initial news release, which was posted on the police department's website and titled "Man Dies After Medical Incident During Police Interaction," may have been both the first and the last word on the subject. Frazier's video laid that narrative to rest and exposed the act for what it was: police brutality. While there have been many key players in the drama of George's murder—everyone from the Floyd family and attorney Ben Crump to Attorney General of Minnesota Keith Ellison and President Biden—Frazier's contribution is singular. Her act of bearing witness—of not looking away at the brutality unfolding before her very eyes—is a profile in real, on-the-ground courage, a tradition carried by too many Black brothers and sisters. Frazier could have kept walking when she saw a Black man lying on the pavement surrounded by police officers. But she didn't. She stopped, raised her phone, and hit Record. Little did she know then that she was filming history.

A Witness to History:
Darnella Frazier

At the time of George Floyd's death, Darnella Frazier was a high school junior at Roosevelt High School in Minneapolis. According to her mother, she was "just a normal teenager with a boyfriend and a job at the mall." That all changed on Memorial Day, May 25, 2020, a day that started off ordinary but ended as anything but.

That evening, Frazier and her nine-year-old cousin went to the store to buy some snacks. As they approached the Cup Foods grocery, they saw police restraining a Black man on the pavement. She'd later reflect on that moment in a Facebook post, writing, "I didn't know this man from a can of paint, but I knew his life mattered. I knew that he was in pain. I knew that he was another Black man in danger with no power." Frazier told her cousin to go inside the store while she stayed curbside along with about seven other bystanders and recorded the incident on her cell phone. Only twenty seconds after she started filming, George said, "I can't breathe." All told, Frazier's video ran over ten minutes long, and captured George's distress and calls for help. As far as photojournalism goes, Frazier's video was the real deal. She posted the video to Facebook at 1:46 a.m. along with the caption: "They killed him right in front of cup foods over south on 38th and Chicago!! No type of sympathy. </3 </3 #POLICEBRUTALITY."

When the Minneapolis Police Department issued their official statement of the incident, Frazier went back at it, writing in another online post: "Medical incident??? Watch outtt they killed him and the proof is clearlyyyy there!!" She returned to the scene of the crime the next day and, standing among a group of protesters already assembled there, broke down in tears, confessing, "It's so traumatizing." She couldn't have known it then, but her personal trauma was just beginning. For several weeks following the murder, Frazier couldn't sleep. When she wasn't fighting off insomnia or night terrors, she was battling a deep sense of guilt and self-blame, staying up most nights to privately apologize to George for, in her words, "not doing more." Trying to avoid unwanted publicity, Frazier and her family moved from hotel to hotel. Police cars made her anxious. Reporters did, too. Her trust in people began to erode. "A lot of people are evil with bad intentions," she wrote.

As the movement for justice for George Floyd gained momentum worldwide, Frazier was publicly hailed as a hero, with her attorney, Seth Cobin, calling her a modern-day Rosa Parks: Frazier, like Parks, had taken a stand to do the right thing at great personal cost to herself and her family. Despite the widespread accolades and attention, Frazier remained a reluctant hero. "I was just in the right place at the right time," she insisted. And yet, it took fortitude to do what she did. She'd later say the experience fundamentally changed her. "It changed how I viewed life," she wrote. "It made me realize how dangerous it is to be Black in America. We shouldn't have to walk on eggshells around police officers, the same people that are supposed to protect and serve. We are looked at as thugs, animals, and criminals, all because of the color of our skin."

A year later, Frazier took the stand as a witness for the prosecution in the trial against Derek Chauvin. She'd just turned eighteen and was one of four witnesses Judge Peter A. Cahill allowed to testify off-camera since they were minors at the time of the incident, a fact that Minnesota Attorney General Keith Ellison jumped on, arguing for a harsher sentence for Chauvin, if convicted, because George was murdered in front of children. During cross-examination, Frazier was asked how what happened to George Floyd had affected her life. Frazier inhaled deeply before replying, "When I look at George Floyd, I look at my dad. I look at my brother. I look at my cousins, my uncles, because they are all Black.... I look at how that could have been one of them." As it happened, Frazier's fears weren't unfounded. In July of 2021, a cop from the same Minneapolis Police Department whose officer killed George was following a suspect in a high-speed car chase. The cop's squad car collided with two other vehicles, killing one of the drivers. That driver was Frazier's uncle Leneal Frazier. The incident, while seemingly accidental, nonetheless highlighted the intimate connections among Black victims. Trauma has long arms. In Black, brown, and other marginalized communities, it reaches out and touches everyone, reverberating generation to generation, until it feels like everyone you know knows someone who's either been harassed or killed by the police, is incarcerated, or getting brutalized in prison. And if you've been lucky enough not to have experienced police brutality firsthand, you most likely have witnessed it.

On the first anniversary of George's murder, Frazier acknowledged her part in a history-making moment, writing online: "Even though this was a traumatic life-changing experience for me, I'm proud of myself. If it weren't for my video, the world wouldn't have known the truth. I own that. My video didn't save George Floyd, but it put his murderer away and off the streets." Because Frazier didn't look away, we were able to see the unvarnished truth of what it means to be Black in America and envision a world in which police are held accountable for their actions.

THREE NUMBERS AND THREE WORDS

I remember when I watched Frazier's video for the first time: I felt waves of anger, sadness, and frustration. Like the footage itself, my emotions ran on an endless loop. Once seen, I couldn't unsee it. I was reminded of Mamie Till-Mobley when she said, "Let the world see what I've seen," and allowed *Jet* magazine to publish photographs of the brutalized body of her son Emmett

Till. There's power in seeing; the private pain of losing a loved one becomes everyone's loss and the failure of humankind, of common, basic decency, becomes a shared burden, something for us all to rectify.

At the trial for Chauvin, prosecutor Jerry W. Blackwell said "nine-two-nine" were the three most important numbers in the case, nine minutes and twenty-nine seconds being the length of time Chauvin kept his knee on George's neck. For me, it wasn't three numbers but three words: "I can't breathe," a sentence George repeated more than twenty times. It was so painfully reminiscent of Eric Garner, who had said the exact same thing only six years prior while another white police officer, Officer Daniel Pantaleo, had knelt on *his* neck, that I almost couldn't believe it. Eric's dying words had been the same as George's. How many other Black men had called out those same words, their bodies pressed to the ground? I knew that if I went to Minneapolis, Gwen Carr, Eric Garner's mother, would have to come with me. Gwen must have been thinking the same thing because she answered my call midring. We jumped right into it.

"You see this?" I asked. Every news show and newspaper was carrying the story.

"Yes," she said. Her voice sounded firm, strong.

"When do you want to go?"

"Reverend, my bags are already packed."

I'd already had conversations with attorney Ben Crump, who'd asked if I would visit the site of George's death to help set a tone of nonviolent resistance because, at that point, tensions were already high. We were concerned that the activism for justice would get appropriated and turn into an excuse for out-of-control looting, some of which did happen. People were hurt and angry. They wanted answers. A lot of young bucks told me I didn't understand their rage, that they were tired of brothers being shot in broad daylight by cops or being put in chokeholds. Are you kidding me? I have just as much rage if not more. The only defense cops like Chauvin have is to say, "See, Blacks are so out of control and violent, I had no choice but to hold him down." I understood the hurt in the community, but any show of chaos or violence would only be held against the family and could negate their quest for justice. We didn't want anything to feed into the racist narrative that our actions were criminal. It was essential that we establish a united, peaceful front. The LA riots following the brutal attack on Rodney King—another crime caught on film by a bystander—were never far from anyone's thoughts; no one wanted a repeat. (It should be noted that George Holliday, the bystander who filmed the attack on King, only released his footage to news station KTLA when the police didn't want to review it.) We also wanted to link Eric Garner's death to George's murder: had the officers in Eric's case been prosecuted and federal legislation passed, George's murder wouldn't have happened or, if it had, action would have been swift and immediate.

Robert Smith, a philanthropic businessman, graciously donated the use of his private plane. Without it, I'm not sure how we would have traveled from New York in the middle of the pandemic. At the time, we didn't know that half of George's family was based in Houston, where he was born. We just knew we had to get to Minneapolis and hit the ground running. When we arrived, we met with members of the community, including South Side Pastor Carmen Means of Christ Presbyterian Church, who ran a community center on the same block as the Cup Foods store, and Tylik McMillan, the youth director for NAN. Together, we were able to put some of the pieces together, including the whereabouts of the rest of the Floyd family. Before I held a vigil at the site, Pastor Means spoke intimately about how the area was a community: store clerks and residents knew one another, and everyone was all too aware of the constant police presence. I'd heard something similar from Eric Garner's friends and neighbors when they talked about their community on Bay Street in Staten Island. Gwen described that neighborhood in her book *This Stops Today*, writing, "You had young men getting their hustle on, trying to make a few dollars; there were shop owners, clerks, even homeless folk down on their luck who hung out in the park…. Everyone looked out for each other…. But there was a dark side…. It was a regular occurrence for the police to show up and give folks a hard time." Every city in America has a neighborhood or a section of town like Bay Street in Staten Island or Brooklyn Center in Minneapolis, which, to my mind, makes it all the more crushing that the store clerk who first suspected George's money was counterfeit only mentioned it to his boss because he, like everyone else in that neighborhood, was just getting by. He didn't want George to be murdered nor could he have anticipated what was going to happen; he just didn't want to risk losing his job or getting in trouble himself.

Aided by the quick on-the-ground efforts of several local clergy, city leaders, and activists, we assembled a sizable crowd for a prayer gathering. "We come to stand with this family and stand with this community," I said, "because this is a struggle that we have all over this country. And let's not tell half the story. The reason why you see the anger in Minneapolis is because this is not the first time, and this is not the first time you ignored the rights of people." Following the vigil, we went to the state capital to voice our support. It wasn't until Gwen and I were leaving Minneapolis, literally preparing to board the plane, that I received another call from Ben Crump. This time, the Floyd family was also on the line.

In the early days of getting to know the Floyd family, I often confused Floyd's cousins with his brothers or sisters. Everyone who comes within the Floyd orbit is treated like a member of the family; there's little distinction between cousins and half siblings or brothers and uncles. If you're a Floyd, you're a Floyd. So, despite them not being near one another geographically— some are in North Carolina where the family originated, others are in Texas—everyone is still close. They're convivial and welcoming and not too dissimilar from other Southern Black families I know, including my own. On that first call, the family asked if I would do George's eulogy. In my lifetime, I've done countless eulogies for too many young Black men. The request never gets easier for me to accept. I keep hoping that the next one will be the last. I'll probably go to my grave with that wish. Because the family was scattered around the country and because we were still in a pandemic, making travel difficult, I ended up doing two of the three services, with filmmaker Tyler Perry arranging for the family's transport.

The night before the first service in Minneapolis, I met George's brothers Philonise and Rodney and his nephew Brandon in person, along with some of the other Floyd family members at a Minneapolis hotel. What I remember most from our meeting was Philonise's curiosity and his sense of engagement. It was as if he showed up for himself the moment he showed up for us. He kept asking questions and sought out advice on everything from the order of events at the memorial service to how to speak in public to how to channel the public's outcry of support into something more meaningful. He was both processing his own emotions, the grief, anger, and sadness of having lost his big brother, whom he called Perry, while mentally preparing himself for the public storm he knew lay in wait.

I don't say this lightly: a spark was lit inside him. From the start, he understood that a burden had been thrust upon the family, one that would require a heavy lift from everyone. He also recognized that the situation was bigger than everyone combined. George's murder was a catalyst, an inflection point, and the spark it lit inside Philonise had also resonated with thousands of Americans across the country who showed their support in a variety of ways. My job was to build a firewall of support around the family, to guide and protect them, and to counsel on matters big and small whenever necessary. The media can be vicious, whether intentional or not. I have thick skin; I'd rather myself, Ben Crump, or another seasoned associate take on their possible attacks than the grieving Floyd family. I can take a few hits. You don't get to push a family when they're already down. I told the Floyds that I would do my best to shield them from any additional outside harm and would use my voice to help amplify and champion their calls for justice. Justice for George meant justice for us all or as Ben said, "My hope is that this case sets a precedent that we will have when we say, 'For liberty and justice for all,' that will mean everybody in America. Black Americans. Native Americans. Hispanic Americans. Asian Americans. It will mean all of us."

During our first meeting, however, not all our talk was about strategy and the fight for justice. We weren't hunkered down and praying all the time. We were simply getting to know one another. Philonise had a way of breaking the tension. After we'd talked about George for a while, the family reminiscing about his life, Philonise turned to me. His face was dead-serious. I thought he was gonna say something profound.

"Rev," he said.

"Yeah?"

"Where do we get some real soul food around here?"

The room cracked up in laughter.

"Well, it's challenging in Minneapolis," I admitted.

Luckily, Barack Obama came to the rescue. The former president called to offer the family his and Michelle's condolences. When Obama heard my voice on the speakerphone, he said, "I knew Al would be there. He's always where he needs to be." I'd last spoken to the former president months previous. My mind reeled by how much the country had changed since his steady tenure. Obama spoke to the Floyd family that night not as the forty-fourth president of the United States but as a Black father himself, someone who genuinely cared for the well-being of another family in pain. It reminded me of when he spoke about the Trayvon Martin ruling at a 2013 press conference, saying, "When Trayvon Martin was first shot I said that this could have been my son. Another way of saying that is Trayvon Martin could have been me thirty-five years ago. And when you think about why, in the African American community at least, there's a lot of pain around what happened here. I think it's important to recognize that the African American community is looking at this issue through a set of experiences and a history that doesn't go away." *Here we are again*, I thought while I listened to Obama speak to the Floyd family.

"If there's anything I can do for you, let me know," he said.

Philonise spoke up. "Well," he ventured, "can you send us some good food?"

Obama gamely replied, "Yeah, of course! What do you want?" I marveled at the scene as a roomful of people gave the former president food orders for a proper Southern meal. To his credit, Obama hooked us up and we ate well that night.

The Brother-Turned-Activist:
Philonise Floyd

Fast-forward to the final funeral service for George Floyd at the Fountain of Praise church in southwest Houston. Everyone from actor Jamie Foxx to Houston Mayor Sylvester Turner and Congresswoman Sheila Jackson Lee were in attendance, along with regular folk, those who knew and loved George or were there to support the immediate family members. Due to social-distancing protocols, we staggered the seating, leaving space between chairs. It was still a heavy turnout, and that was inside the church. Outside, spectators were lined up for miles. The public viewing lasted longer than six hours. It looked like all of Houston had showed up to pay homage to their city's fallen son. Some mourners wore crimson and gold—the school colors of the Third Ward's Jack Yates High School, where George was a member of the class of 1993. With a golden casket nestled inside a glass-sided carriage drawn by a pair of white horses, you'd have thought a dignitary had died.

When it came time for Philonise to speak inside the church, he took to the podium cautiously. It isn't every day that you're called upon to speak to an audience of entertainers and politicians, people who speak in public and to the media as part of their daily jobs. On that day, though, none of those distinctions mattered. Everyone who showed up at George Floyd's funeral was there because, as American citizens, they were outraged, saddened, and humbled by this man's murder. Philonise spoke about the love he had for his older brother, a man who was as generous as he was loving, and who, like their mother before him, welcomed everyone into their family's embrace. On a day that would have broken most families, I saw the Floyds rise.

After the service, the family, friends, and supporters, along with Ben Crump and I, congregated upstairs in the church. Philonise approached me.

"How did I do?" he asked quietly.

I told him the truth. "You were good," I said.

He started peppering me with questions: What should he do differently? What worked? What didn't? What should he cut from his speech? What should stay? He wanted a critique. Whether he liked it or not, he knew he'd be thrust onto the public stage again and wanted to be ready, polished. In a way, he reminded me of a younger version of myself. I thought of the many mentors I'd had growing up: Bishop Washington, Adam

Clayton Powell Jr., James Brown, and Jesse Jackson. I used to watch them with an eagle eye, hoping to glean some of their finesse and power. I loved the way Adam Clayton Powell Jr. spoke, the boom of his voice and his oratorial style, the way he delivered his missives while chomping on a cigar. True leaders aren't good, they're great, forever honing their message to stay on point no matter the public critique or opposition. They hold the public's attention. The truly great ones deliver their messages like they're preaching sermons from the top of the mountain. I gave Philonise some notes, which he incorporated as he saw fit.

Over the course of a year—from the time of his brother's murder to the conviction of Derek Chauvin in 2021—I watched Philonise transform from being George's brother to being an activist, an advocate for social change. Prior to his brother's murder, Philonise wasn't particularly motivated by social justice or politics, but this life-changing event brought everything into focus. He went from being shy, self-effacing, and laid-back to being a motivated leader, someone others could turn to for advice. In time, he gained the confidence that comes with public speaking and the passion that goes hand in hand with activism. Without sounding too cliché, I believe he found a sense of purpose and meaning in life, a cause that may have been sparked by his brother's murder but was nurtured by his own moral clarity and the support he got from a community of fellow activists and from other families whose lives had also been touched by police violence. His contribution to the success of what some people now call the George Floyd movement was substantial. The fact that it was embraced and accepted by unlikely allies in the general American public was unquestionably aided by Philonise's persona, humility, and his sense of sincerity. He helped set the tone for the movement.

In a way, he was the perfect messenger. If his style had been more abrasive, I don't think the message of justice would have been as effective. Instead, by God's grace, Philonise was gifted with both humility and authenticity and so, whenever he called on us to say George's name, we did so in unison and without question. While I obviously didn't know George, I'm not alone in saying that whenever I saw or spoke with Philonise, I felt that I understood who George was. I think that telegraphed to the rest of America: this was a real family going through real pain caused by the systemic failure of a policing system created to work for the benefit of the few and to the detriment of the many.

Philonise's evolution was and still is empowering to behold. He hasn't let up. He's been a consistent presence on The Hill, taking meetings with various politicians, testifying before the House Judiciary Committee at a hearing on policing and accountability, and pushing to get support for the George Floyd Justice in Policing Act, a legislative bill that combats police misconduct and reins in excessive force and racial profiling in policing. His testimony before Congress, only a day after burying his brother, was one of brotherly love as spoken from the heart of an activist. "This is 2020. Enough is enough," he told lawmakers. "The people marching in the streets are telling you enough is enough. Be the leaders that this country, this world, needs. Do the right thing. The people elected you to speak for them, to make positive change. George's name means something. You have the opportunity here to make your names mean something, too."

In 2020, Bridgett, George's sister, along with Philonise and other members of the family, started the George Floyd Memorial Foundation, a group dedicated to eliminating the systemic obstacles of racism, addressing everything from economic disparities to working to build a fair legal system. They've already created several programs to help mobilize communities, including an internship program with Texas A&M called the Be His Legacy Internship Program that provides hands-on community outreach experience and a scholarship program for law school students. As much as I'm encouraged that the Floyd family is helping to advance the next steps in our march to justice, I'm also saddened by how they got here. Too many activists are born out of heartbreaking personal tragedy. Prior to George's death, many members of the Floyd family—like most Americans today—were concerned citizens. Like everyone else in this country, they, too, had seen the newspaper headlines, stories that detailed the deaths of too many Black men and women, cases that reached as far back as Emmett Till and up to Breonna Taylor. George's murder, however, tipped the scales and changed their general sense of concern and worry into full-fledged activism. They may have unwillingly been thrust into the media's eye, but they decided to make use of it. Philonise instinctively understood that his private pain—the loss that came from saying goodbye to his big brother—could be channeled into public activism. In offering up his brother's name to the cause of justice, we might all be transformed, too.

Over this tumultuous time, Philonise and I have stayed in regular contact with one another, so much so that his brother Rodney and his nephew Brandon tease him, saying, "You gonna grow up and be just like Rev." As much as they joke around, calling him Baby Al or Lil Al, I know Philonise will be who he's gotta be. His is a strength of character that can't be taught.

Black America's Attorney General:
Ben Crump

In my line of work, it's wise to have a roster of lawyers on hand. I never know whose expertise I'll need for what and when. In my life, lawyers have come and gone but three have withstood the test of time and stand leagues above the rest albeit for different reasons. I first met Michael Hardy, my longtime colleague and NAN's primary attorney, in the early years of my activist work after I'd just led a march in Howard Beach. Hardy prefers to work behind the scenes, something I deeply admire and appreciate. His consistent and steady hand has helped shape NAN into what it is today: one of the nation's preeminent civil rights organizations with over 120 chapters. Johnnie Cochran, who actively sought out the limelight, was the near opposite of Hardy. I first worked with Johnnie in the 1990s on the Abner Louima case. A slick, Hollywood-type lawyer, with impeccable suits and a flair for fashion, Johnnie was a master of the sound bite: "If it doesn't fit, you must acquit," "If it doesn't make sense, you should find for the defense," and so on. I've often wondered how he would have managed in today's social-media-savvy world. Some of his quips were Twitter-world ready even back in the day. Sadly, Johnnie left our world too soon, but his work, style, and legacy live on. Not long after Johnnie's death to cancer in 2005, I received a call from a lawyer I didn't know. He told me he was from

Florida but spoke with an unmistakable Southern accent. His name was Ben Crump.

"The reason I'm calling, sir," Ben said in what I would soon learn was his typically polite manner, "is on account of Martin Lee Anderson, a fourteen-year-old boy who died at a boot-camp-style detention center."

He went on to explain: upon arrival at the Bay Country Boot Camp, which was operated by the sheriff's office out of Panama City, Florida, Martin was forced to run track and, within two hours, became fatigued and stopped running. A gang of seven guards beat him, forced him to keep running, and covered his mouth while forcing him to inhale ammonia tablets. He collapsed and died. It was determined that his cause of death was by suffocation due to the actions of the guards. The forced inhalation of ammonia fumes had caused a spasm of his vocal cords, which then internally blocked his airway. Security cameras had recorded the beating. The on-staff nurse had watched the beating happen in real time and failed to intervene.

"Heavy stuff," I said.

"You kill a dog, you go to jail. You kill a little Black boy, nothing happens," Ben said. It was a line he'd use again to decry the guards and nurse once they were acquitted in Anderson's death. We didn't know then we'd lose the case, though. I asked, "What do you need me to do?"

"A group of local college students are organizing a sit-in at Governor Jeb Bush's office," he said. "They'd appreciate your show of support."

Next thing I knew, I was on the next plane to Florida, speaking at rallies, drumming up public support and media attention, and helping to lead a march out of Tallahassee. I met Ben at that march. From the get-go, I got the sense that he was a humble man, a true Southerner. He was nattily dressed but, unlike Johnnie Cochrane, not ostentatious. I got the feeling that for Ben style came second to substance. An eagle of justice pin is permanently perched on his left lapel. For as long as I've known him, I've rarely seen him without it, a personal reminder of his work as a crusader of justice. When we shook hands, he looked me straight in the eye. Here was a serious, sober man unbowed in his sense of duty, and yet, when he spoke, he was as welcoming, kind, and approachable as any one of my Southern cousins. After the march, we kept in touch. In this line of work, it's good to keep your allies close, especially in the courtroom.

I had a difficult time shaking the loss of the Anderson case in 2007. Ben did, too. Five years after the acquittals he said, "I will go to my grave feeling that justice didn't happen for Martin Lee Anderson's family." I don't think either one of us will forget seeing the all-white jury come back in less than two hours of deliberations. We both thought it was an open-and-shut case: video footage of seven grown men savagely beating a fourteen-year-old boy at a state-sanctioned center while medical personnel failed to intervene. He and I both learned some important lessons in that fight, however, lessons that we'd apply to future causes like the killing of Trayvon Martin. In civil rights battles, you can't assume victory. You also can't expect to attack and not be attacked in return. Your work has to be better than meticulous. It's gotta be bulletproof.

Today, Ben is the go-to lawyer for racial justice. As a kid growing up in North Carolina, he hadn't anticipated that he'd one day wield the power of the pen nor that he'd help usher in an era of racial reckoning in America. But anyone who knows Ben knows that he had no choice but to become a lawyer. As Reverend R. B. Holmes Jr., pastor of Bethel Missionary Baptist Church, said, "I don't see law being his career. I see law being his calling. It's pastoral. He has been used to give people their voice, and a sense of hope and purpose, how to turn literal pain into purpose." Like most Black lawyers, Ben's journey toward becoming a changemaker began when he first recognized racism and racial disparity. For Ben, that realization came early.

When Ben was about six or seven years old, he witnessed his uncle being brutalized by the police, allegedly for speeding. It was only when he was older and had a clearer understanding of the way the world works that he guessed that his uncle was harassed because he was a Black man driving a nice car. "They were making an example that it doesn't matter who you are, where you go, because you will always be a second-class citizen," he said. Another childhood experience left a permanent mark, and altered the course of his life forever.

In 1978, the schools in Ben's hometown of Lumberton, North Carolina, were being integrated for the first time. Ben soon learned that it was because of the work of a lawyer named Thurgood Marshall and his series of cases that culminated in the landmark legal victory *Brown v. the Board of Education of Topeka* that he was able to attend the L. Gilbert Carroll Middle School. Ben's mother was overjoyed that her son could now attend the best schools their town had to offer. Ben himself was thrilled to have access to new books and resources. At the same time, he began to wonder why the people on the white side of the tracks had it so good when he'd had it so bad.

Kids being kids, Ben quickly formed friendships with his new white peers. Their fraternity stopped during lunchtime, however, when the students were divided into three categories: free lunch, reduced-price lunch, and something called "à la carte" that had the best options but, priced at two dollars, the most expensive ones, too. One day Ben and one of his friends from a neighboring government housing project were complaining about how slowly their line was moving when a white girl named Jenny pulled out a hundred-dollar bill, her weekly allowance. Ben and his Black friend couldn't believe the money belonged to her. To prove her point that the money *was* hers, Jenny bought lunch for a group of kids, including Ben and his friends. He wrote in his book *Open Season*: "I was stunned that a ten-year-old girl had an allowance that was the equivalent of my mother's weekly income working *two* jobs—one in a hotel laundry room during the day and another at the Converse shoe factory at night.... I wanted to understand this money and ownership disparity that seemed to be very much tied up with economic justice and race." In time, Ben realized that a lot of people wanted to uphold these economic and racial disparities and, had it not been for federal legislation, Ben would have been denied the benefits that came with his newly integrated school. School integration was a significant chink in the armor of white supremacy. Marshall became his personal hero. His goal quickly came into focus, writing, "I would become an attorney like Thurgood Marshall, and I would fight to make life better for the people from my side of the tracks." And so began his long journey toward becoming a crusader for social justice.

Ben launched his career with medical malpractice and personal injury cases, which his firm still handles, winning substantial payouts that help subsidize the gru-eling, high-risk civil rights cases that all too often yield nothing but heartache. Even these workaday cases, however, are meaningful to him—a way, he says, of "try-ing to get justice for the underserved." While fighting for justice for George, for example, he's also filed a class-action suit against Johnson & Johnson on behalf of the National Council of Negro Women, citing the com-pany's specific marketing of talcum-based baby pow-der to Black women, despite links to ovarian cancers.

Ben is the attorney for our times. Like Johnnie Coch-rane, he understands the media component of big-time trials and is just as comfortable arguing in front of a judge as he is doing a press conference on cam-era. Without public attention, a lot of cases are swept under the rug: Anderson's case, for example, didn't get the kind of coverage it should have but then most civil rights cases don't. To counter that, Ben often courts the media outright. He knows that the media is often a more powerful tool in effecting broader social change than whatever happens in the courtroom.

Ben says he often feels compelled to argue two cases for every one: a sound legal argument for the courtroom and another, more emotional one for the public. My job is to help him win in the court of public opinion, getting the media to shine a light on a par-ticular injustice. There are some things I can say and do that Ben Crump can't and vice versa. We know and understand our roles, and how our personalities and strengths can be played to full effect. If Ben made half of the statements I do—or publicly showed his outrage—he'd risk undercutting his legal arguments and would be doing a disservice to the families who entrusted him to represent them in court. I can give voice to their outrage; I can speak for the families when doing so themselves may jeopardize their standing in court. I can stand front and center to take the criticism and heat. I've been doing it for so long I may as well be fireproof.

While Ben knows how to navigate the media, he's also careful about not letting the substance of his legal argument turn into a stylish hashtag. If a hashtag can help amplify his legal message, he'll utilize it to full effect. If it detracts from the energy of the movement or from any possible gains he can make in the courtroom, however, he won't use it. Everything he does is in service of dismantling systemic social injustice. He's a hard worker who never gives up even when the chips are down. In the many years I've known and worked with him, I've known him to step down only once, and that was for a very good reason.

One of the biggest organized protests of 2020 was unquestionably the Get Your Knee Off Our Necks Commitment March. Ben represents about 80 percent of the victims' families who were either going to be in attendance or speaking at the march. The night before the march, he and I were returning to our Washington, DC, hotel after being interviewed for the Bravo reality television show *Marriage and Medicine*, which planned to highlight the COVID-19 testing protocols we'd instituted for the event. Ben received a call from his family. From the hushed tone of his voice, I could tell that the news wasn't good.

Ben hung up and turned to face me. "I can't go to the march," he said.

"What do you mean you can't go to the march?" I asked. "Your clients are there. It's gonna be huge."

"My aunt is in the hospital with COVID," he said. "I

have to leave immediately." And he did—no more conversation about it. When news broke that Ben had to leave to be with his aunt, none of his clients faulted his absence. By then, everyone knew well enough that family came first for him; it was one of the reasons they were his clients in the first place. Sadly, his aunt died a few days later. He is the rare example today of a lawyer who understands the political aspects of the social justice movement because, deep down, the work is deeply personal for him. He believes in what he does because he does what he believes in. His values are rooted in his love for family, his understanding of faith, and the morality of what it means to be a decent, caring person. Shows you how much of an ambulance chaser he is not. It's also telling that, even in his absence, he was still very much present at the march by virtue of the victims' families and his staff. If you would have asked anyone, they would have sworn to you that they just saw Ben even though he was miles away, sitting bedside with his aunt. His is a presence that can be felt and, in the sea of supporters, Ben's fingerprints were all over that march.

When I get a call from Ben, I know that he's tapped into something larger than himself. He doesn't work in a vacuum; his social justice mission overlaps with mine. So, even though he's not a civil rights leader per se, he's still helping to lead the struggle for civil rights, taking on only those cases that, in his words, will "shock the conscience" of the American people. He's not trying to be a politician or a celebrity. His almost pastoral devotion to fighting for social justice is one of the reasons why Scott Carruthers, a managing partner at Ben's firm, calls him a "lawyer-preacher." Call him what you want—a lawyer-preacher or a lawyer's lawyer—with over two hundred wins in police-violence cases, I like to think of him as Black America's Attorney General.

AN ORDINARY BROTHER

George Floyd's story has been the story of the treatment of Black folks in America since its founding days. The nearly last ten minutes of his life encapsulated our national history—from his assumed criminality to the escalation of violence from the police to his very identity as an ordinary brother. He could have been any Black man living in America today.

George grew up in Houston's housing projects where he had a somewhat promising future as a potential athlete, a dream that never landed. As an adult, he moved to Minneapolis where he cobbled together a living, working security jobs at the Conga Latin Bistro and the local Salvation Army and as an occasional truck driver, making just enough money to send a portion of his pay to support Gianna, his then-six-year-old daughter who lives with her mother. George mattered to the people who knew him. By all accounts, he was a gentle giant with a big heart, a description Gwen Carr also used to describe her own son Eric. Philonise told me that his big brother was "like a general," shouting friendly directives to friends, family, and neighbors. He was frequently surrounded by people and could command a group—not because he was imposing or mean but because people wanted to do good by him. When the Cleveland Cavaliers, his favorite basketball team, won the 2016 NBA championship, George was overjoyed. "I feel like *I* won a championship," George told Brandon, his nephew, whenever he asked him how he was doing. He was a man who cheered for others' successes even when he couldn't experience them himself.

To the Minneapolis police, however, George fit the stereotypical description of a Black criminal and was treated with immediate aggression. The police escorted white supremacist Dylann Roof to Burger King after he opened fire at the Emanuel African Methodist Church in Charleston, killing nine Black people, but George, who may have been in possession of a counterfeit twenty-dollar bill, was treated no better than an out-of-control animal, killed on the spot. George's murder magnified the disparities all Black Americans face. His neck represented all of ours. How he suffered is how we all suffer, which is why it's not enough to solely talk about police reform when we talk about George Floyd. We must also talk about voter suppression, the wealth gap, affordable housing, redlining practices, and health care. We must talk about the discrepancies in the education system and in environmental justice. The failures that plague Black America are foundational.

There are many different forms of racism—from the blatant to the hidden to the systemic. Each form represents a different way to struggle, a different way to die. In his book *Open Season*, Attorney Ben Crump writes that there are many ways to kill a race of people. "You can take away their hope for a better life. You can deny them access to quality food and health care. You can flood their community with drugs. You can take away safe, decent housing. You can lock them up for crimes they did not commit. In short, you can kill their spirit so they become the walking dead." The ability to inflict such a death is that knee on our neck: deep-seated yet casual in its power and hatred. Too many of us have been cast away, disregarded, and told we don't matter, but as I've said many times before, "God took the rejected stone and made him the cornerstone of a movement that's going to change the whole wide world."

George Floyd was that cornerstone. Darnella Frazier and Ben Crump are cornerstones, too. And Philonise and every member of the Floyd family, and the thousands of protesters who stood to demand justice for George. We are the cornerstones and, together, we will build a better future.

2

TURNING PAIN
INTO PURPOSE

"I'm going to put up a fight every day because I'm not just fighting for George anymore. I'm fighting for everybody around this world."

—PHILONISE FLOYD

Joe Biden's first trip from his home state of Delaware during the pandemic was to meet with the Floyd family in Texas. At the time, he was running as the Democratic Party's nominee for president. Remember all that Republican chatter about how Biden was stuck in his basement during the 2020 presidential election season and here Biden—not President Trump—is the politician who meets with the grieving family. Never mind George's murder happened on Trump's watch. The week George died, Trump delivered mixed messages on the subject, first saying it was "very sad and tragic" only to switch his focus to the Minneapolis protesters, calling them "thugs." He later tweeted, "When the looting starts, the shooting starts"—a reference to an incendiary phrase first coined in 1967 by Walter E. Headley, a Miami police chief long accused of using racist tactics to patrol Black neighborhoods.

I interviewed Philonise for my show *PoliticsNation* not long after the Floyd family first spoke to President Trump. About their conversation, Philonise said, "He didn't give me the opportunity to even speak. It was hard. I was trying to talk to him, but he just kept pushing me off like, 'I don't want to hear what you're talking about.'" A few weeks after George's death—he'd yet to be buried—Trump celebrated the country's economic numbers in a Rose Garden news conference, saying, "Hopefully George is looking down right now and saying this is a great thing that's happening for our country. This is a great day for him. It's a great day for everybody." Trump's disconnect was deeply troubling, though hardly surprising from a man who famously said there were "very fine people on both sides" of a violent clash in Charlottesville, Virginia, between white supremacists and activists protesting racism.

The day before George's funeral service in Houston, the Floyd family, Ben Crump, and I, along with members of Biden's campaign, including Cedric Richmond, who is now a senior adviser to the White House, met with Joe and Dr. Jill Biden at a soul food restaurant. The restaurant was closed to the public, and because of the pandemic we sat socially distanced from one another, with Joe seated to my left. No one ordered food. We weren't there for the chicken; we were there to talk. The family wanted to avoid turning George's funeral into a media circus more than it already was and so, at the request of the family, Biden decided he wouldn't attend the service but would instead record a message of support. During our hour-long meeting with the Bidens, Philonise, in his typical fashion, asked lots of questions. Some were easy to answer. Others, not so much, questions like: When will we see justice? How do we stop police brutality? What do we tell Gianna now that her daddy is gone?

Toward the end of the meeting, Gianna tiptoed into the room.

She clung to her mother, her wide eyes scanning the room, taking in the scene. Joe Biden saw her immediately and rather than having her come to him, he went to her. They stood off to the side of the room, huddled in a private conference of their own, though everyone could overhear their conversation.

Biden told her, "I'm here because of what happened to your dad."

"My dad's gonna change the world," she said, her voice unwavering.

He looked at her and said, "You're right."

It was one of the most touching exchanges I've seen in my life. Biden repeated their exchange in his prerecorded message that played at the service.

As we left the restaurant, I turned to Philonise and said, "You realize that man's probably going to be the next president of the United States, don't you?"

"You really think he's gonna win?" he asked.

I nodded yes.

"And I'm talking to him like that?" he exclaimed, and we both laughed.

"Get used to it," I said. I could have reminded him that he had told Barack Obama to order us some brisket, but I didn't. While traveling back to New York City, it dawned on me that the only person in that room who had the answer to Philonise's questions was his six-year-old niece. Her declaration was a kind of road map.

We had a long road ahead of us. If my past experiences have taught me anything, it's to temper my sense of hope and optimism. I've seen far too many wrongful deaths and have sat in too many courtrooms where justice wasn't slow, it simply never arrived. The grand jury failed to indict Ferguson police officer Darren Wilson, who shot and killed Michael Brown. George Zimmerman was acquitted after shooting and killing Trayvon Martin. The grand jury failed to indict Cleveland police officers

Timothy Loehmann and Frank Garmback for killing twelve-year-old Tamir Rice. The list of heartbreak goes on. I was in the Albany courtroom when the four police officers who killed Amadou Diallo were acquitted in 1999. More recently, the grand jury failed to indict police officer Daniel Pantaleo for the killing of Eric Garner in 2014. It took more than five years from Eric's passing for Pantaleo to be fired from the force. To this day, the grand jury proceedings have remained sealed. The New York Civil Liberties Union among others have been unsuccessful in their attempts to have that information released.

As I watched Philonise pepper the soon-to-be president of the United States with questions big and small, I could tell that he was stepping into the role of an activist; he was thinking outside himself. He was thinking of George, yes, but he was also beginning to think about all the other Black men and women who hadn't seen justice, the other families who'd unnecessarily suffered because of systemic racism. His burgeoning transformation reminded me of someone else I knew: Gwen Carr, Eric Garner's mother. She, like Philonise and so many others before them both, had been thrust onto the stage of social justice while fighting the deep wounds of personal tragedy. The ability to turn pain, sadness, and anger into something positive requires Herculean personal strength. It takes courage, faith, and grit, and if anyone best personifies those three qualities, it's Gwen Carr.

Mother Justice:
Gwen Carr

I remember July 17, 2014, the day Eric died, as if it was yesterday. I was in Nevada speaking at a labor convention. I'd spent most of the day either on stage or sequestered in conference rooms away from my phone, so I'd missed the headline already dominating the evening news in New York City. Besides being on television, the video of Eric Garner's death was also circulating online. It was only when I arrived at Las Vegas's McCarran International Airport and spoke with Cynthia Davis, president of the Staten Island office of NAN, that I got brought up to speed. She called and told me what had happened: New York Police Department officers had approached Eric on the suspicion that he was selling loosies, single cigarettes from packs without tax stamps. Several witnesses, however, said this wasn't true and that Eric, instead, was simply breaking up a fight and had gotten the attention of the cops. Whichever version was correct, it was a fact that police from the 120th Precinct knew most of the people who gathered on Bay Street. The Staten Island neighborhood was the kind of place where retirees played board games out in the open, kids sold loosies now and again to make a few bucks—few residents could afford a whole pack of cigarettes anyway—and the occasional fight broke out but was never so bad someone couldn't intervene and get everyone to calm down. The police were a regular presence, always circling with their squad cars, making inquiries, and harassing residents. For most poor Black and brown residents of Staten Island, this was—and still is—the way of life.

Even if Eric wanted, he couldn't hide from the police. Over six feet tall and weighing over three hundred pounds, he was hard to miss, and because he'd already been in trouble before for selling loosies, he was a prime target. The police singled him out, surrounding him in front of the Bay Beauty Supply store. Ramsey Orta, Eric's friend, started recording the scene on his phone despite being told several times by police to stop. On video, Eric told the cops he was tired of being harassed and wasn't selling any loosies. The officers still tried to arrest him. Officer Pantaleo swung his arm around Eric's neck from behind and, with the aid of the other officers, pushed him to the ground, putting him in a chokehold, a maneuver that's been banned by the New York Police Department since 1993. Another of Eric's friends, Taisha Allen, pulled out her cell phone and started filming, too.

With multiple officers pinning him down, Eric repeated the words, "I can't breathe," eleven times while Pantaleo put him in an illegal chokehold. Eric lost consciousness and lay facedown on the sidewalk for another seven minutes, with no one attempting to perform resuscitation of any kind, before an ambulance arrived. The cops drove away, leaving everyone on Bay Street stunned. When they returned a short time later, it was to string up yellow police tape. The area was now subject to a homicide investigation.

Cynthia explained that she'd happened to be in the neighborhood on another case when one of the witnesses found her. She made her way back to the scene of the crime where she spoke with the commanding officer as well as with several bystanders and fellow caseworkers who had been with clients in the nearby park. Part of NAN's mission is community outreach and I was thankful Cynthia was already on the ground and putting together the pieces, making sure the atmosphere stayed calm.

"Good," I told her. I said I'd take a red-eye flight and would be back in Manhattan the following morning to deal with everything. Cynthia's next words caught me off guard.

"Would you speak with his mother?" she asked.

"Now?"

"Yes. A few words," she coaxed. I hadn't realized Cynthia was already in touch with Eric's mother, too. I said yes, and Cynthia connected us.

When I first heard Gwen's voice, I could tell she was in a state of profound shock and disbelief. Behind her voice, however, I detected the steely nature of a mother's love. I couldn't help but think of Gwen's suffering as the pain that flowed through too many generations of Black mothers. My heart ached; I thought of my own mother, and how she wore a brave face even in the most troubling of times. She did that so I wouldn't falter myself. I understood that Gwen was trying her best to keep herself together. Her composure understandably quickly melted to tears when she retold the story of what had happened to her son as she best understood it. Her voice shook but she pressed on, saying, "I want you involved, Rev. I want you to help. I remember when you were a boy preacher. You used to preach at Charity Baptist Church," which was one of the churches I used to preach at way back when. She told me she'd seen me do a sermon and still remembered it all these years later. I was struck that, even in her darkest hour, she'd extended this kindness to me, offering up a memory she knew meant something to us both. She also may have thought that sweetening me up would make me more inclined to want to help her. The truth was, I'd already wanted to help, but having her give consent to my help meant that we were going to be in this thing together.

"I tell you what, Mrs. Carr," I said, "tomorrow I'll make an announcement on my radio show during our Saturday service at the House of Justice in Harlem. We're gonna march to Staten Island to the site where your son was murdered. Come to the morning service. Bring your family and anyone else who wants to join, and we'll get ready from there."

"I'll be there," she said.

Unsure of our commitment and her own fortitude, Gwen arrived at the House of Justice with Cynthia that following Saturday and cautiously introduced herself. We loaded fifteen buses full of supporters and traveled to Staten Island together where we led the first of what would become many marches, rallies, and organized events to protest the death of her son. I'll never forget when we arrived in Staten Island for that first march.

Gwen put her hand in mine, and we stood at the center of the march. The rest of the family linked arms, forming a chain that fanned out beside us. I've been doing this kind of marching for so long I often forget how powerful it is the first time someone else does it. There's something energizing and life-affirming about the simple act of coming together, unified in purpose, voice, and step. I could see that Gwen felt it. Her jaw was clenched and, whether she knew it or not, her hand had become a fist inside mine, a rock. She was determined. It was a decisive moment; it was the first indication I had that Gwen was a fighter. She wasn't going to let her son's death be swept under a rug, forgotten.

"Let's go," I said, and Gwen took her first tentative step toward justice for her son.

That evening, Gwen had found the strength of a new community and had gained back some of her footing. We'd be with her every step of the way. She and I have been marching together ever since, raising our voices in unison, still fighting for justice in Eric's name. Marching gave Gwen a sense of purpose; it helped her channel her discomfort and pain into something motivating. The more attention she got for her activist work—interview requests, other families reaching out to her for support, reporters seeking her out for her comments and thoughts—the stronger she became so that, by the time of George Floyd's murder, she was forceful in her demands for justice. The quest for justice for Eric had broadened by 2020, and Gwen knew she wasn't fighting for her son only. She was fighting for all of us when, during an interview addressing issues of police violence, she said, "The struggle is real. There's a lot of work to be done and to do this work you really have to be about change. And to be about change is not always a comfortable thing. We have to be in uncomfortable situations to make America and the government uncomfortable—to make them see that there is a problem—because if they don't admit there's a problem, we can't begin to get to a solution. It's a fight that we must fight."

One of the reasons why Gwen is such an inspired and impassioned activist is because she lifts people up. A true matriarch, she brings everyone into the fold and, so, it was only a matter of time before she'd found other activists with whom she could unite. She needn't look far: in the fall of 2014, while attending the Congressional Black Caucus (CBC) convention in Washington, DC, she met Sybrina Fulton, the mother of Trayvon Martin, who, about two years prior to Eric's killing, had been shot and killed in Sanford, Florida, by George Zimmerman, a neighborhood watch volunteer. She also met Lesley McSpadden, the mother of Michael Brown, who'd been killed by police just a month before the convention in Ferguson, Missouri. The three women shared similar experiences with one another. As Gwen wrote in *This Stops Now*, "The three of us were all members of an unfortunate club, a club that no one would ever choose to join." Sadly, that club expanded each year, and soon came to include Maria Hamilton, mother to Dontre, whose son was killed by Milwaukee police; Lucy McBath, mother to Jordan Davis, who was killed in Jacksonville, Florida; and Cleopatra Cowley-Pendleton, mother to fifteen-year-old Hadiya, who was shot at Harsh Park in Kenwood, Chicago, only a week after performing at Obama's second inauguration in 2013. Whenever the women were at activist events together, people informally referred to them as "the mothers" and then "the Mothers of the Movement." They weren't an actual organization per se, but the public came to see them as a core activist group, each member relentless in her pursuit for justice. Whether appearing alongside Hillary Clinton at the 2016 Democratic National Convention or with Beyoncé in her 2016 short film *LEMONADE*, today the Mothers of the Movement are a vital force in the world of activism and in raising social awareness of police violence. In 2020, Gwen's circle widened even further as she embraced the Floyds like they were her own family.

Of the many travelers I've met on this long and winding road toward justice, Gwen stands out. She never misses a rally. On the rare occasion that she misses a service, it's because she's out of state staging a march of her own or helping to bring awareness to someone else's plight. It hasn't been easy: she'd be the first to tell you that she's faced many dark days. But she's also found the light, becoming an active participant in her life. When I asked her how she does it, she had an answer at the ready, saying, "I had to change my mourning into movement, my pain into purpose, and my sorrow into strategy." Would that we could all be so courageous.

A GOOD KID

About two years before Eric died, an unarmed, seventeen-year-old boy named Trayvon Martin was shot and killed in Sanford, Florida, by George Zimmerman. The case struck a nerve in the country's psyche, especially since Florida's Stand Your Ground statute protected Zimmerman from arrest. Not long after the case broke, Ben Crump brought Trayvon's father, Tracy, to meet me at my MSNBC office, where we discussed how to get national coverage. At the time, there was all kind of talk in the news about what kind of kid Trayvon was, the typical conversation that gets thrown around whenever a Black boy is murdered—that he was a criminal or looking for trouble, et cetera. The first thing Tracy said to me was, "Reverend, this was a good kid."

"Go on," I said.

"He'd just gone to get some iced tea at the store and was coming home. He wasn't trying to do nothing. I promise you, he did not have a weapon." Tracy paused. I noticed he was tearing up. Then he looked at me and, with a firmness in his voice, said, "I know my son." Father to father, I knew Tracy's love for his son was real and enduring. As I'd later discover, Sybrina's love for her son was just as fierce. Tracy continued, saying, "All I want is justice. They won't even arrest this guy. They act like my son doesn't mean anything, that his life is nothing."

"Let's tell your story to the world and get the country to rally behind you," I said. We put together a rough plan, one we'd later finesse.

I often see families when they are at their most vulnerable—in shock, angry, or in pain. When Tracy left my office, however, I was more shook up than usual. I found myself thinking about my own father, and how I'd wished he'd showed up for me the way Tracy was fighting for his son Trayvon. My father had left the family when I was a young boy, and so I'd never had a man like Tracy in my life. I looked at Tracy as if I was one of the millions of Black boys in this country who never had a daddy like that, never felt that kind of love. I privately promised myself that I'd fight for justice on behalf of all the lost sons. Zimmerman, of course, was famously acquitted. Don't think I don't think about that every day when I get up in the morning to attend the next trial or the next funeral, the next wake for another Black boy or man shot in the back, choked on the ground.

But I tell this story because it's impossible for me not to think of Tracy, Philonise, or Gwen, for example, as members of my own family, and to find healing in my relationships with them. In this line of work, you end up forming lasting relationships forged in hardship and battle-tested. I consider Michael Hardy, NAN's attorney for over thirty years, to be like a brother. Jesse Jackson is more than a mentor to me; he's like a father and brother both. When I think of Gwen, I think of my own mother. Like Gwen, she had a steely inner reserve, was devout in her faith, and tireless in her love. I wonder if my own father is watching me in heaven same as Trayvon is watching his daddy.

These relationships branch outward. So, as I got to know Tracy, I also got to know Trayvon's mother Sybrina. As I've gotten closer to Philonise, I've also gotten to know his sister Bridgett better. Besides Gwen, I've had the pleasure of knowing her husband, Ben, who was as good a man as any I've met. Sadly, Ben died of a heart attack only nineteen months after Eric's daughter, Erica, died from the same cause. In the midst of such sorrow, we draw strength, love, and healing from each other, knowing that we're in it together.

The Heart of an Activist:
Erica Garner

Before Erica Garner, Eric's daughter, died at the age of twenty-seven after an asthma episode precipitated a major heart attack, she, too, was an activist. She'd sometimes call me up, asking me for advice. I remember she once planned a protest across the Verrazano Bridge in her father's name. She was hoping she'd get arrested if only to draw some mainstream media attention to the event. When she and a group of about a hundred protesters, including my daughter, got to the bridge, however, nothing happened. No arrests. She called me and said, "Uncle Al, what should we do?" They were just rerouting the traffic around the group.

"Guess you gotta regroup," I said.

And she did. The next major march she organized was a success: she staged a "die-in" at the exact location where her father had been choked, lying down on the sidewalk where her father drew his last breath. A group of protesters marched with her to the location and lay down, too. The gathering was small but impactful and got media attention. She later told me that she'd felt a strong connection with her father while lying where he had died. She imagined the last minutes of his life as if they'd been her own.

Erica learned how to be an activist the hard way— by getting out there and doing it. There are books written on the topic and you can listen to someone like me who can tell you war stories about the things I did, what did and didn't work. Or you can do what Erica did and learn on the job. It's a harder route but one with greater rewards, and a steeper learning curve. She'd later hold other successful protests and die-ins, refusing to let the governing politicians off the hook. Only a few weeks before her death, she'd taken Mayor Bill de Blasio to task, demanding that he do more for his Black constituents.

I did Erica's eulogy same as I did for her father and, later, for her step-grandfather. When I saw her two children—her eight-year-old daughter and her four-month-old son—at the funeral, I thought of something

Erica had written for the *Washington Post*: "Even with my own heartbreak, when I demand justice, it's never just for Eric Garner. It's for my daughter; it's for the next generation of African Americans." Lotta people don't know how much grief and rage Erica carried over the death of her father. While she may have died from a medical heart attack, her mother, Esaw Snipes, and I believed that her heart had been under severe emotional strain since the day of her father's death. Trauma is a heavy load to bear, and poses real threats—emotional, mental, and physical. Her mother called her a warrior. She was. In Esaw's words, "Erica's death is just the first fight in twenty-seven years she lost."

A Witness to Injustice:
Ramsey Orta

When I think of the Eric Garner case, my thoughts naturally turn to Gwen, but there are other individuals whose bravery made a substantial contribution to the ongoing fight for justice in Eric's name. One such individual is Ramsey Orta.

Ramsey lived in the Tompkinsville neighborhood of Staten Island since 2009, an area known for its constant police surveillance. He'd gotten so used to being stopped and searched by the police that he often recorded his interactions with them. His phone was a kind of weapon, filming a form of self-defense. So when the police surrounded Eric on July 17, 2014, it didn't take long for Ramsey to reach for his phone and press the recording button. When he watched the ambulance carry away Eric's lifeless body, he was briefly consoled by the thought that he had the one piece of evidence—video proof of the crime—that would surely bring justice to his friend's death. Later that same night, his heart sank: he also knew that the video would put him at risk for more police harassment or worse. He'd noticed a black Crown Vic car as he'd walked home from the crime scene. Had it tailed him or was he imagining it? By morning, police cars flanked the street in front of his apartment. Were they there for him? He was unnerved, to say the least, and had every right to be, knowing that the police could be a brutal, mobilizing force, especially against someone like him, who'd already had significant run-ins with the law.

In the months that followed Eric's death, things got difficult for both Ramsey and Taisha Allen. (While Ramsey's video was the footage that circulated most widely, Taisha's video also made the rounds, which put her at risk as well.) The police began targeting Ramsey, and with each interaction alluded to the fact that they knew he made the video. I'm sure Ramsey felt that he was a wanted man; I would have felt that way, too. By August 2014, Ramsey had been arrested three times, the first time for criminal possession of a handgun he allegedly tried to give a seventeen-year-old. At the time, I urged the Justice Department to start a civil rights investigation. In both prosecuting Ramsey and calling him as a witness in the Garner case, the Staten Island district attorney's office would create a conflict of interest. I wanted the federal government to step in so there'd be no question about the objectivity of the investigation. My pleas got little traction. The second and third arrests were on drug charges, the third arrest coming when he was accused of selling MDMA to an undercover cop. A lab test later showed that the alleged MDMA was fake, and the charges were reduced.

In 2015, his home was raided, and he was arrested

on a drug charge that resulted in him taking a plea deal. At the Rikers Island Correctional Facility, where he was sent, everyone at intake knew who he was. According to journalist Chloé Cooper Jones, the correction officers taunted him about the Garner video, saying things like, "You're ours now," and "Not so tough without your camera." According to Jones, he was denied visitors, ticketed for petty or falsified offenses, beaten, called racist names, had his food tampered with, put in solitary confinement, and moved from one facility to another, making any kind of access difficult for his family and friends. Ramsey's treatment hasn't been coincidental. It's been intentional, targeted, and extreme.

It's easy to dismiss Ramsey—to say that he's a criminal, someone who surrounds himself with drugs and guns, someone who's made the wrong decisions in life. But his life, like that of any other poor Black or brown man in America, has been stacked against him from the get-go. And yet, it was this so-called criminal, this rejected stone, who stood up and did the right thing, filming the crime of a police officer who, I would argue, by virtue of the powers granted to him by his badge and gun and training, has a greater responsibility than the average citizen to uphold the law. Ramsey bore witness to Officer Pantaleo's betrayal of the badge. Eric's death was its ultimate failure. I am humbled by Ramsey in the bravery of that moment and in his ability to steel himself as truth and goodness contorted themselves into something toxic and grotesque. I know he's had doubts in having done what he did, telling *Time* magazine in a 2015 article, "Sometimes I regret just not minding my business. Because it just put me in a messed-up predicament." His contributions to the social justice cause came at great personal cost and yet his courage undoubtedly helped pave the path toward a better future, a world when, only six years later, another witness to a heinous crime, Darnella Frazier, would be lauded as a hero.

Ramsey Orta was just as courageous as Darnella, as Rosa Parks. He knew the risks of and the potential consequences for filming the police, and he did it anyway. He did the right thing when the cops failed in every way to do right by Eric.

A Witness to the Black Experience:
Spike Lee

Long before people were using their own phones to document police harassment and abuse, Spike Lee was doing it with his movie camera, bearing witness to the entire breadth of the Black experience but especially to the realities of the urban Black community.

Spike and I go way back. I met him during a pivotal moment in my early adult life, back when I was traveling with James Brown and trying to decide whether I should go into show business, maybe work as an agent, or double down on my activism. I didn't know what kind of person I wanted to be and here was Spike, a guy who already knew who he was, a filmmaker through and through. He was also a Black man from Brooklyn, both of us around the same age. We shared a language and a perspective of the world that needed no translation. Our rapport was instantaneous.

By 1986, I'd dug into my activism in earnest, marching on Howard Beach to seek justice for Michael Griffith, who was killed by a speeding car after being chased by a mob of whites. That same year, Spike released *She's Gotta Have It*, his first feature-length film. When I decided to run for the US Senate in 1992, Spike rented out the Fort Greene Tennis Club in Brooklyn, so my staff and supporters could watch the returns together. I lost the race but won about 70 percent of the Black vote, an affirmation that I was doing something right with at least one segment of the state's demographic.

Spike's the kind of guy who, outta nowhere, will call me up and ask, "Where's the march tomorrow?" and then show up. He's not interested in doing speeches or being out front. He wants to be with the people. And it's the same with his art. Most of his films, certainly his earliest ones, document the lives of everyday people going about their business. He's interested in portraying the lives of Black and brown people—their struggles and hardships, their beauty and power. Until Spike came along, we weren't used to seeing ourselves like that on screen. We were treated as minor characters. As Spike has said, "People of color have a constant frustration of not being represented, or being misrepresented, and these images go around the world." Spike changed that, and he did it in a way that was authentic to our experiences. He didn't flinch.

For those of us in the activist movement, Spike was—and is—essential: he put a lens on the Black condition and revealed the emotional components and complexity of police brutality, racism, and oppression. These are issues that, up until Spike was able to portray them, activists like myself had to explain to the mainstream politicians, journalists, and CEOs of white America. My heated rhetoric about police brutality is one thing, and I can back it up with stats and figures and we can debate certain aspects of key legislation for hours. Watching the police murder Radio Raheem, a character in Spike's 1989 film *Do the Right Thing*, is another. You cannot watch that film without having a better understanding of how something like this can and does happen in real life whereas you might not be able to envision it when I preach the same truth at a press conference. You can't visualize something that was never your reality in the first place. Through Spike's films, white audiences were able to see the Black experience through *our* eyes and...guess what? We live in different realities. While Spike's worlds were fictional, Black America knew they captured the truth and the brutality of our everyday lives long before Ramsey and Darnella filmed Eric's and George's deaths.

If it hadn't been for Spike, how would we have, in the 1980s and 1990s, even approached an understanding of the normalized behavior that Blacks had to deal with that was actually racist and bigoted in origin? Before Spike, white audiences were comfortable with the character of the polished Black man as exemplified by actor Sidney Poitier, a persona we needed during the era of integration. When so much of the country was on edge, white audiences wanted to see examples of nonthreatening Black men, and Poitier, in his trim suits and with his calm, measured way of talking, put them at ease. But in the next wave of cinema, Spike took the baton and ran with it, elevating the urban, hard-core Black man to a more mainstream position and, with him, raising issues like police harassment and oppression to a more prominent platform. Spike helped bring the civil rights movement out of the South and showed us that oppression, though different from our Southern brothers' experiences, was also alive and well in the North. Suddenly, the struggle for civil rights didn't exclusively feel so Southern. This made a lot of the power brokers in New York City uncomfortable. It's one thing to call out Southern hillbillies for their racism, it's another to point a finger at the liberal New York elite, many of whom don't consider themselves racist. The inherent institutional racism that pervades our society makes it difficult for those who don't consider themselves racist to reconcile themselves to that fact that they have nonetheless benefitted from racist structures.

As the Southern civil rights movement of the 1950s and 1960s became the Northern activism of the 1980s and 1990s, the players shifted, too. The Northern urban Black of the 1980s and 1990s wasn't Sidney Poitier. Activists from the North had a more in-your-face kind of style. I should know; I was one of them. I liken the 1950s/1960s era of the Dr. King movement to Sam Cooke and B. B. King type of music. I was in the era of the Last Poets, Gil Scott-Heron, and the beginning of rap and hip-hop, Biggie Smalls, Russell Simmons, and Public Enemy. Our differences in style—from the way we dressed to the music we listened to—reflected our urban environment. The style didn't negate the substance. We didn't need the validation of white America, but we demanded the same rights, the same access to power, and the same services that they enjoyed. The civil rights chant went from being "I Am Somebody" to "No Justice, No Peace." That's a massive psychological shift from the image that had been projected to white America of the safe Black man. Spike helped force the conversation. Even when his films dealt with the era of integration, his cinematic approach was fueled by a modern-day understanding of racism. Had he been a filmmaker working in the 1950s and 1960s, he wouldn't have been able to show us what he did.

With his 1997 historical documentary *4 Little Girls*, for example, Spike turned his lens to the 16th Street Baptist Church bombing of 1963 that killed fourteen-year-olds Addie Mae Collins, Cynthia Wesley, Carole Robertson, and eleven-year-old Carol Denise McNair.

That bombing was the third in eleven days after federal order came down to integrate Alabama's school system. A well-known Klan member, Robert Chambliss, was charged with murder but was cleared of the charge, receiving only a six-month jail sentence and a one-hundred-dollar fine for the 122 sticks of dynamite he'd used to blow up the church. J. Edgar Hoover blocked the prosecution of the three men who'd helped Chambliss, and it was only until 1977 that the case was reopened and Chambliss sent to prison. During post-production, Spike discovered the postmortem records, which included photographs of what the dynamite had done, in Spike's words, "to those four beautiful Black girls." After much thinking and praying, Spike decided to include the images in the film. The family members of the four girls didn't like it, but they understood why Spike had made the decision that he did. It wasn't unlike the decision made by Mamie Till-Mobley, who had an open-casket funeral for her son. There is power in witnessing and in confronting the horror and pain of a system of oppression that otherwise renders Black people invisible. His 2006 documentary *When the Levees Break* showed the country what was happening to the Black and brown communities of Louisiana after Hurricane Katrina. Whether it's a documentary, a historical drama, or a straight-up, modern-day comedy, his films always capture the soul of Black America.

He reminds me, in many respects, of a war photographer. During some of humanity's most gruesome moments, most of us instinctually look away. Spike is the opposite. He goes in for the close-up. It's a lesson we can all learn from: our humanity lies in our ability to see and validate one another. As Spike has said himself, "I think it is very important that films make people look at what they've forgotten."

Spike's enduring commitment to the act of bearing witness made him the perfect person to honor Darnella Frazier with the PEN/Benenson Courage Award in 2020, an award that celebrates acts of courage and bravery by those who stand up to oppression. Speaking about Frazier, Spike said, "I am so proud of my sister. She documented the murder of George Floyd, our brother. And that footage reverberated around this God's earth, and people took to the streets." Other luminaries expressed their words of gratitude to Frazier, with Deray McKesson saying, "Your bravery changed this country." Frazier would also go on to receive a 2021 Pulitzer Prize Special Citation, proof that a lot has changed since Ramsey Orta's day. Today, the whole world is watching.

WITNESSES TO CHANGE

New York never embraced the Eric Garner case. It didn't get the same kind of traction and movement that George Floyd's case did. Amazingly enough, a year after Staten Island's District Attorney Daniel Donovan had failed to indict the officers involved in Eric's killing, Donovan was elected to Congress, replacing Michael Grimm, the representative who resigned after pleading guilty to federal tax fraud. Think of how Staten Island—a largely conservative borough almost two-thirds white—treated the Garner case compared to that of Baltimore, a majority Black city, where District Attorney Marilyn Mosby charged six officers with murder in the death of Freddie Gray, who died while being transported in a police van after being arrested for the possession of a knife. It took until the summer of 2020 for the New York state assembly to pass the Eric Garner Anti-Chokehold Act, which stipulates that any police officer in the state of New York who kills somebody using a chokehold can be charged with a class C felony, punishable up to fifteen years in prison.

While there are obvious similarities between Eric Garner's death and the way George Floyd was murdered, there are significant differences, too. A lot had changed in America—culturally and politically—between 2014 and 2020. In 2014, we had a Black president and a Black attorney general, Eric Holder. Issues surrounding police brutality were mainly discussed among activists, the young Black men and women who experienced that kind of harassment daily, their families, and their lawyers. Beyond this community, however, police brutality was something hinted at— in films, hip-hop lyrics, and the occasional news report where deaths were treated as isolated incidents and not the racialized pattern we now see them to be. Under President Obama's leadership, it was inevitable that some of these issues would begin to see the light—and he was able to address them from his unique experience as a Black man—but we were also riding the coattails of his initial campaign promise: we hoped things would get better. We hoped, just by having him as our president, that the killings and the attacks would stop. We couldn't be a racist country if we'd appointed a Black man as our president, could we?

In 2016, we replaced the country's first Black president with a man who promised to Make America Great Again, a campaign slogan that was a blaring dog whistle appeal to white America. By 2020, Trump's priorities were clear: he cared about the economy (so long as he could take credit for its success), his base of white male Republicans, and himself though not necessarily in that order. By March of that year, the nation was under lockdown, suffering through a pandemic that made the nation's racial disparities painfully clear. As COVID-19, job loss, and police brutality cases racked the country's Black communities, the *New York Times* declared a "pandemic within a pandemic," with Mike Griffin, a Black community organizer, telling a *Times* reporter, "I'm just as likely to die from a cop as I am from COVID." Racial disparities in the COVID-19 death rate contradicted the idea that COVID was "the great equalizer." According to a 2020 data report in the *New York Times*, Latino and Black residents of the United States have been three times as likely to become infected with COVID as their white neighbors and are nearly twice as likely to die from the virus as white people.

By the time of George's murder, people had been on edge for months: jobs had been lost, child-care responsibilities were taxing families, schools were closed, and people were literally dying from COVID, unable to breathe. Most of us were stuck at home, anxious and consuming media at an alarming rate. According to Nielsen, the data and market measurement firm, news was the most popular TV genre viewed in 2020, with consumption increasing in the second quarter to over 47 percent of American households watching or streaming news shows. It was in the context of this national climate that the video of George's murder spread like wildfire. Not only was the video egregious and emotionally disturbing but it also fit inside a pattern of abuse and hostility that more Americans were acknowledging publicly: in February of 2020, Ahmaud Arbery, a twenty-five-year-old Black man, had been killed while jogging. And in March, Breonna Taylor was shot and killed by Louisville police officers during a botched raid on her apartment. Taken back-to-back, the message was clear: Black men and women were targets. It didn't matter whether you were going for a run, sleeping in your own bed, or being arrested. It was as good a time as ever to rise up. All our usual distractions—championship games, concerts, blockbuster Hollywood films—were gone. There was nothing else going on *but* this. Our collective attention was focused on George Floyd in a way that it wasn't for Eric Garner. Justice for George became a catchall, a stand-in for all the brothers and sisters whose due process had been delayed or overlooked.

Gianna may have said it best when she said her daddy was gonna change the world. She was right. It was incumbent on us to shepherd through that change, turning, as Gwen would say, our sorrow into strategy so that George's day in court would make us witnesses to change ourselves. His victory would belong to everyone.

3

THINGS WORSE
THAN DEATH

"Our lives begin to end the day we become silent about things that matter."

—MARTIN LUTHER KING JR.

I first met Mamie Till-Mobley in Chicago in 1997 when I attended a meeting with her and PepsiCo officials to discuss an ad campaign they planned to run that contained offensive rap lyrics about the 1955 murder of her son, Emmett Till. The ad also featured questionable content about the history of civil rights. The meeting was less about wanting to punish individual rappers than it was about trying to turn the controversy into a cultural teaching moment. It ended up being a positive meeting, with PepsiCo apologizing to the Till family, and Mamie and I spending some time together. I had many questions I wanted to ask Mamie about her life, but it wasn't the appropriate time nor place to voice them. We kept our conversation to the issue at hand.

One year later, James Byrd Jr. was murdered by three white supremacists in Jasper, Texas; they dragged Byrd in chains three miles behind their pickup truck, dismembering his body. It was a heinous crime, a modern-day lynching-by-dragging. We flew in Mamie and other members of the Till family for Byrd's funeral at the Greater New Bethel Baptist Church in Jasper, the pews filled with small-town family and friends and big-city politicians and celebrities. Basketball star Dennis Rodman paid for the family's funeral expenses and fight promoter Don King later helped start an education fund for Byrd's children. Two of Byrd's killers, Lawrence Brewer and John King, were sentenced to death by a jury of eleven whites and one Black, making Brewer and King the first white men to receive such a sentence for killing a Black person in the history of modern Texas. The third killer, Shawn Berry, was sentenced to life in prison. Eleven years later, in 2009, President Obama signed the Matthew Shepard and James Byrd Jr. Hate Crimes Prevention Act, commonly known as the Matthew Shepard Act, into law. (Matthew Shepard was a gay University of Wyoming student, who was beaten, tortured, and left tied to a barbed-wire fence to die in Laramie, Wyoming, in 1998.) Though it was eleven years late in the making, the legislation was still a victory.

At Byrd's funeral, Reverend Jesse Jackson and I both took to the pulpit. Jesse's voice reverberated in the small church as he spoke. He said, "Dr. King would say that unearned suffering is redemptive, that there's power in the blood of the innocent. Brother Byrd's innocent blood alone could very well be the blood that changes the course of our country, because no one has captured the nation's attention like this tragedy." The same thing could have been said about the blood of Emmett Till or the extinguishing breath of George Floyd. Perhaps because of the emotional nature of us being together at Byrd's funeral, Mamie and I spoke a bit more freely with one another this second time around. She told me the broad strokes of her son's murder, a story intimately known to most Black Americans and certainly, by that time, to me.

I was born in 1954 and Emmett had been murdered the following year. It wasn't until I was in middle school that I first heard the story of his killing in church. Mamie Till-Mobley and I both happened to belong to the same denomination. She was a member of Bishop Louis Henry Ford's Church of God in Christ in South Side Chicago and, before becoming a Baptist, I was a boy preacher at Washington Temple Church of God in Christ in Brooklyn. The Emmett Till story had been passed down from one generation of the denomination to the next, with an important distinction: our church was woven into the story itself. In 1955, Church of God in Christ wasn't particularly active in civil rights and politics and so, when Bishop Ford broke rank to help politicize Emmett's murder, allowing Mamie to hold the open-casket funeral at the South Side Chicago church where he was bishop, it was a big deal. For us, the Church of God in Christ's involvement in the Emmett Till story solidified the fact that we, as believers and congregants, were working on the right side of the Lord. Bishop Washington often preached the story from the pulpit in Brooklyn. My mother, being a devout, church-going woman, took the man's words to heart, and made sure I did, too. My ears pricked up whenever he talked about Emmett. How could they not? The story of his murder was both horrific and riveting.

Till, a fourteen-year-old Black boy from Chicago, was visiting relatives in Money, Mississippi, for the summer when he encountered Carolyn Bryant, a white woman, who was tending her family's shop. Whether Emmett really flirted with Bryant, whistled at her, or unintentionally touched her hand—something not allowed in the South—when he exchanged his money for candy it mattered less than the fact that four days later, Bryant's husband, Roy, and Roy's half brother, J. W. "Big" Milam, both known segregationists, seized Emmett from his uncle's house under the cover of darkness. Three days later Robert Hodges, a teenage fisherman, found Emmett's corpse in the Tallahatchie River. A seventy-five-pound metal fan, the kind used to ventilate cotton gins, was tied around his neck with several feet of barbed wire. Besides having been shot in the head, his body had been brutally beaten and was waterlogged almost beyond recognition. He was identified by the silver ring on his finger that had belonged to his deceased father, Louis Till, and bore the initials "L.T." Mamie and I didn't talk about those painful details, nor did we speak about the trial of her son's murderers, the not-guilty verdict delivered by an all-white, all-male jury after sixty-seven minutes of deliberation. (One juror indicated they would have been done sooner but were encouraged to take their time to make it look like more deliberation took place.) Instead, we spoke about the importance of bearing witness to atrocities like the murder of her son and that of James Byrd Jr.

James Byrd Jr.'s sister Carol and other members of his family had been made uncomfortable by the public attention and media storm that followed Byrd's death. Their feelings of discomfort, and of wanting to be left alone, were understandable given their grief. Mamie's stance had been the exact opposite of theirs when Emmett was killed: not only did she demand an open-casket funeral for her son, but she'd also actively pursued the Chicago media, encouraging journalists to pick up the story and giving her permission to *Jet* magazine to publish photographs, both close-ups and a full-body shot, that showed the horrific remains of her son's corpse. "I want the world to see this, because there's no way I can tell this story and give them the visual picture of what my son looked like," she'd said. Those photographs changed everything. They were passed around at barbershops, beauty parlors, college campuses, and Black churches, affecting millions of people, Black Americans especially. As Representative Charles Diggs said in 1987, "I think the picture in *Jet* magazine showing Emmett Till's mutilation was probably the greatest media product in the last forty or fifty years." Television coverage would also help turn the story into an international media circus, with countries around the world asking how America, which was supposed to represent the lofty ideals of equality and freedom, could maintain such a blatant system of racism and hatred upon its very citizens.

In many respects, Mamie's decision, and the way it would galvanize the civil rights movement of the 1950s and 1960s, became the playbook for another generation of leaders like myself, who came up in the aftermath of that first wave of activism. The spark that Mamie Till had lit worked: in confronting the gruesome truth of her son's murder, Emmett became a son to us all. He, like George Floyd would nearly seventy years later, became a martyr for the movement, a reason for us all to work together. Or as Mamie put it, "I have invested a son in freedom and I'm determined that his death isn't in vain." Transportation Secretary Rodney Slater had expressed a similar statement at James Byrd Jr.'s funeral, addressing Byrd's sister Clara and saying, "We know, Clara, that you wanted to be left alone. But we can't. We have to be with you. We have to be with this family and we have to be here in Jasper. Because we can ill afford to have what has happened here happen any place else across this land."

Listen, I get it. The Byrd family had to continue living in Jasper among their white neighbors and colleagues long after the media and people like myself had left town. The family's discomfort spoke to a larger historical pattern of fear and intimidation that was particularly prominent in the South: it wasn't uncommon for Black folks to go "missing" only to turn up later found in dark rivers or hung from bridges. It also wasn't uncommon for victims' relatives and friends, out of fear for their own lives, to stay quiet about it. Once common in the South, the days of the old spectacle lynchings were gone but not forgotten. Victims' body parts used to be taken as souvenirs by mobs, bands played and politicians barnstormed before mass lynchings, and photographs of the bodies were bought and sold. By Till's time, these mass spectacles had disappeared. In their place, it was expected that the lynching or beating of any individual would

be a more discreet affair, a secret kept between the perpetrators and the victims' families. Several witnesses in the Till case
were forced to leave Mississippi for their own protection, having broken the unspoken code of the South. The sad fact that
so many generations of Southerners had stayed quiet about the
violence they witnessed or experienced for themselves firsthand
had the effect of making it seem like race relations weren't really as bad as they were.

Before she'd refused to give up her seat on that bus in Alabama, Rosa Parks was a member of the Montgomery branch
of the NAACP, working as its secretary and as a youth council adviser for the area. In a transcript of cut remarks she made
for Henry Hampton's 1985 multipart documentary *Eyes on the
Prize: America's Civil Rights Years (1954–1965)*, she noted that one
of the reasons Montgomery was considered to have better race
relations than some of the other cities in the South was because
witnesses to crimes and victims' family members were often
"too intimidated to sign an affidavit, or to make a statement to
let it be known what had happened." Emmett was undoubtedly
in Rosa's thoughts when she performed her now-famous act of
civil disobedience, but she was also thinking about the other
unknown Black folks who'd been beaten, tortured, and killed.
After all, Emmett was far from being the first Black boy or man
killed by white men who wanted to uphold the racist traditions
of white supremacy. His murder was one in a long line reaching
back to the earliest days of American slavery and continues still
today. Only thirteen years before Emmett's murder, the South
had been rocked by another particularly gruesome crime: two
fourteen-year-old boys, Charlie Lang and Ernest Green, were
seen playing with a white girl near a bridge in Mississippi. After
being charged with rape, a white mob seized them from the
jail in Quitman, brutalized their bodies, going so far as cutting
off their reproductive organs and using pliers to pull off their
flesh. They were then hung from the same bridge where they'd

been with the white girl, which happened to be a well-known lynching site in Clarke County. A story like that doesn't just disappear, though at the time white newspapers tried to bury it. Black newspapers, however, printed photos of the boys' lynching. Even if they wanted to, it was impossible for Black families to forget so much pain. It adds up to a form of generational trauma that haunts us still.

In that same documentary, Parks commented on another murder she'd heard of that happened in Montgomery months before Emmett had died. The man who'd been killed was, according to Parks, "a young minister who had a singing group."

"My husband knew him and his mother," she explained. She went on to tell the production team that, for reasons not entirely known but most likely arising from the Black minister working with a white woman on church songs, "some white men took him out to the Alabama River on a bridge and he supposedly jumped over into the river. They told his mother she'd better keep quiet about it, which she did." The difference between the Emmett Till case and this one was, in her words, because "Emmett Till came from the North and the media picked it up." Being from Chicago, Mamie didn't abide by the same kind of rules that governed the Southern way of life. People have argued that, for the same reason, Emmett was particularly vulnerable. Not knowing the ways of the South, he could have been more cavalier in his attitude toward Carolyn Bryant, and that could have been the very thing that got him killed. But Chicago had its fair share of racism, too, with a long history of racial upheavals, most notably the race riot of 1919.

On July 27, 1919, a Black teenager named Eugene Williams accidentally drifted his wooden raft into a segregated beach on Lake Michigan. A white man threw a rock at Williams's head, and he drowned. Rather than arresting the white assailant, the police instead hauled off a Black bystander. The spark of injustice fanned to five days of rioting, with the police shooting seven

Blacks dead, white mobs killing sixteen, and Black mobs, in return, killing fifteen whites. More than five hundred citizens were injured, two-thirds of them Black, and thousands became homeless because of arson. By the time of Emmett's murder in 1955, these events may have felt like ancient history, but the damage had been done. Violence—the threat of it, the memory of it, the anticipation of it—had become the undercurrent that fed into the lives of most Black Americans, whether you were from the North or the South. That said, there were unmistakable differences in the style, deployment, and codes of racism between the two. Listen: racism is racism. A possible wolf whistle doesn't warrant the murder of a fourteen-year-old boy. William Faulkner wrote, "If we in America have reached that point in our desperate culture when we must murder children, no matter for what reason or what color, then we don't deserve to survive, and probably won't." Roy Wilkins of the NAACP put it more bluntly: "The state of Mississippi has decided to maintain white supremacy by murdering children." In 1981, Clarksdale NAACP leader Aaron Henry told an interviewer, "Emmett Till was, you know, that sort of strange phenomenon. White folks have been killing Black boys all my life, throwing them in rivers, burying them... Just why the Emmett Till murder captured the conscience of the nation, I don't know. It could have been that it was the beginning of television and people could see things. The fact that a Black boy was killed by white men wasn't nothing unusual."

MAKE A WAY OUTTA NO WAY

The third time I met Mamie Till-Mobley was when I brought her and James Byrd Sr. to the House of Justice in Harlem, New York, to help drum up support for memorial and education funds for James Byrd Jr.'s children. It was at this third meeting that Mamie and I talked at length about civil rights and the impact her son's murder had had on the movement at large. Mamie reminded me of Coretta Scott King in that I always felt I had to be on my best behavior around both women. Mamie had what I affectionately call a church mother's voice—she sounded powerful, determined, even when she whispered. I halfway expected her to either break out in prayer or a gospel song in the middle of us talking, and you'd better believe I sat up straight in my seat whenever she was around. She sounded so much like a preacher that I found myself doing more listening than talking; it's never good to have two preachers at the same pulpit. At that time in her life, she favored African print dresses and colorful geles that she would tie atop her head, a regal-looking outfit that conveyed authoritative respect. Even dressed in African garb, however, Mamie still looked the part of a classic, churchgoing woman, same as any I'd known my whole life. Hers was a steady presence, solid.

Mamie had known I'd become a Baptist, but she still thought of me as her compatriot in the Church of God in Christ, saying things like, "He might look like a Baptist and he might sound like one, too, but you know deep down he still belongs to us!" She and I talked about the fact that there was no civil rights movement before she opened that casket. Yes, *Brown v. Board of Education* had passed the year before her son's murder, and its passage definitely got things moving. But there were no large-scale civil rights marches, no Freedom Riders, no Montgomery bus boycott, until Mamie, with little formal support or experience of her own, championed her son's story, visiting churches and town halls across the country to share her outrage, sadness, and her determination for a better future. While she did much of the initial heavy lifting on her own, the NAACP, under Medgar Evers's charge as field secretary for Mississippi, was also involved in the case, with Evers, along with field workers Ruby Hurley and Amzie Moore and local doctor and businessman T. R. M. Howard secretly searching for Black witnesses to stand up and testify. They eventually found Willie Reed, the prosecution's only witness who could tie Milam and Bryant to the scene of the crime. (Reed had heard someone being beaten in Milam's barn during the night in question, and then saw Milam go in and out of the barn.) Before the NAACP's involvement, however, Mamie largely shouldered the cause on her own. There was no Southern Christian Leadership Conference (SCLC). No PR team swooped in to help her manage the media as myself and other civil rights organizations have in place to help victims' families today. Beyond the counsel she sought out herself, there were no strategy meetings. The thing I couldn't wrap my head around was how, with no crowds to stand up to and a civil rights movement straining to catch up to her, she'd found the courage within herself to look hatred in the eye.

"How did you do it?" I'd asked her. "Where did you get the strength?"

Her answer was movingly simple. "It was only because I believed in God and only because I'm a true believer that I knew God would make a way," she'd said. She'd acted on raw faith. It made sense to me then why she'd been so elated that she and I had belonged to the same church: the church had been her foundation. Because of the support she'd had from other believers, she'd been able to both keep her belief strong and keep herself strong in her belief, and thank God she had because the Emmett Till case was a watershed moment in our country's history. It was a gamechanger, helping to inform much of the strategic playbook that civil rights leaders like myself still use today. Mamie modeled how to leverage media attention into on-the-ground, grassroots activism while pressing for victory both in the legal courtroom and in the court of public opinion. The Emmett Till case was ground zero for our future work. We took her model and built on it. Today, we partner with political allies as well as with on-the-ground activists and faith communities because we know it's not enough to focus on victory in the courtroom: we must win the heart of the people while pushing for lasting legislative change.

None of that is possible if we choose to look the other way. If Mamie hadn't done what she did, her son would have been just another murdered Black boy, his story drowned out by the muddy backwaters of the Tallahatchie. She didn't stay silent. She spoke up. She said, "Look at what you did to my boy," and, just as I did when she visited me in my Harlem office, the world stopped to listen.

Our conversation stayed in my thoughts for several days. I was humbled and awestruck by the traits in Mamie that I would later see expressed in both Gwen Carr and Philonise Floyd. They reminded me of one another, sharing a similar sense of determination. All three—Mamie, Gwen, and Philonise—had a fire inside them, a restlessness that told me they wouldn't give up until justice was served. Mamie wasn't going to rest until the rest of the world saw what had happened to Emmett. The same can be said for Gwen and Philonise with respect to Eric and George. They were ordinary people, going about their normal lives, working, raising their families, and trying to navigate life as best they could, who were then thrust into extraordinary circumstances. In the pain of losing their loved ones, Mamie, Gwen, and Philonise could have shrunk from the moment. Instead, they discovered their calling and built a movement. In aligning themselves with a newfound sense of purpose, they found life in the death of their loved ones. Mamie could have been speaking for them all when she said, "Mine is not just the passion of an aggrieved mother. This should be the sentiment of an entire nation. As long as the Emmett Till murder is unresolved, this case will sit there like a thorn in the side of our sense of justice and fair play.... Without a resolution, we can never be at ease."

As amazing as Mamie's bravery was, hers was not the only profile in courage. Reverend Moses Wright, Emmett's uncle, had not only personally known Emmett's murderers, but also testified against them before a courtroom filled with hostile white neighbors and known segregationists. The fact that Wright, a man the townsfolk called the "Preacher," did so is somewhat unbelievable. How did he summon the inner fortitude to break the Southern code of silence and how was he not killed himself?

The Preacher:
Reverend Moses Wright

Known simply as the Preacher because he often held mass at the Church of God in Christ, a simple one-room rural church building not far from his home, Reverend Moses Wright was a sixty-four-year-old sharecropper who'd lived his entire life in the Mississippi Delta. His son Simeon said this about his father in a 2011 interview for *American History TV*: "Well, my father, he was what we call kind of a hard man. Fair. Someone that's tough but fair.... He loved farming. He was honest.... He was a hard worker and he enjoyed to see when cotton would begin to grow in Mississippi, he just became excited. And I couldn't figure out why. But that's the kind of man he was. He enjoyed the farming and told my mother, said, 'Hey, I was born and bred in Mississippi. Mississippi I'm going to die.'" According to Timothy B. Tyson, author of *The Blood of Emmett Till,* Wright had never had trouble with white people before the incident with Emmett. Maybe that's because he was seen as being the model Southern Negro, still working the cotton fields and staying outta people's business. As if to confirm this, at the murder trial District Attorney Gerald Chatham addressed him as Uncle Mose or Ole Man Mose.

Rows of cotton stretched out behind the Wright family's simple-looking four-bedroom house, the nicest of all the tenant houses on the G. C. Frederick Plantation. In August 1955, the Wright house was cramped. In addition to himself, his wife, Elizabeth, and his three children, three other boys were visiting for the summer: two of Wright's grandsons and his nephew Emmett, or "Bobo" as the family called him. It was Wright who had first encouraged Emmett to come visit Mississippi for the summer, enticing the young boy with his stories of lazy-day fishing in the nearby lakes or from one of the rivers, the Yazoo, the Sunflower, or the Tallahatchie. Wright put all the boys to work in the cotton fields when Emmett arrived. On Wednesday, August 24, the boys had spent the day picking cotton before making their way to Bryant's Grocery and Meat Market in Money.

Despite the drowsy atmosphere of the Delta, news traveled fast, and by evening, Wright had already heard about Emmett's brushup at the store from several Black witnesses who'd been outside visiting with one another, playing checkers and passing the time. It didn't sound like anything serious, though, so Wright didn't give it much thought. It was only when Wright heard the unmistakable thud of heavy work boots on his front porch at two in the morning on Sunday, August 28, that he knew Emmett was in trouble. Elizabeth later told reporters, "We knew they were out to mob the boy." She tried to hustle Emmett out of the house and into the cotton fields, where he could hide, but the sleepy boy was too slow, and probably didn't understand the urgency. Wright, meanwhile, tried to stall Bryant and Milam, who stood on his doorstep carrying US Army–issued .45 automatics and reeking of whiskey. In the distance, Wright saw a third man, whom he said in the trial transcript of his testimony "acted like a colored man," most likely one of the Black men who worked for Milam.

"We want to see the boy from Chicago," Milam said.

Wright slowly let the men inside. The scene quickly turned chaotic as they marched around the rooms, flashlights beaming and pistols blared. Elizabeth offered the men money to leave Emmett alone. Wright suggested they rough him up with a good whipping and be done with it. According to Simeon, Milam asked Wright how old he was.

"Sixty-four," the man answered.

"If you tell anybody about this, you won't live to see sixty-five."

Emmett, who was still rousing himself from the bedroom, didn't say a word. Bryant and Milam hauled him to a car waiting outside.

"Is this the boy?"

A voice from inside the car answered, "Yes." It's later been speculated, though never proven, that this voice belonged to Carolyn Bryant. If so, she'd be an accessory to the crime.

The car pulled away with its headlights off. Simeon said, "We never saw Emmett alive again. But in that house that night, I never went back to sleep." Elizabeth feared for their lives, and convinced her husband to take her to Sumner, Mississippi, where her brother lived. She stayed there until Emmett's body was found. Then she left for Chicago. She never set foot in that house again. Simeon said, "So we was there in Mississippi with no mother. No one to sing [to us]. It was terrible.... We got through it. But it was tough. It was tough."

Moses Wright was the first witness called in the trial. He took the stand, and when questioned as to whether the men who kidnapped Emmett were in the courtroom, he set a precedent in Mississippi history. According to Ellen Whitten of the Winter Institute "not only did he identify Milam and Bryant, but he rose from his seat on the witness stand and extended a crooked finger in Milam's direction, saying simply, 'Thar he. And thar's Mr. Bryant.' The already imposing air in the courtroom thickened, as did the blood in the veins of every white man there. Moses Wright had not only testified against a pair of white men, but had looked into their faces and pointed them out." A photographer by the name of Ernest Withers captured the moment when Wright accused Bryant and Milam on film, Wright's long, skinny finger pointing at the men in a gesture of defiance. No doubt everyone in that courtroom knew the gamble Wright had just taken with his own life. He knew the risks as well as anyone. His son explained, saying, "The neighbors were trying to convince him not to testify. They said, 'They'll kill you.' Of course, Medgar Evers encouraged my daddy. They would do all they could to protect him.... He did something that no other Black man had ever done in Mississippi and lived to tell about it." As he testified, Wright did something else remarkable for the time and place: each time Defense Counsel Sidney Canton asked him a question, Wright answered but refrained from addressing the white man as "sir." Maybe Ole Man Mose had more fire in his belly than they'd thought.

Remarkably, Wright didn't go into hiding for the rest of the trial. He didn't hightail it to Chicago. He stayed put, and saw the trial through to its sad end. Tyson wrote, "Every day of the trial he could be seen around the courthouse, wearing blue pants and a crisp white shirt, his pink-banded hat tilted back on his head. Wright seemed transfigured by his bravery on the witness stand." Author Dan Wakefield confirmed this imagery, writing for the *Nation*, "He walked through the Negro section of the lawn, with his hands in his pockets and his chin held up with the air of a man who has done what there was to do and could never be touched by doubt that he should have done anything less." The day before Mamie Till took the stand, Wright stood alone outside the courtroom. Some members of the United Packinghouse Workers of America delegation from Louisiana came up to him and one, a man by the name of Frank Brown, asked Wright where he'd found the courage to testify.

"Some things are worse than death," he replied. "If a man lives, he must still live with himself." Wright knew with near-absolute certainty who butchered and killed his nephew. He also knew that the men would likely get away with it. But Wright didn't back down; it wasn't his way. "I wasn't exactly brave and I wasn't scared," he said later. "I just wanted to see justice done."

Convinced no one would be convicted, Mamie wasn't in the courtroom when the verdict was read. She was already making her way to Tunica, Mississippi, and planning her next move. Simeon said, "Daddy was crushed at that verdict. Yet from what I learned later, he had an idea what was going to take place. But it still crushed him." Wright wanted to stay in Money long enough to harvest his cotton crop, telling *Jet* magazine, "I'm going to keep praying for the day when there's a hollering 'Preacher, Preacher' out my door. And when I look out, I want to see them two white men on their knees begging forgiveness for killing my boy." Milam and Bryant never paid Wright that visit but they were run out of town themselves as their patrons boycotted their places of business. Milam tried to change his line of work to farming but wasn't given enough land to farm on; he was finally able to rent 217 acres in Sun-flower County, but no Blacks would work for him. The Milams eventually moved to Orange, Texas, but didn't last long in the Lone Star State and later returned to Greenville, Mississippi. After a Black boycott forced his store to close only three weeks after the trial, Roy Bryant bounced from job to job, eventually working as a welder and going legally blind as a result of the hazardous conditions of his job. The family also moved to Orange, Texas, and then relocated to Ruleville, Mississippi, the Bryant marriage eventually ending in divorce.

After the trial, Willie Reed, the surprise witness for the prosecution, seemingly went about his daily routine, changing into his work clothes to pick cotton. When he got to work, though, he took off running through the fields, trying to get away. Haunted for decades by the beating sounds he'd heard from Milam's barn, he later had a nervous breakdown and was hospitalized in Chicago, telling a reporter in 2007, "That's something you never put out of your mind. I remember it like it happened yesterday." Wright wrestled with leaving Mississippi himself. He went back to work, however, he and his sons picking his twenty-five-acre cotton crop, a shotgun and rifle close at hand. He told folks that the night after the trial, he'd had a dream in which he was told to get out. So, that first night, he left the house and slept in his car about a half mile away near the Church of God in Christ. When he'd returned to his house the next day, he'd discovered it had been ransacked. For a while, he continued to sleep in his car, moving its location from between a rural cemetery and other secret hideouts. It didn't take long for him to finally come to the awful conclusion, telling his boys, "We can't stay here any longer. We have to leave." The family packed up and headed to Illinois, where they met up with Elizabeth.

When asked if Wright ever spoke about Emmett or the trial after they'd left Mississippi, his son said, "No. He never talked about what happened at that store. We never brought it up. Even Emmett's mother—we never talked about it. But Daddy, he put his life on the line. He was so devastated. You know, it's like sending your son to care with someone else and your son come up killed or murdered. It destroys you. It tears your heart apart. He was willing to die to bring justice for Emmett Till."

Wright never returned to Mississippi and stopped preaching, though he remained a man of faith. He worked odd jobs and lived a quiet life outside of the public eye, except for having gone on a month-long speaking tour with the NAACP in November 1955. Big-city living proved difficult, but Wright made the most of it, gardening a small parcel of land near the railroads. Wright's son Simeon still visits Mississippi every now and again, telling a reporter, "Well, in one sense, it's a place of horror, but in another, it was a place where I was born and raised and all of my childhood, the good memories, they are still there. And the bad memories. And if I go down a dark-filled road my wife says a whole new spirit comes over me. I told her one day, 'I'm from this dirt.'" Simeon said he never understood why his father had loved sharecropping so but he had. No doubt Wright must have missed his plot of Southern land, the acres of dirt he'd transformed into white seas of cotton. On the one hand, sharecropping had made Wright a relic to the old Southern way of life, but his bravery had set him apart, helping to loosen the ties that bound. He died at the age of eighty in 1977.

The Civil Rights Showman:
Theodore Roosevelt Mason (T. R. M.) Howard

T. R. M. Howard was an unlikely civil rights hero. A wealthy Black surgeon and businessman, he was known for his expensive Cadillacs and impressible wardrobe. Howard gambled on horses, owned a one-thousand-acre plantation, hunted big game in Africa, and, despite the outsized ego that often accompanies a larger-than-life personality, also remained deeply committed to the community, running a successful hospital that offered quality affordable health care. He'd been born into poverty in Murray, Kentucky, where his father worked as a tobacco twister and his mother worked as a cook for Will Mason, a prominent white doctor. Hiring him to do menial medical jobs, Mason soon saw potential in the boy, and eventually helped pay for his formal medical education. Howard was so grateful that he added "Mason" to his name. Before settling in Mississippi, Howard attended three Adventist colleges: the all-Black Oakwood College in Huntsville, Alabama; Union College in Lincoln, Nebraska; and the College of Medical Evangelists in Loma Linda, California. His activism began in earnest while he was in California, where he wrote a regular column for the *California Eagle*, the main Black newspaper of Los Angeles.

In 1935, he married the Black socialite Helen Boyd and became chief surgeon at the hospital of the International Order of Twelve Knights and Daughters of Tabor, a fraternal organization, in the all-Black town of Mound Bayou, Mississippi, where he also made a name for himself in the world of business. Within five years, he'd founded an insurance company, a hospital, a home construction firm, a restaurant with a beer garden, and a large and prosperous farm on which he raised cattle, quail, hunting dogs, and cotton. He also maintained a thriving personal practice, where he performed discreet illegal abortions to both Black and white patients, a practice he advocated as being a matter of individual rights and family planning. A man of eccentricity, he also built a small zoo, a park, and Mississippi's first Olympic-sized swimming pool for Blacks between Edwards and West Main Street. God calls on some people to do big things in life, and Howard, I believe, got that special calling. In the grand sweep of history, he seemed to be in the right place at the right time for greatness.

In 1952, Howard hired the recent Alcorn College graduate Medgar Evers as an agent for his Magnolia Mutual Life Insurance. Evers visited plantations in his insurance territory near Clarksdale and, with Howard's full backing, promoted an agenda of civil rights as he sold policies and collected premiums. When Howard later cofounded the Regional Council of Negro Leadership (RCNL) with Amzie Moore and Aaron Henry, the charismatic Evers became one of the group's first officials, helping to launch what would become several successful boycotts against segregated service stations. The RCNL was a kind of homegrown NAACP that sought to appeal to white neighbors as much as to Black folks, with an added emphasis on improving the economic conditions for every citizen in the Mississippi Delta. For their first large-scale boycotting effort, Evers and Howard distributed over fifty thousand bumper stickers with the slogan Don't Buy Gas Where You Can't Use the Restroom. Howard soon hired Evers's wife, Myrlie, to be his secretary and, truly a businessman and a doctor both, delivered two of her three children. Speaking of Howard, Myrlie said, "One look told you that he was a leader: kind, affluent, and intelligent, that rare Negro in Mississippi who had somehow beaten the system." Howard would go on to similarly mentor the young Fannie Lou Hamer, the voting and women's rights activist.

Perhaps more impressive than the boycotting campaign were the RCNL's rallies, which took place under a massive circus tent on Howard's plantation. The affair was akin to a Southern church revival, complete with barbeque ribs and fried chicken, speakers, and musical performances. Author Timothy B. Tyson writes: "At the RCNL's first conference in 1952, Representative William Dawson from Chicago became the first Black congressman to speak in Mississippi since the Reconstruction, addressing a crowd of seven thousand. The great gospel singer Mahalia Jackson appeared alongside him. At the third conference, only ten days before the historic victory in *Brown*, Thurgood Marshall spoke to roughly eight thousand attendees, accompanied by eight school bands and the sixty-piece marching band from Tennessee A&I State University, which led the 'Great Freedom Parade' down Main Street while Howard and Moore waved from a convertible."

By the time Emmett Till was murdered, Howard had already amassed a certain amount of clout in the Black activist circles, his council having been instrumental for countless rallies and voter registration pushes, drawing speakers like Representative William Dawson and alderman Archibald Carey, both of Chicago; Representative Charles Diggs of Michigan; and Thurgood Marshall of the National Association for the Advancement of Colored People (NAACP). When Mamie Till-

Mobley came to Mississippi to testify in her son's trial, Howard offered up his home to her as a command center, where Black journalists and other out-of-state observers gathered. Not only did Howard bankroll and assist in the investigation, but he also acted as an informal chief of security, shepherding witnesses and supporters to and from the courthouse under the cover of a heavily armored caravan. During the trial, Howard's home was like a compound, with Howard himself sleeping with a Thompson submachine gun at the foot of his bed, a .357 Magnum revolver on one bedside table, and a .45 semiautomatic on the other. A rifle or shotgun stood in all four corners of the bedroom and throughout every other room in the house. An armed man sat twenty-four hours a day at a guardhouse stationed on the driveway. Howard always believed that more people had been involved in the crime than the two white half brothers, Milam and Bryant. Upon their acquittal, Howard commented that a white man was less likely to be punished for killing a Black boy than for "killing deer out of season."

Weeks after the trial, Howard embarked on a cross-country speaking tour, demanding a federal investigation into the murder. It was while he was speaking to an overflow crowd at Dexter Avenue Baptist Church in Montgomery, Alabama, the host of which was a largely unknown twenty-six-year-old pastor named Martin Luther King Jr., that audience member Rosa Parks first heard Howard's powerful firsthand account of Emmett's murder. She'd read about the lynching and had seen the photographs in *Jet* magazine, but it was another thing entirely to hear about it from someone who'd been there. Four days later, Parks refused to give up her seat on a segregated bus in Montgomery. Howard's tour culminated in a rally for twenty thousand at Madison Square Garden, where, as the featured speaker, he shared the stage with Adam Clayton Powell Jr., A. Philip Randolph, the former first lady Eleanor Roosevelt, and Autherine Lucy, the first Black student to attend the University of Alabama in 1956. Facing death threats upon himself and his family, Howard sold off nearly eight hundred acres of land and moved, first to California and then to Chicago, where he opened a medical practice and went into politics, helping to found the Chicago League of Negro Voters and being an early contributor to the Chicago chapter of the SCLC's Operation Breadbasket under Jesse Jackson.

Howard made a lot of people uncomfortable—most famously J. Edgar Hoover, director of the FBI, whom Howard blamed as being too slow to address the murders of Blacks in the South. Hoover released an open letter denouncing Howard for his "intemperate and baseless charges" and for his "disservice to common decency." Thurgood Marshall occasionally bristled against Howard, attacking him as a "rugged individualist" and a maverick with too strong a military tone. Others, like Jesse Jackson, disliked the fact that he continued to perform abortions throughout his career. (He was arrested, though not convicted, twice in Chicago for providing the service.) Howard regarded this work as being complementary to his civil rights activism, viewing both as fights for freedom; in Howard's work and life, civil rights and women's rights converged. In 1972, he funded the multi-million-dollar Friendship Medical Center on Chicago's South Side, the largest privately owned Black clinic in the city. He died on May 1, 1976, in Chicago, with Jesse Jackson, who'd once picketed against Howard's medical clinics, officiating his funeral.

TURNING MOURNING INTO MOVEMENT

At a rally in Cleveland, Ohio, on September 18, 1955, at the Antioch Baptist Church, Mamie shared her story of how Emmett's death turned her maternal grief into a call for action on a global level. She said, "Two months ago, I had a nice six-room apartment in Chicago. I had a good job. I had a son. When something happened to Negroes in the South, I said, 'That's their business, not mine.' Now I know how wrong I was. The death of my son has shown me that what happen[s] to any of us, anywhere in the world, had better be the business of all of us." Her words would help galvanize a civil rights movement that, up until Emmett's murder, had been building but hadn't yet found its footing. Things moved quickly: two days after the verdict had been reached, A. Philip Randolph, president of the Sleeping Car Porters, organized a protest rally in a Harlem church. Protests began to spring up all over the country. In short order, the Women's Democratic Council, under Jo Ann Robinson, called for a citywide bus boycott and asked a young, twenty-six-year-old minister to help. That minister's name was Reverend Martin Luther King Jr.

King had been deeply moved by the Emmett Till case, delivering a sermon called "Pride Versus Humility: The Parable of the Pharisee and the Publican" at Montgomery's Dexter Avenue Baptist Church, saying, "The white men who lynch Negroes worship Christ. That jury in Mississippi, which a few days ago in the Emmett Till case freed two white men from what might be considered one of the most brutal and inhuman crimes of the twentieth century, worships Christ.... The trouble with these people, however, is that they worship Christ emotionally and not morally. They cast his ethical and moral insights behind the gushing smoke of emotional adoration and ceremonial piety." Eight years later, on the anniversary of Emmett Till's murder, Dr. King would stand at the base of the Lincoln Memorial to deliver his "I Have a Dream" speech. The Emmett Till case still rivets today: following Keith Beauchamp's documentary *The Untold Story of Emmett Louis Till*, which claimed that at least seven people were involved in Till's murder, the United States Department of Justice reopened the case in 2004 though eventually determining there was no federal jurisdiction; in 2007, a state grand jury in Mississippi, to which the case had been referred, decided not to issue charges. In 2018, the Till family pushed for a new investigation, the results of which are still pending. Beyond the case's legal reverberations, however, was the lasting shock and impact of the crime itself. As recently as 2014, when the local grand jury decided not to prosecute the police officer who had fatally shot Michael Brown in Ferguson, Missouri, hundreds of protesters gathered in front of the White House and across the country, chanting, "How many Black kids will you kill? Michael Brown, Emmett Till!"

Today, the Emmett Till of our time is George Floyd. Neither Emmett nor George knew anything about being a symbol for change, but they were, nonetheless. The nation lifted them up. Similarly, the Mothers of the Movement are today's equivalent of Mamie Till. Just as Till became a driving force for change in the civil rights movement of the 1950s and 1960s, our collective mourning for George has likewise become a modern-day movement for justice.

It was impossible for me not to think of Eric Garner and Emmett Till as I prepared to head to Minneapolis to lend my support to the Floyd family during the 2021 trial of Derek Chauvin. Despite the overwhelming evidence, the perpetrators in the killings of both Eric and Emmett had gotten away with murder. I comforted myself with the reminder that, at least in the case of James Byrd Jr., the murderers were brought to justice. As I packed my suitcase for Minneapolis, I steeled myself for what would undoubtedly be a difficult journey.

4

A RECKONING

"We must rebuild, restore, and reimagine the relationship between law enforcement and the communities they serve. We must tackle racial inequalities in every corner of society—from health to home ownership to education. We must come together around our common humanity."

—MINNESOTA GOVERNOR TIM WALZ

March 8, 2021, marked the first day of the trial for Derek Chauvin, the *State of Minnesota v. Derek Michael Chauvin*. The Floyd family, Ben Crump, and I planned to hold a press conference in front of the Hennepin County Government Center after opening statements were made on March 29, 2021. As we approached the government center that day, I was shocked by the level of lockdown. We already knew security was going to be tight but extra precautions had been put in place because of the insurrection at the US Capitol in January. Barricades surrounded the perimeter of the center and barbed wire had been added to the fencing. The place looked like a fortress, and it felt as if we'd entered a war zone. Few people were out and about and those who were were dressed in uniform, standing guard or checking for people's identification. Days before jury selection had begun, the enclosed twin-tower government building was closed off to just about everyone, including the twenty-five hundred people who normally work there. As Chief Hennepin County District Judge Toddrick Barnette said, "The fear of having the government center overrun is real."

The courthouse had cleared out a room on another floor for the Floyd family and its legal counsel, including Ben Crump and his assistants, to convene. It was in this so-called Family Room that I joined them to prepare for the day's press conference. A room was also made available for the defense. The prosecution was overseen by Attorney General Keith Ellison. His team included lead prosecutor Assistant Attorney General Matthew Frank, Jerry Blackwell, Steven Schleicher, and Erin Eldridge. A separate team of attorneys assisted in shaping the legal strategies and motions. In the lead-up to the trial, Ellison invited Gwen Carr to speak to the prosecution team. Neal Katyal, who heard her, said, "It was so spellbinding to listen to her say, 'You're giving me something my son and me never got, a day in court.'" On the other side, Chauvin was represented by attorney Eric Nelson, who was compensated by the Minneapolis Police and Peace Officers Association. The defense was also given a separate room in which to meet, but Chauvin had little visible family support throughout the trial, so I assume it was largely left unused except by Nelson and his associates.

It was the first criminal trial in Minnesota to be televised in its entirety and the first in the state court's history to be broadcast live. Because of COVID-19 and public safety precautions, physical access to the eighteenth-floor courtroom was restricted to about thirty people, including the jurors, defendant, judge, clerks, lawyers, a live cable-television crew, and two rotating seats for the media. The state and defense were permitted a single observer each. Members of the Floyd family would take turns watching the trial, but the duty would largely fall to Philonise, who attended several days of the trial alone, his thoughts, he later told me, often drifting to memories he had of George, and his emotions running wild. A petite, older woman assumed to be related to Chauvin would arrive late in the trial but the observer's seat for the defense would be empty most of the time. I would watch the trial unfold on television like everyone else.

Before starting the news conference, the Floyd family, Ben, and I took a knee for eight minutes and forty-six seconds—the amount of time we'd thought Chauvin had had his knee on George's neck. (Turned out, he'd done so for about a minute more.) I marked each minute aloud as it passed. Standing, I told the journalists that the trial wasn't just about any one white man; America itself was on trial. The world was watching to see whether our country could hold police accountable if they broke the law. The law is for everybody. Policemen aren't above it. Ben elaborated, saying the trial would be a moment for America to show the rest of the world that it remained the "standard-bearer when it comes to liberty and justice for all."

In the first week of the trial, the prosecution called many of the witnesses who had seen the arrest of George in person, their words helping to give a clearer account of the last moments of George's life. The witnesses ran the gamut—from Donald Williams, a security guard with a long background in mixed martial arts, to Christopher Belfrey, a forty-five-year-old man from South Minneapolis, to Genevieve Hansen, an off-duty Minneapolis firefighter, who'd asked the officers to check Floyd's pulse and begin chest compressions. It also became clear just how emotionally jarring it was for them to have seen the murder, with several witnesses, including sixty-one-year-old Charles McMillian, breaking down in tears. The court took a break so McMillian could regain his composure while testifying. He later told the jury that he'd begged George to get up and get into the police cruiser, because, in his words, "Once the police get the cuffs on you, you can't win." Christopher Martin, the young cashier at Cup Foods who'd first suspected the twenty-dollar bill George used to pay for cigarettes was counterfeit, said that he'd wished he hadn't taken the money to begin with. When asked what went through his mind when George was loaded into the ambulance, Martin said, in a soft-spoken voice, "Disbelief and guilt."

Besides the bystanders, use-of-force experts, forensic patholo- gists, medical examiners, doctors, and paramedics took the stand. So did police officers, active and retired, whose job titles ran up and down the chain of command. Of the many individuals who bravely testified, Minneapolis Police Chief Medaria Arradondo stood out. He was unwavering in his condemnation of Chauvin's behavior, a rare rebuke from another officer and a break in the so-called blue wall, the unwritten Code of Silence that exists be- tween officers who don't report abuses of power committed by other officers. Before the trial had even begun, Chief Arradondo had already called Chauvin out. Less than a day after George's death, he fired Chauvin and the three other officers, Thomas Lane, J. Alexander Keung, and Tou Thao, who were present at the scene. He publicly stated that Chauvin's use of force was con- trary to department policy and training. He also addressed the Floyd family directly, expressing his position that all four offi- cers were at fault and called on the FBI to investigate. Chief Ar- radondo is the kind of officer we think of when we talk about a "good cop." His is a lesson in character and compassion both.

The Guardian:
Chief Medaria Arradondo

As the first Black police chief in the history of Minneap- olis, Chief Medaria Arradondo is a fifth-generation Min- nesota resident who worked his way through the police ranks, starting out as a patrol officer in the Fourth Precinct until being named the inspector for the First Precinct. He was appointed chief of police in 2017 after his predecessor, Janeé Harteau, resigned, following the shooting of Justine Ruszczyk by police. Long before he'd taken the stand in the Chauvin trial, Chief Arradondo had already been in the habit of breaking the Code of Silence. He, along with four other Black officers, sued the department in 2007, accusing its leadership of tolerating racism in promotions, pay, and discipline. As police chief, he'd already begun implementing significant changes in the department like requiring officers to turn on their body cameras as soon as they start responding to 911 calls. After the Chauvin trial, he's continued to make changes, acknowledging the distrust between law enforcement and Minneapolis's Black community.

At a news conference on June 10, 2020, Chief Arradondo announced the withdrawal of contract negotiations with the city's police union and restarted an effort to identify troubled police officers through early warning signs, with a particular emphasis on rooting out bad cops and improving the supervisory structure. Recognizing that there's a long road ahead, he admitted, "This will not be accomplished overnight. It will take time. But I am confident that in being both vulnerable in shaping a new paradigm in peacekeeping and courageous in identifying and tearing down those barriers that have crippled the relationships with our communities and that have eroded trust, we will have a police department that our communities view as legitimate, trusting, and working with their best interests at heart." He continued, saying, "American policing in this nation—we have to address the race issue head-on. We are the most visible, first face of government in our communities, and our communities are crying out. They've been doing it certainly with Mr. Floyd's death, but decades before that. We must do better. We have to do better. We have an opportunity not only to change how we do business in terms of being peacekeepers in Minneapolis, but across this nation."

His words are a remarkable assessment on the state of policing today as seen from the point of view of an officer working to change it for the better. He's readily acknowledged that change needs to happen, and that the kind of large-scale reform that's needed depends on common-sense legislation: the enforcement of recent bans on restraints, eliminating the kinds of barriers in place that shield officers from misconduct charges, and police union contracts that allow officers who have been fired or disciplined to get arbitration. As he sees it, it doesn't make sense to demolish the police when the institution can be changed by the good cops already working from the inside, saying, "Our men and women will continue to show up and respond and be guardians of that community when they call us for help." If only more officers would approach their jobs with a peacekeeping mentality—protecting citizens and not harming them, asking questions first and practicing de-escalation techniques before shooting—we may have a police force worthy of their own Oath of Honor, which underscores "the importance of treating all individuals with dignity and respect and ensuring the preservation of human life."

BELIEVE YOUR EYES

Over twenty-three million people watched the verdict being read live on television on the last day of court, April 20, 2021.

Wanting to both offer my support to the Floyd family and to help set a tone of nonviolence no matter the outcome of the verdict, I went to Minneapolis for closing arguments.

Attorney General Keith Ellison provided continual updates to the Floyd family, delivering them in his signature style of measured calm. You got the sense that everyone was walking on eggshells. So, while the fortified exterior of the government center conveyed the public's nervousness about the case, an anxiety about what was about to unfold, inside, the operations were largely carried out with extreme care, with each member of the court acutely aware that they were being watched, which only amplified the seriousness of their proceedings. I was reminded of the supposed decency of Judge Curtis M. Swango in the Emmett Till case; the *New York Post* described him as "a quiet man firmly and graciously committed to a fair trial whatever the verdict." The man's demeanor, however, did little to sway the substance of that trial, starting with jury selection. The *Jackson Daily News* declared: "No Negroes will serve on the jury. Women do not serve on Mississippi juries either." I comforted myself with the thought that at least the jury for the Chauvin trial was more representative of today's population: six white, four Black, and two multiracial jurors. Five of the jurors were men, seven were women. They included a chemist, a nurse, an auditor, and a grandmother, among others.

I didn't know much about Judge Peter Cahill, except that he was a fourteen-year veteran of the bench in Hennepin County, and had previously worked as a public defender, private defense lawyer, prosecutor, and was chief deputy under Amy Klobuchar when she'd served as the county attorney. Judge Cahill had agreed that once closing arguments were made, the court would alert the Floyd family if and when a read-back of the testimony should occur. (A read-back is a request to literally read back all or part of the testimony, a process that's often time-consuming.) If there was a verdict, we'd receive a two-hour warning so the family would have enough time to travel from the hotel to the courthouse.

The day before closing statements, California congresswoman Maxine Waters stirred things up when she called for protesters to "stay on the street" and "get more confrontational" if Chauvin was acquitted. While I understood she was referring to confronting the justice system and not about outright violence, her words, given the events of January 6, were suddenly open to misinterpretation and political manipulation. For the Floyd family, there was too much at stake for even the slightest misstep. When Judge Cahill dismissed Mr. Nelson's motion for a mistrial, saying that Ms. Waters's "opinion really doesn't matter a whole lot," I won't lie: I exhaled, relieved that Judge Cahill hadn't let the fervor of the case affect his big-picture judgment of it.

Prosecutor Steve Schleicher made a compelling and emotional closing argument, asking the jurors to trust what they saw in Frazier's video, saying, "This case is exactly what you thought when you first saw it.... You can believe your eyes.... It's what you felt in your gut. It's what you now know is in your heart. This wasn't policing. This was murder." After four years of listening to Trump, a president known for his gaslighting tactics, it was almost comforting to hear those words: "You can believe your eyes." Schleicher was asking the jurors—and the rest of America—to listen to the higher calling of their heart and do what was right.

In 2011, Simeon Wright, Moses Wright's son, was asked by a journalist how to measure the wider legacy of the Emmett Till case in our nation's history; he responded by saying, "I've seen a lot of change. The Emmett Till case brought a lot of changes in the laws, federal law mostly.... Men's hearts, I don't see too much change there. Law can't change a man's heart." He's right: real change, the kind we can feel in our hearts and in our guts, requires a higher calling and for generations of people—

individuals like Chief Arradondo, Attorney General Keith Ellison, and Ben Crump, for example—to continue to push for incremental advances until our society reflects what we know is right in our hearts and minds.

SAY HIS NAME

After the defense's closing statement, the family and I were met by a throng of journalists waiting outside the courthouse. Because we didn't want anything said that could possibly further inflame the situation, I said a prayer. There was no reason to add any hype. I knew my prayer had to be simple but strong. It was a time to stay calm, to be intentional with our words and actions, and to keep the family's dignity intact. It felt like we were all holding our breath underwater, waiting for the next big wave to crash overhead. When could we surface? I stood on the courthouse steps and asked God to deliver justice and to be merciful. I thanked Him for His good graces in letting us do His work. Inside the courtroom, the jurors were sent to deliberate and, later that evening, we were told to go home.

After lunch the following day, Ben called to tell me that the jurors had reached a verdict.

"No read-back?" I asked.

"They said verdict," he confirmed.

I paused, unsure of myself. "I think that's a good sign," I said confidently. Suddenly, I wasn't so sure. "Right?" I asked nervously, realizing my emotions were swinging from one extreme to the next.

"Whatever it is," Ben said, "it's not a hung jury, and I doubt they got everyone to acquit. Doesn't mean we win everything. Could be a compromise verdict."

"There's no compromising justice," I said, and we laughed a little.

The Floyds had set up another Family Room inside one of the conference rooms at the local Hilton Hotel. It became the

family's main control center, where close friends and supporters came to keep vigil. A large television screen dominated the
center of the room and kept everyone tuned in to what was happening in a courtroom only a few miles away. We decided to
divide up the family members, friends, and supporters so everyone would have someone to lean on: Philonise, Ben, and Ben's
team of attorneys would head to the courthouse. We were concerned that, if the verdict didn't go the way we'd hoped, riots
would break out. We needed to keep everyone together and safe.
The rest of us would make our way to the Family Room at the
Hilton, and after the reading of the verdict, Ben, his team, and
Philonise would join us there.

To say that the atmosphere was tense in the Family Room at
the hotel would be a massive understatement. Everyone was nervously biding their time, scrolling the screens of their phones,
and uneasily chatting with one another. Someone occasionally
broke out in prayer, but quietly; it was the kind of praying you
do when you're having a private conference with God. The general scene was what you'd typically find at a hospital, a room
full of anxious fathers or partners waiting for the birth of their
firstborn. People paced back and forth, sighed, and checked the
time. Then they'd do it again. We were waiting to see if justice
was going to be alive and kicking or stillborn. When I entered
the Family Room, I made my way to Jesse Jackson, who, despite
his health, had still traveled from Illinois to be there.

Jesse and I have been in this place before, waiting with a heartbroken family for a verdict that might deliver justice but rarely
brought peace. Even if a jury found in favor of the family, the
road toward healing was long and the journey often exhausting.
He and I both knew that the Floyd family was perched at an
emotional precipice. The next hour would determine whether
they'd be able to fly off the edge or would be forced to climb
back down, one painful step at a time. Jesse and I exchanged
words with one another.

"Hey, Young Buck," he said to me jokingly, using his long-ago nickname for me.

"Hey, yourself," I said, and took a seat. "Everyone know you're here?" I asked, and he shot me a look. I should have known better not to ask—there's no way he'd miss something like this. It was a reckoning, in many respects, of everything he'd worked toward his entire life. He and I both, I suddenly realized. *Here we are*, I thought, *the last in a long line of peaceful warriors.*

Jesse turned to me and said, "I want you to know that whatever happens today, you done good, Al." Coming from him, a man I consider to be as much a big brother as he is a mentor or a father figure to me, his words were particularly meaningful.

I knew he was referring to the broader sweep of our activism. He'd meant that I'd remained faithful to Dr. King's path of nonviolence. Regardless of whether the jury found in favor of Chauvin, I'd stayed true to those ideals. That in and of itself was a victory. I thanked him and we sat for a while in silence, both of us marveling at how far we'd moved to the front row seat of history.

I decided to pace the room myself and took my leave of Jesse. The atmosphere in the rest of the room was supercharged. The longer we waited, the more it felt as if we were locked in suspended animation, simultaneously keyed up and frozen in time. We had about another hour until the verdict would be read. You could have cut the tension with a knife.

I wanted to tell the family that I thought it was a good sign that the jury had returned so quickly, but I was also reluctant to say anything at all because I've also been in plenty of situations when the verdict was its own form of injustice. You don't have to go as far back as the Emmett Till case to see justice deferred. All three of the police officers who'd killed Sean Bell were found not guilty. A total of fifty rounds was fired by the police in Sean's death. Unbelievable. The police officers who killed Amadou Diallo in the vestibule of his home were let off. I could go on and on, and I realized that doing so wasn't going to help the Floyd family nor myself. For once, I decided to bite my tongue. I privately held on to my optimism but didn't say a word of hope aloud; I wanted to shield the Floyd family from disappointment if Chauvin was acquitted. Inwardly, though, I prayed like a man who'd just discovered the power of prayer. I prayed for justice. I prayed for peace. I prayed for the blood of Emmett Till. I offered up the names of those we'd lost: Michael Brown, Ahmaud Arbery, Breonna Taylor, Freddie Gray, Sandra Bland, Jordan Davis, Dontre Hamilton, Blair Holt, Trayvon Martin, Tamir Rice, Hadiya Pendleton, Amadou Diallo, Sean Bell, Ramarley Graham, Eric Garner. I prayed for a reckoning. I prayed for healing. I prayed for hope. Just twenty minutes prior to Judge Cahill's reading, sixteen-year-old Ma'Khia Bryant was shot and killed by the police in Columbus, Ohio. I prayed for her, too.

We directed our collective attention to Judge Cahill as he adjusted his microphone on the television screen. Everyone in the room tensed.

"Members of the jury," he said, "I will now read the verdicts as they will appear in the permanent records of the fourth judicial district." He continued, "We the jury in the above entitled manner as to count one unintentional second-degree murder while committing a felony find the defendant guilty." In that moment, I lost control of my arms. They shot overhead and I began to cry. It was only over the wails and the uncontrollable cries of everyone else in that room that I heard the rest of the verdict: guilty down the line. There wasn't a dry eye in the place. Our emotions were a combination of relief and victory but also deep pain. I looked at Jesse and suddenly it hit me. The weight of all the years that he and I, along with other civil rights leaders, activists, and lawyers, have spent inside courtrooms and at rallies, in funeral homes, and beside too many grief-stricken Black mothers came crashing down on my shoulders. I hadn't realized how much I'd been carrying until the moment it was lifted from me.

I've marched and advocated for the most basic of rights—equal protection under the law—for so long that the struggle has defined my very life. The relief in hearing the verdict was overwhelming. It was jarring, a real shock to the system. I know everyone in that room felt something different. For George's family, there was undoubtedly the feeling of personal justice. For me, it was a sense of validation. I've dedicated my life to activism, and on that particular April day, all the marching, advocacy work, and late nights spent organizing and planning for press conferences worked. Justice was delivered. I don't say this lightly: change does happen. It may not come overnight, but it does happen. I finally got to see one crack of light in this dark tunnel.

I felt elated one minute and then, strangely, in the next I was heartbroken. Waves of disappointment and a conflicted sense of remorse washed over me—to think of all the other victims and their families who didn't get to see justice. It was almost too much to bear. I also didn't want to rejoice in the fact that an ex-policeman was going to prison. Yes, he had committed a crime but the mere fact that the crime had been committed in the first place, and with such impunity, indicated that our system of policing was deeply corrupt. Its failure was not something in which I delighted.

A short time after our initial celebration, Philonise, Ben, and Ben's team of attorneys joined us in the Family Room at the hotel. We embraced one another, fist-bumped, and wiped away our tears. The room fell quiet again when Attorney General Ellison began the first press conference. "I would not call today's verdict justice," Ellison said. "Because justice implies there is restoration. But it is accountability, which is the first step toward justice." He mentioned the Kerner Commission, a group appointed by President Lyndon B. Johnson in 1967 to investigate the causes of uprisings over racial injustice in American cities. "Here we are in 2021 still addressing the same problem," Ellison said. "This has to end. We need true justice. That's not one case. That is a social transformation that says that nobody is beneath the law and no one is above it."

As we listened to the rest of Ellison's remarks, the White House called: President Biden wanted to know if the Floyds preferred that he give a statement to the nation before or after the family held a press conference of its own. It was decided that the family would speak first. George's cousin Rodney, who was like a brother to him, suggested that I start the press conference with a prayer—not only would it help set the tone, but I'd also been praying with the family for the past year at particularly crucial moments. We all agreed: this was a particularly crucial moment. It was the right thing to do and the right time to do it.

When we stepped in front of the pool of reporters, Ben raised his arm in the air. "Say his name," he called, and we dutifully responded, "George Floyd." It was a rallying call we'd done several times before, a chant that the country has picked up and employed at various marches, subbing in the names of other victims of violence and police brutality. As a civil rights activist, I know that the call-and-response is a way to keep the movement alive; it invites group participation. As a preacher and as someone who knows the pain of losing a loved one, I also know that saying their name aloud is one way of keeping their spirit alive. When thousands of demonstrators chant George's name, it's as if George himself is standing shoulder to shoulder with us, helping to lead the march. Saying his name, and the names of other victims, is both healing and a form of activism in its own right.

Ben repeated the call and we answered him in kind, our voices joining together. We may not have been in church, but it felt like we were. I stepped up to the podium, we locked arms, and I began the prayer: "Dear God, we thank You for giving us the strength to stand together. Sometimes we would question each other. Sometimes we'd say, 'This is just going to be a waste of time.' But somehow You touched us in the midnight hours and taught us to hold on and that if we would be faithful over a few things, You'd give us the victory over many. We thank You because we know it was not any doing of ours but Your loving kindness and Your tender mercy that made tonight possible. Bless those that worked, that made this prosecution something they couldn't deny. Bless those policemen who got on the stand and testified against another policeman. Bless the jury that listened to the evidence and didn't listen to those who may have criticized them for doing so." I went down the line, thanking Attorney General Keith Ellison and Ben Crump, for the civil and human rights leaders who stood up, but I reserved my closing thanks for the "nameless grandmas and grandpas who got on their knees to ask God to give us a victory this time." George's name will go down in history. He will forever be known as a figure who brought change, whose death led to the first conviction of a white police officer killing a Black civilian for the first time in the history of the state of Minnesota, a victory that helped to lift the knee from our collective neck.

Before my tears of relief had dried, I was already getting ready for another wake the very next day. Another Black man had been fatally shot by Brooklyn Center police in Minnesota. It's almost like behind every Barack Obama, there's a Donald Trump lying in wait, which is why we can't stop pushing for change. In life, there are times when you may feel tempted to kick back and enjoy your wins. In my experience, it's best not to give in to that kind of temptation. You may win one today, but tomorrow's another day.

THE PRINCE OF BROOKLYN CENTER

Daunte Wright, a twenty-year-old biracial Black man, was shot and killed while resisting arrest during a traffic stop just ten miles away from the courthouse where the jury was deliberating the Chauvin trial. The shooting was characterized as "accidental," with officials saying that the responding officer, Kimberly Potter, mistook her handgun for her Taser. I'd say the eulogy for Daunte's funeral in the same county where George was murdered, my celebration for justice short-lived. I'd also later discover that George Floyd's girlfriend had been one of Daunte's high-school teachers. The world is so small, sometimes it's suffocating.

The jury convicted Chauvin on Tuesday, April 20. On Wednesday, I met with the Wright family, who was devastated by their loss, and accompanied them to an informal wake for their son. While I was with them, I answered a call from Philonise, expecting for him to say his goodbyes—I knew he had to return to Texas after the trial. Instead, he told me that he was planning to stay on. He wanted to attend the funeral for Daunte. It was at that moment that Philonise made the full transition into being an activist. Like Gwen Carr, he crossed over from being a "member of the victim's family" to becoming an agent for change. He now understood both sides—how to be a support system for a grieving family and how to channel that emotion into positive action. Besides being grateful for his transformation, I was also deeply appreciative that I wouldn't have to be alone.

While headed to the Shiloh Temple International Ministries in north Minneapolis to say the eulogy at Wright's funeral, Ben Crump called to tell me that the police had shot another Black man: Andrew Brown Jr., in Elizabeth City, North Carolina. One victory here and two tragedies there. So far in 2021, I've personally said eulogies at five funerals, all for victims of police killings—and, as of this writing, the year ain't over yet.

By the time we reached the temple, my mind was reeling. Still buoyed by the fact that justice was served for George, I was also gutted by the ongoing struggle. I was humbled that so many people around the world rose up to support the Black Lives Matter movement yet I couldn't shake the worry that it might not be enough. My heart was already heavy when I entered the temple. A host of politicians were in attendance, everyone from Senator Klobuchar to Governor Tim Walz. More striking, however, was the appearance of other families who'd also lost their loved ones to police violence. Standing at the church pulpit, I saw the families of Oscar Grant and Philando Castile, along with three or four other families, besides members of the Floyd family. It was both heartwarming and wrenching to see this community of survivors banded together under the banner of yet another funeral. During the trial of Derek Chauvin, there were four high-profile deaths of Black civilians by police officers: Ma'Khia Bryant, Daunte Wright, Adam Toledo, and Anthony Thompson Jr. Daunte was killed on the day of Chauvin's summation. You'd have thought that police forces across the country, especially in the same county where George was murdered, would have been extrasensitive and cautious during the Chauvin trial, but the fact that six Black men lost their lives in the midst of one of the greatest trials of police violence in our nation's history tells me that our work is far from over.

The Wright family had requested an open casket. As I watched the family members line up one by one to say their last goodbyes, I thought of the open-casket funeral of Emmett Till where an estimated one hundred thousand people lined up for two days to bear witness to the brutality of white supremacy. I thought of George's funeral, too, with what felt like all of Houston lined up to see him off. I took my turn and said a final private prayer over Daunte's body but the words I said weren't only for him. I prayed that his death would be the last of its kind. After I performed the Rite of Committal, the family asked if I would join them for the cremation and push the button.

"What button?" I asked, not understanding. They explained that Daunte was to be cremated—something I'd never witnessed before. "Pushing the button" began the process of cremation; I advocated for one of his sisters to do this instead of myself. Perhaps it was the cumulative stress of the past week, but in all my years of preaching funerals, I've never experienced what I did while attending Daunte's cremation. It was surreal to say the least. Something shifted inside me; I didn't know whether to cry, scream, fall to my knees, or stand stock-still. I'd felt something similar earlier that week when the Chauvin verdict was read aloud: tears had streamed down my face while, at the same time, my arms had shot up in elation. Each funeral exacts an emotional toll on me, but Daunte's was the first that rendered me completely speechless. I was a silent witness in the truest sense and hoped that God, in His good graces, would know my silence spoke volumes.

I don't think I've ever lived a week of my life quite like that one, where there were so many highs and lows, everything compressed and emotional. I may preach about the glories of heaven but, every so often, it's one hell of a week. I found my solace in the families and in the words of the Bible. Each morning, I thanked God to have been given another day to do His work. But by the time I got to Sunday, the Lord's day, I was ready to rest, too. I got my first full night of sleep in I don't know how long. I, along with many other Americans, had had several restless nights ever since the May 25, 2020, murder of George Floyd. I'm used to grieving with families of victims of police brutality, but the situation surrounding George's death was different—not only had it sparked a national awakening and conversation about policing, but it also affected me deeply on both an emotional and psychological level. I've been saying eulogies for Black men and boys for decades, and each funeral hits me with the sad reality that the person I'm praying over could have been me or one of my loved ones—my grandson or a dear friend. I've never gotten over that realization, and don't think I ever will.

To me, these Black men and women, these boys and girls whose lives are cut too short, are beautiful. They are kings and queens, princes and princesses. It's like I said at Daunte's eulogy, "The reason why the temple is decorated in purple for

Daunte is because the color represents royalty. You thought he was just some kid. He was a prince. So, take your seat, Daunte. Tell George Floyd who you are. Take your seat, Daunte. Shake hands with Philandro Castile. There's a special place in heaven for those who shed innocent blood because God will use you to straighten out the world. Daunte played center on his high school's basketball team. Well, the game's changed. Now, he's the center of a movement of God."

VISIBILITY AND COMMUNITY GIVE YOUR ISSUE CREDIBILITY

Throughout my life, I've been involved in any number of police brutality cases. How do I know which one is going to resonate with the American public? How do I know which spark is going to burn brightest? I don't, but I go in and do the work anyway because what's the alternative? To do nothing? And if I do nothing, how can I sleep at night? How can I turn from life's suffering when I know there's a better way? I can't.

After Daunte Wright's funeral, I was called upon to do another eulogy, this time for Andrew Brown Jr., the Black man who was shot and killed in Elizabeth City, North Carolina, while being served a search warrant. The cops surrounded Brown's pickup truck like they were a posse, armed with AR-15 and Glocks. Brown attempted to flee by driving away. The police fired, hitting Brown two times, once in the back of his head. In my book, that's an execution. Legal doctrine and departmental policies indicate that officers can only use deadly force if a suspect poses an imminent threat of injury or death to the officers or others. District Attorney Andrew Womble said that Brown's flight posed a threat, but he was driving away from the officers when he resisted them.

Womble, who's announced that he's running for superior state court in 2022, decided not to prosecute the deputies. There's no way he's going to indict police in light of him wanting to move up the judiciary ranks. At Brown's eulogy, I said, "I know a con game when I see one." Womble released some of the body cams but not all of them. They've allowed the family to watch twenty seconds and then eighteen minutes of the interaction, but there's over two hours' worth of edited tape. Imagine what else is on those tapes. Visibility gives your issue credibility: it's why we have body cams in the first place. If the cops abided by the law, then show us. Let us see good cops doing their jobs. If they didn't, well then, we have the right to see that, too.

Andrew Brown Jr.'s death may or may not spark national interest. But I know a family in pain when I see it and, as a reverend, I'm called to perform my duty: to look them in their eyes and address their suffering. Because their suffering is all of ours. There are thousands of cases like Andrew Brown Jr., because the systemic racism and oppression that has infiltrated all aspects of American life is real pain that puts each and every one of us at a disadvantage.

The good part of the Chauvin trial was that we were able to secure three convictions. The bad part was that we had to worry, even with video evidence, that we might not get one conviction. It is never over. Black Americans are getting taken down one at a time. It's a death by a thousand cuts, and until police know that they can go to jail, that their lives can be impacted by their own harassment, change is going to happen too slowly.

Throughout history, people have witnessed crimes being committed by the police against Black folks on a daily basis. The difference today is that most people have cameras in their back pockets and can film what they see. Yet, even with video evidence, witnesses are often told they didn't see what they saw or that the killing was somehow justified. Black folks have been told time and time again to simply move along. There's nothing to see here, nothing to do. Think about the message that conveys. Up until the very moment that the Chauvin verdict was announced, for example, the Floyd family and I were comforting each other about how we were going to deal with the defeat. If that doesn't tell you something about the psyche of our nation, I don't know what does. Think about it: a relatively clear-cut case, with video evidence, and supporting testimony of dozens of witnesses and experts, and we *still* thought we might lose. Why? Because if you are Black in this country, you are conditioned *all the time* to think you'll lose. Lose what? You name it: your house. Your job. Your money. Your life. Why? Because, as a people, we've been conditioned to think about how to make the best out of a bad situation rather than demanding that the situation not be bad in the first place. Dr. King used to say it makes a person maladjusted. Reverend Jesse Jackson once told me something I've never forgotten. He said, "Al, it's bad enough to be enslaved. What's worse is when you accept it." If you think of yourself as a second-class citizen, that your life doesn't matter, then I may as well say your eulogy, too. We have got to break that mental bondage.

One of the reasons I'm still an activist, why I still link arms and march, is because I don't want anyone to accept being treated like a slave, someone "less than." I protest that very ideology. You have to be out front and raising your voice for someone else to understand that they, too, don't have to accept that kind of thinking. In this respect, marching is a form of mental conditioning. You may not be responsible for being put down, but you are responsible for getting up. And if you're waiting on people who knock you down to lift you up, you'll never get up, 'cause if they wanted you up, they wouldn't have knocked you down in the first place. Even if you don't have the power or the strength to get up right now, roll over and look up until you build up the strength to do it. Do not accept staying down. It's not an option. Remove it from your thinking. The hardest thing about my job is convincing people that they can get up and, in getting up, they can succeed in life and pursue their dreams. They can win.

Black folks have known about police brutality and harassment for decades. We live with it. But I think it's to everyone's benefit that the rest of America sees what we've been dealing with—for decades. It proves we haven't been making it up. We've been talking about police brutality for years. Video after video bears the truth of our words. To anyone who's looking, it's clear as day that our policing system is fundamentally broken. To anyone who's looking, it's clear as day that racism is real and pervasive.

Over the years, I've learned how to simultaneously deal with the public outcry over racism while pushing for pragmatic legislation and comforting a victim's family at the same time. It's a balancing act. You're playing to three different situations at three different levels of engagement. If any one is off-kilter, everything comes crashing down. If you don't deal with the public outrage, the situation could easily get out of hand. If you don't make the legislative piece pragmatic, then you've let anger win the day. And if you don't sufficiently comfort the family, then the larger social moment can be lost entirely. At the end of the day, these are people's lives we're dealing with and their real, raw emotions. As a pastor, it is absolutely essential to me that the family is able to move forward, and can begin the healing process. It's complicated, though, because healing, in many of these cases, doesn't mean acceptance. Rather it means working through the anger and the frustration and turning those negative feelings into energy for positive change. That's a tall order for anyone to do on a good day but on a day when you've lost your son or daughter because of the color of their skin? It takes an inner reserve that most people have rarely had to call on before. It takes faith and fortitude, two qualities I'm fortunate to be well-versed in myself. It also takes a community: a church, close family and friends, trusted work colleagues, an organized group, or any combination thereof. My community rests squarely on the shoulders of my faith, my family, and NAN, which I founded in 1991. I could have never envisioned that NAN would grow into the organization it is today. Back in the 1990s, I was just looking for an answer to the Slave Theater.

FROM THE SLAVE THEATER TO THE HOUSE OF JUSTICE

In the 1980s and 1990s, I used to meet with a group of activists at a place called the Slave Theater in the Bedford-Stuyvesant neighborhood of Brooklyn on Fulton Street. The name has always made people a little uneasy, and that's exactly why its owner, Judge John L. Phillips, chose it. It was originally called the Regent, and had been around since 1914, one of Brooklyn's many theaters. The larger Fulton Theater was a few doors down. The story goes that Judge Phillips made a film about an inter-racial love story and when no theater would show it, he bought the Regent in 1984 and ran it there. He also purchased the Black Lady Theater, at 750 Nostrand Avenue. People used to call Phillips the "Kung Fu Judge" because, unbelievably enough, he had a black belt in martial arts. That, and the fact that he was also one of the only Black judges on the civil court bench in Brook-lyn made him known in the community. Phillips changed the name to the Slave Theater, he said, to remind everyone in the neighborhood, including himself, where they came from.

The inside of the theater was colorful. Hand-painted murals covered the walls and depicted Black heroes throughout history, some from other countries: Toussaint Louverture, Marcus Garvey, Dr. King. If I remember correctly, there was also one of Bruce Lee. There were hand-painted quotes, too, all affirmations of Black culture: "The Real Black Man's Creed: I would rather die in dignity than live without honor as a coward." By the 1980s, Bed-Stuy was struggling: most of the neighborhood's manufacturing jobs had left in the 1960s, and the area's commercial center was dying. Drugs were rampant. Poverty was everywhere. Woolworth's shuttered their doors. It was in this climate that the Slave Theater became a hub for activism. I coordinated a lot of my early marches and protests from there. We always met on Wednesday nights, and before the place fell into disrepair, the Slave Theater was one of the most popular places in Bed-Stuy, and not just because of the kung fu double features. A church rented out the offices upstairs. At any given moment, a rally, movie, or church service could be going on. Sometimes, all three. The activist groups that met there were an amalgam of Black nationalists, civil rights leaders, community organizers—everyone.

In 1991, I was stabbed in the chest while leading a march in Bensonhurst in support of Yusef Hawkins, a teenage Black boy who'd been killed by a white mob there. While recovering at Coney Island Hospital, I had what I like to call a Meeting with Al, one of many I've had over the years with myself. My injury wasn't life-threatening, yet it was a moment of personal reckoning nonetheless. I privately vowed to redouble my activist efforts. I decided to become much more serious about working within the nonviolent King tradition. As fate would have it, I got out of the hospital a few days later and went to the weekly Wednesday night meeting at the Slave Theater. Someone stood up and made a motion: the group didn't want any press in the meeting, and, at the time, I'd attracted the attention of a few journalists, some of whom were white. What they meant when they said they didn't want press was, they didn't want me, and they didn't want any whites in the Slave Theater.

"How are we going to get word out about our rallies without the press?" I asked.

"No whites allowed."

A heated discussion followed, and I voiced my concern: How could we confront racism and our community issues in a vacuum? After much back and forth, I finally said, "I'm out." Of the

250 people gathered there, about twelve stood up and came with me, one of whom included a young journalist named Michael Hardy. Everyone kept saying, "Al will be back. He just needs to calm down." Well, I didn't go back and I didn't calm down.

Over the course of the next month or so, I created a more formal organization, one dedicated to the King tradition, and centralized our operations in Harlem. I decided to host our rallies every Saturday morning, in part because I knew that was what Reverend Jones used to do in Brooklyn, back when I was a little boy. It's what Jesse Jackson did in Chicago and Dr. King had done, too: the weekends give enough time for people to come together for mass and then afterward to organize for community action work. I worked to get the Black radio stations to broadcast us live on the weekends—Dr. King did something similar, and used the Black church and the Black radio as his community outreach program and megaphone both. I named the organization National Action Network. Integrated into our incorporation papers is the statement—and the promise—that NAN was created "in the spirit and tradition of Dr. King, a movement for the North." Our formal incorporation letter was signed by many up-and-comers in New York's political and business worlds like Eric Adams, for one, who back then was a transit cop and a member of the Black police organization, the Grand Council of Guardians.

Reverend Jesse Jackson attended the ribbon-cutting ceremony for our permanent home on 145th Street in Harlem, where he whipped the crowd into a frenzy. I remember it as if it was yesterday. Former Mayor Dinkins was there and, next to him, the chairman of our board, Wyatt Tee Walker, who'd been chief of staff to Martin Luther King Jr. Jesse didn't even need a microphone. He delivered the keynote speech but, with his voice full of the spirit of God, it sounded more like a good, old-fashioned, rollicking sermon. As he reached the climax, he boomed, "What we need is a house of justice, where grieving mothers can come when the courts refuse to listen to them. We need a house of justice, where young Black boys and girls can learn the power of their worth. We need a house of justice, where outcasts can come and feel loved. I know the commissioner won't listen to you, but the house of justice hears your cries. I know the police may have shot your son, but now you can come to the house of justice." The crowd was already riled up, but he kept on.

"We need a house of justice!" he said, and the crowd responded with cries of, "Yes, sir!" and "Amen!" Then he said, "*This* is the house of justice!" and, like that, the House of Justice, NAN's Harlem headquarters, was born, blessed both by Reverend Jesse Jackson's good graces and his impromptu oratorial skill. I've been doing Saturday meetings at NAN's House of Justice ever since. I like to say that the rejected stones of this world are the cornerstones that built the House of Justice.

Today, NAN is a multipronged organization, covering everything from crisis intake and victim assistance programs to criminal justice reform and police accountability to voting rights and corporate responsibility to tech programs for youths. We have chapters around the country and, while many of our chapters are associated with local Christian churches, NAN is welcome to anyone looking to advance the social justice principles of Dr. King, no matter your creed, color, gender identity, or background. Over the years, we've hosted a multitude of speakers, everyone from Barack Obama to Hillary Clinton, Wynton Marsalis to Aretha Franklin, Winnie Mandela to Coretta Scott King, all of whom know that when you come to the House of Justice, you're coming to both listen and to be heard yourself, because real justice requires us to lift every voice.

5

TRUE GRIT

"These things do not happen all of a sudden. They grow out of feelings that have been developing over many years. Human beings reach a point.... 'This is as far as I can go,' and from then on it may be passive resistance, but it will be resistance."

—ELEANOR ROOSEVELT

Reverend William A. Jones, the pastor of Bethany Baptist Church in my hometown neighborhood of Brooklyn, and Reverend Jesse Jackson taught me that the biggest wins of the 1960s civil rights era were legislation, namely the Civil Rights Act of 1964 and the Voting Rights Act of 1965, because they changed the social and legal landscapes of the time. If federal legislation hadn't passed, there's a good chance we'd still be in the back of the bus. Moments pass, but the law is the law. Dr. King rode the crest of several moments, building them into a broad non-violent social justice movement. Black Power was a moment, too. Both have receded. But laws last.

These thoughts were fresh in my mind after hearing the Chauvin verdict. The American public may know George

Floyd's name today but three or four generations from now, if his name isn't attached to a meaningful bill that protects his daughter or his granddaughter, then we'll have squandered our collective energy for positive change. It took fifty years for some of the teeth to be taken out of the Voting Rights Act with 2013's *Shelby County v. Holder*. And yes, it's under attack again today. But listen, *Shelby County v. Holder* was roughly fifty years after the passage of the Voting Rights Act. If we can get federal laws passed in George's name, even if the opposition tries to undo some of them later, well, I'll take those odds. I'll take the passage of real legislation over a hashtag trend any day. Yes, there may come a day when, like today's battle over voting rights, we'll have to defend the legislation, but let's first get the bill passed.

The George Floyd Justice in Policing Act of 2021 is an expansive civil rights and police reform bill drafted by Congressional Democrats working in concert with members of the Congressional Black Caucus and others. Its scope is sweeping. The provisions I find most important include: getting rid of qualified immunity, making it a requirement for federal uniformed police officers to wear body cams and for every marked federal police vehicle to be outfitted with dashboard cameras, establishing a federal registry of police misconduct, prohibiting federal police officers from using chokeholds or other carotid holds like the kind that led to Eric Garner's death, and changing the threshold for permissible use of force by an officer from "reasonableness" to only when "necessary to prevent death of serious bodily injury."

Getting rid of qualified immunity would make an impact; it would help make police more personally accountable. Right now, most cops in this country think they can get away with murder. One of the most shocking and impactful images from the Chauvin trial was the look on Derek Chauvin's face when he realized he was being sent to jail. Every cop should pause and reflect on that moment and think to himself or herself: no one is above the law. The Chauvin trial showed us a new reality, a world where the actions of the police have lasting legal consequences. It's a reality that, for many Black and brown citizens, has come too late. The Chauvin trial also demonstrated the impact video footage can have on the outcome of a case. It's one of the reasons body cams and dashboard cams are so important. While the bill passed in the House, it struggled in the US Senate, with Senator Tim Scott of South Carolina negotiating for the Republicans. Many conservative Republicans today are trapped in a party that, because of Trump's iron grip, is forcing them to play a hand that's further right than what's politically comfortable for them. I'm holding out hope that their better angels will guide them toward a morally conscionable solution.

The greatest threat to the social justice movement today is the lack or absence of meaningful legal change. It's one thing to build a movement; it's another to transform that momentum into federal legislative change. What made the civil rights movement of the 1960s so successful is that once activists and civil rights leaders got through the drama—the sit-ins and the arrests, the marches and the Freedom Rides—they passed legislation, so Blacks were no longer legally forced to drink from the Colored drinking fountains. They could check into proper hotels and could go to restaurants. They could vote. They could attend better schools with white children. The laws literally changed the way we lived and not just immediately but also in the decades that followed.

The United States Supreme Court's 1954 decision in *Brown v. Board of Education*, the landmark case that declared the racial segregation of children in public school unconstitutional, was major both for its immediate backlash among segregationists and for its lasting impact in giving generations of Blacks a more equal foothold in the American dream. Author Timothy B. Tyson wrote that Mississippi Circuit Court Judge Thomas Brady "speculated that the mandate…would compel right-minded white men to commit violence against foolhardy Black boys." Brady wrote a manifesto called *Black Monday*. In it, he predicted that violence would start with the "supercilious, glib young Negro, who sojourned in Chicago or New York, and who considers the counsel of his elders archaic." He went on, writing that this Black child "will perform an obscene act, or make an obscene remark, or a vile overture or assault upon some white girl." Brady's play-by-play seemingly sanctioned the conditions under which a white Southern man's violence had permission to erupt—and neatly described the conditions under which Emmett Till was murdered, one year after *Brown v. Board of Education* was handed down. In this respect, Emmett's murder could be seen as a gruesome result of the rising anger felt among certain Southerners losing their grip on their segregationist way of life as precipitated by *Brown v. Board of Education*. In the months leading up to Emmett's death, there'd also been a concerted push in the South, and in Mississippi in particular, to get Blacks to the polls—another threat to the system of segregation that had effectively filtered political power into white hands for generations.

I was born the year that *Brown v. Board of Education* became a legal mandate. Unlike my parents, both of whom dropped out of school to work in the fields, I was able to attend an integrated school. My parents never knew what it meant to go to school let alone to have white classmates. They didn't get to experience some of the benefits that come from a mixed-race school environment. I was part of a generation who directly benefitted from the legislative wins of the previous generation. And yet, these benefits disappeared once my family moved from our middle-class neighborhood in Queens to a lower-class one in Brooklyn, where I attended a majority-Black public school. That experience opened my eyes: I witnessed firsthand how the racism of redlining overlapped with class issues, and how it all played out in the classroom. Racism isn't tidy. It bleeds over everything.

When Ben Crump and I first met, we talked about our shared life experiences, and how *Brown v. Board of Education* was a point of intersection for us both. Without it, Ben wouldn't have attended the newly integrated middle school in his hometown of Lumberton, North Carolina. It's also highly possible that Ben may not have become a lawyer himself. But he did, and his decision to do so was largely influenced by the admiration he had for his mentor, Thurgood Marshall, who, besides becoming the first Black Supreme Court justice, had also argued *Brown v. Board of Education.* If Ben and I were the branches, Marshall was the root. Marshall is to Ben what Dr. King is to me. In the early days of Ben and I getting to know one another, we traded war stories, and he'd been delighted to know that one of the last cases Marshall sat on was mine.

Mr. Civil Rights:
Thurgood Marshall

Thurgood Marshall grew up in Baltimore, Maryland, during the Jim Crow era when state laws codified racial discrimination and segregation in nearly every way possible. His ancestors had been slaves. Marshall liked to tell people that his great-grandfather had been captured as a slave from the toughest part of the Congo—although relatives argued he may have been from a Sierra Leone tribe—and taken to the Eastern Shore of Maryland, where he was eventually freed. One of his grandfathers, Isaiah Olive Branch Williams, operated a Baltimore grocery store, but was perhaps better known for joining a local, Black-led campaign against police brutality and discrimination—back in 1875. Thurgood got his name from his paternal grandfather, Thorney Good Marshall, the only grandparent of his who wasn't free when the Civil War broke out. In second grade,

"Thorough-good" famously shortened his name to Thurgood, a less difficult name for him to write.

His father, William Canfield Marshall, once worked as a Pullman railroad car waiter and later as a steward at the Gibson Island Club, an exclusive, whites-only club on Chesapeake Bay. His mother, Norma Arica Williams, was an elementary school teacher. The family moved into a house that belonged to Marshall's uncle Fearless, or "Fee" for short, on Baltimore's Division Street when Thurgood was around six years old. Both his sets of grandparents owned grocery stores; the one on the corner of Dolphin and Division was the largest Black-owned one in the city. Despite it being a prominent family neighborhood, Marshall later told biographers Roger Goldman and David Gallen that "we lived on a respectable street, but behind us there were back alleys where the roughnecks and tough kids hung out. When it was time for dinner, my mother used to go to the front door and call my older brother. Then she'd go to the *back* door and call me." Marshall's habit of hanging out with the local troublemakers didn't sit well with the principal of his elementary school who made him study the US Constitution as punishment. "Before I left that school," Marshall later said, "I knew the whole thing by heart."

William and Norma raised Marshall with an eye toward justice, and the family regularly debated the days' current events and topics at the dinner table. According to author Howard Ball, Marshall's father loved to debate and would challenge his son to back up his "youthful assertions." His father never told Marshall to become a lawyer, but he clearly helped pave the path toward him becoming one, taking Marshall to the Baltimore courthouse to watch various criminal trials. William had been the first Black man to serve on a grand jury in Baltimore. Perhaps this experience had instilled in him a love for the judiciary. Whatever the reason, the father turned the son into a lawyer. "He did it," Marshall said, "by teaching me to argue, by challenging my logic on every point, by making me prove every statement I made."

When Marshall was seven years old, however, he experienced something that no logical argument could explain. He recounted the incident to a reporter years later, saying, "I heard a kid call a Jewish boy I knew a 'kike' to his face.... I asked him why he didn't fight the kid. He asked me what I would do if someone called me 'nigger'—would I fight? That was a new one on me. I knew 'kike' was a dirty word, but I hadn't known about 'nigger.' I went home and wanted to know right that minute what all this meant. That's not easy for a parent to explain so it makes sense to a kid, you know." After a discussion about the definition of the word and an explanation of the history of slavery, Marshall's father got straight to the point.

"Anyone calls you nigger," William said, "you not only got my permission to fight him—you got my orders to fight him."

In a sense, Marshall spent the rest of his life fighting the racist name-callers of the world. He attended a segregated high school in Baltimore and Lincoln University, a historically Black university near Oxford, Pennsylvania. Because his first-choice law school, the University of Maryland School of Law, was segregated, he attended the historically Black Howard University School of Law in Washington, DC, instead, where he was mentored by the law school's then vice-dean, Charles Hamilton Houston, and graduated first in his class in 1933. (His mother pawned her wedding and engagement rings to pay for the law school's entrance fees.) Houston was the first Black lawyer to win a case before the Supreme Court. Under his tutelage, Marshall became the face of civil rights litigation, arguing thirty-two cases before the Supreme Court, winning twenty-nine of them, and participating in hundreds of other cases in lower courts nationwide. As he moved up the legislative ranks, a federal court clerk once told Marshall that he "could look at a pleading filed by a lawyer and tell from looking at it whether it was done by a white or Negro lawyer." It was a message that stayed with Marshall. "From that day until I stopped practicing law," he later said, "I never filed a paper in any court with an erasure on it. If I changed a word, it had to be typed all over, because I didn't want that on it." Marshall understood early on that the bar was set higher for a Black lawyer; the system was *looking* for ways to obstruct him. He knew that his work had to be perfect—he couldn't afford to give anyone ammunition to use against him, and in the world of legal briefs, a misplaced comma or misspelled word could be disastrous.

As head of the NAACP Legal Defense Fund in New York City, Marshall would occasionally speak at Washington Temple, the church I grew up in. Even then, he was a larger-than-life legal persona, but he wasn't church baked; I could tell the difference. He was more erudite than the pastors of the church and, since I never wanted to be a lawyer, I didn't follow him around like some of the other kids did. Even as young as four years old, I already knew I wanted to be a preacher. Now if Marshall had been a reverend, well, maybe my excitement would have matched theirs when he'd come around. Everyone in the congregation knew when Marshall made an appearance. You didn't have to look around to know he was there. There'd be a kind of buzz in the church, people excitedly whispering his name, gawking but trying to play it cool.

It was a big deal when President Lyndon B. Johnson nominated him to replace retiree Justice Tom C. Clark to the Supreme Court in 1967. President Johnson famously remarked that putting Marshall on the bench was "the right thing to do, the right time to do it, the right man, and the right place." If he was a larger-than-life figure before the appointment, he became epochal afterward. I'd never introduced myself to him as a boy at Washington Temple, but as an adult, I'd met him a few times in passing. It was fortunate that the last time I encountered him was when I needed him most.

In the early 1990s, I was in the midst of my own personal court battle over taxes. Thankfully, I won my suit. Marshall, on his very last day as a presiding judge in New York City, was one of three judges who saw to it that my case wouldn't be subjected to further scrutiny in Albany. When news got out that Marshall and I would be in the same courtroom together, tons of spectators came, filling the small room to occupancy. I don't know what people were waiting for—Marshall, by that time in his life, had long been known as the Great Dissenter because he either said "no" or said nothing at all to most legal questions. As for me, I knew when to keep my mouth shut. There were no sparks from either of us that day. Along with mine, Marshall heard four other cases that day. He finished and left without a word. When I told this story to Ben years later, we both laughed a little: Marshall had loomed large in both of our imaginations, and in the one meaningful interaction I'd had with him, he loomed larger still. A silent force. That long black robe. I think it was affirming to us both that Ben's childhood hero had helped me out and, some thirty years later, that Ben and I were working together. Marshall once said, "You do what you think is right and let the law catch up." I see my role as helping to effect change on the street level—with the culture and the people—so the lawyers and the politicians can follow up with the next wave of change.

In 2016, President Obama invited me to watch an advance screening of Reginald Hudlin's film *Marshall*, starring Chadwick Boseman in the titular role. It was more than a little surreal to watch the film in the private theater of the White House with Cecilia and Thurgood Marshall Jr., Marshall's widow and son, along with President Obama and the first lady. I kept sneaking glances at Cecilia to see how the film registered with her. After the movie ended, we talked a bit, and I related the story about how I'd been one of Marshall's last cases on the bench.

Cecilia said, "I remember. I was in court that day." Cecilia had gotten in the habit of taking him his lunches and checking in on him, and she'd spoken to Marshall about me after he'd seen to my case. As she spoke in more detail about her late husband, I realized I was awestruck: I could not believe I was speaking with the widow of the first Black Supreme Court justice while standing in the same room as the first Black president and first lady. I was humbled by the moment. Not bad for a kid who came out of the welfare system in Brooklyn. In too many ways to count, I had Marshall to thank for helping to change the social landscape of the America I'd grown up in.

Thurgood Marshall is undoubtedly one of the most

significant changemakers of the twentieth and twenty-first centuries. There's a clear delineation—a before and an after—in both our legal system and in American culture that's a direct result of his influence. He was our line in the sand. He, along with Charles Hamilton Houston and Fred Gray before him, was one of the early principal architects of the civil rights strategy of using the courts to provide what the political system would not: a definition of equality that assured Black Americans the full rights of citizenship. Paul Gewirtz, one of Justice Marshall's former law clerks, wrote a tribute to Marshall after he retired from the court: "Thurgood Marshall had the capacity to imagine a radically different world, the imaginative capacity to believe that such a world was possible, the strength to sustain that image in the mind's eye and the heart's longing, and the courage and ability to make that imagined world real."

Beyond having a heroic imagination, Marshall also had an expansive legal mind, formulating arguments that addressed systemic racism and oppression using the same system and legal language that had helped to codify such hatred in the first place. To break that up required a painstaking knowledge of the law, broad, visionary thinking to imagine how it could be different, and the audacity to pull it off. Marshall had a mix of all three characteristics—so, too, does Ben Crump. Most people today know Marshall either because of his appointment to the Supreme Court or his landmark win, *Brown v. Board of Education*. To the end of his days, however, Marshall credited the ruling on *Brown* to the brilliance of his mentor, Charles Hamilton Houston. If Crump is the branch and Marshall the root, then Houston was the seed. While I never met Houston—he was before my time—I did have the pleasure of meeting

Houston's successor, Fred Gray, at one of the anniversary marches in Selma. You have to be someone who's been involved in the movement to truly understand who Fred Gray was, and his impact on the American legal system.

Gray was *the* lawyer of the civil rights movement. He was the lawyer to Rosa Parks and Claudette Colvin, the Selma marchers Vivian Malone and James Hood, who'd both been denied admission to the University of Alabama, the victims of the Tuskegee Syphilis Study. The list goes on and on. In 1960, he successfully defended Dr. King from charges of tax evasion and won an acquittal from an all-white jury. If we're talking sports or entertainment: before Blacks could play Major League Baseball, you had the Negro League, with players like Satchel Paige and Cool Papa Bell. And before the Negro League, on the entertainment side, you had the Chitlin' Circuit, with artists like Tiny Bradshaw and Snookum Russell entertaining Black audiences long before James Brown, Sam Cooke, and Otis Redding broke into popular culture. If Gray had been a musician, he'd have been on the Chitlin' Circuit. If he'd played third base, he would have been in the Negro League. He was the man who played until Thurgood Marshall could become Jackie Robinson.

In all the years I've participated in the marches in Selma, I never once heard Gray give a speech. He doesn't showboat. In fact, I don't think he considers himself a civil rights leader per se, though he is. In his mind, he's a lawyer first and foremost, a lawyer's lawyer. As a lawyer, he was as humble as he was determined, fighting cases well into his old age. A common refrain among activists is that we never retire. Well, Fred Gray fixed that script. Originally, he'd wanted to become a preacher, but found his calling in law instead, delivering closing arguments that sounded like sermons. The jury was his clergy.

Besides Gray, Houston, and Marshall, there's another legal mind, lesser known but equally as significant— a hidden seed—who rewrote the American legal system. Not only did she have a profound impact on the argument that Marshall used to build the case around *Brown v. Board of Education*, but she also helped advance feminist issues while challenging popular notions about gender conformity. She did so by dint of living her own life as a Black woman to the fullest. That woman was Pauli Murray.

The Firebrand:
Pauli Murray

Pauli Murray never got the widespread credit she deserved. Had she not written a paper in her final year of law school stating that segregation violated the Thirteenth and Fourteenth Amendments of the Constitution, would Marshall have been able to successfully argue *Brown v. Board of Education* as well as he did? Would Ruth Bader Ginsburg have been able to convince the US Supreme Court that the Equal Protection Clause applied to women? Murray's fingerprints are on both cases.

Ever since the ruling of *Plessy v. Ferguson*, the landmark decision made by the US Supreme Court in 1896 that codified racial segregation laws, lawyers had been trying to land an argument against it by focusing on the "equal" part of the "separate but equal" doctrine. In a Howard University classroom in 1944, Murray suggested the opposite. Rather than trying to prove why a Black school wasn't the equivalent of a school for white students, for example, why not argue that segregation itself violated the Thirteenth and Fourteenth Amendments of the United States Constitution?

At the time, Murray was the only woman in Professor Spottswood Robinson's law class. Her fellow students laughed at her suggestion, calling it impractical. It was more than that. Murray's argument was a bull's-eye dart: simple, direct, and elegant. It was also radical. Undeterred, Murray bet Robinson ten bucks that *Plessy* would be overturned in twenty-five years. She short-changed herself: it was overturned in a decade when, only a few years later, Robinson presented Murray's paper on the subject to Thurgood Marshall's legal team, who referenced it to successfully argue *Brown v. Board of Education*. Marshall would later come to describe Murray's 1951 book *States' Laws on Race and Color* as the bible for civil rights litigators.

In the 1970s, Ginsburg would give Murray coauthor credit, along with Dorothy Kenyon, another pioneer in the field, on the legal brief that formed the basis of her argument for *Reed v. Reed*, the 1971 precedent-setting case that held that the Equal Protection Clause of the Fourteenth Amendment protected women's rights. Murray didn't author that paper herself, but Ginsburg acknowledged that, without Murray's work, she wouldn't have had a foundation for her own winning legal argument; such was the debt these two legal titans owed Murray. Ginsburg would also go on to draw heavily from Murray's *Jane Crow and the Law*, written with Mary Eastwood, to create material for one of the first law school courses devoted to gender discrimination. Murray's outsized influence and accomplishments changed the course of American history, yet hers was a life few among us know.

Anna Pauline Murray was born in Baltimore on November 20, 1910, the fourth of six children. Her mother, Agnes Fitzgerald Murray, a graduate of the Hampton Training School for Nurses, was thirty-five years old and seven months pregnant when she suffered a massive cerebral hemorrhage while standing on the staircase of the family home at 1330 Argyle Street. At the time, Murray was around four years old and, recovering from a recent bout of chicken pox, was isolating from the rest of the family. Her mother died within the hour. Upon learning of her mother's death, Murray insisted, "You just wait till my aunt Pauline comes. She'll straighten things out."

William, her father, was a bright scholar, a graduate of Howard University, and, later, a teacher and principal in the Baltimore public school system. Anxious and depressed after his wife's death, he struggled to make ends meet. Unable to care for his children, he split them up: the three eldest children stayed on with him and the two infants were sent to live with his sister Rose, on West Lanvale Street, a short distance away. Murray was a special case. In a sort of strange warning before she'd died, Agnes had written to her sister Pauline: "If anything happens to me, I want you to have little Pauline. She is not like the other children and I'm afraid they will ruin her disposition." It was decided that Murray would be sent to Durham, North Carolina, to live with her aunt Pauline along with another aunt, Sallie, and grandparents Robert George, a former Union soldier who went blind late in life, and Cornelia Smith Fitzgerald, a proud woman who frequently delivered impassioned sermons to neighbors and passersby from her porch step. Sadly, only three years later, back in Baltimore, William, still suffering from anxiety and depression, no doubt made worse by the long-term effects of typhoid fever and from the loss of his family, was committed to Crownsville State Hospital for the Negro Insane. With their father locked away in an asylum, the eldest children joined their brothers and sisters with their aunt Rose. Murray had little contact with this side of her family.

Growing up in the segregated world of the South, Murray was nonetheless surrounded and absorbed by a diversity of people from her mother's side. Cornelia, Murray's grandmother, had been born into bondage; her mother, Murray's great-grandmother, had been a part-Cherokee slave named Harriet. Murray's great-grandfather had been the white slaveowner's son and Harriet's frequent rapist. The Fitzgeralds, in fact, were a prominent white family in North Carolina—Cornelia was the granddaughter of Dr. James S. Smith of Chapel Hill, a member of the US House of Representatives from 1818 to 1820 and a former member of the board of trustees of the University of North Carolina. Cornelia's aunt, Mary Ruffin Smith, created a permanent trust fund for the education of students there called the Francis Jones Smith Scholarships. Where Cornelia was 100 percent Southern stock, a product of the kind of unspoken racial intermixing that the segregation of slavery and Jim Crow didn't curtail but perversely encouraged—so long as the intermixing was done by white men to Black women—Robert George, Murray's grandfather, hailed from the North. Raised in Pennsylvania, he'd attended antislavery meetings with Harriet Tubman and Frederick Douglass, and fought in the Civil War. His days as a military soldier informed his disciplinarian style as a grandparent. Being blind, he often made Murray read the newspaper aloud, prompting her to start an article from the beginning if and when she'd stumble over the words.

The resulting extended family was a mix of all different types of skin tones, religions, and economic backgrounds—from light-skinned to dark, Episcopalian to Quaker, impoverished to wealthy. Murray later said that her family looked "like a United Nations in miniature." Despite their diversity, Murray knew they had to keep to themselves—not even the more fair-skinned among them could cross the rules of Jim Crow. She wrote, "Surrounding and intersecting our segregated world at many points was the world of 'the white people.' It was a confusing world to me because I was both related to white people and alienated from them." It wasn't uncommon that the Ku Klux Klan would visit her grandmother's farm near Chapel Hill, brandishing torches, yelling, and circling the house with their horses. Lynchings were a regular fear.

In 1923, when Murray was nearly thirteen, she received word that her father had died and that his body was being sent home for burial. A white hospital guard named Walter Swiskoski had taunted her father with racist epithets, dragging him to the basement of the hospital and beating him to death with a baseball bat. When the gray casket arrived in Durham, no one was prepared for the sight of its gruesome contents. Murray wrote, "The body we saw was not recognizable as my father... His face was purple and swollen, his head was shaven, and his skull had been split open like a melon and sewed together loosely with jagged stitches crisscrossing the blood-clotted line of severance." Murray struggled to reconcile herself to her father's brutal death, writing, "I always believed that my father was a victim of racial antagonism." Swiskoski was convicted of manslaughter and sent to prison for ten years. William joined Anna in the Murray family plot at Laurel Cemetery. Years later, the cemetery went bankrupt, the family's gravestones vandalized and overrun. A new developer later erected a shopping center on the spot.

Murray struggled with her father's death and focused on her academics, eventually working her way through Hillside High School, where she graduated first in her class despite having received spotty grades for conduct, a result, she'd later say, of her fiery temper. At the time, most Blacks in North Carolina attended the North Carolina College for Negroes, but Murray felt that the entirety of her life up to that point had been defined by segregation. Longing for the promise of freedom in the North, she set her sights on Columbia University in New York City, until she learned that the college didn't admit women. She eventually ended up at Hunter College, which, at the time, was a women's college, financing her studies with various jobs and living at the Harlem YMCA where she met and befriended some of the Harlem Renaissance's most notable figures: Langston Hughes, W. E. B. Du Bois, and civil rights activist Mary McLeod Bethune, among others. It was during this time that Murray changed her name from "Anna Pauline" to "Pauli," and investigated possible gender reassignment treatments, including hormone therapy, which she was denied.

Both during and after her education at Hunter, Murray became increasingly more active in the world of civil rights, working for the Work Projects Administration (WPA) and becoming a teacher at the New York City Remedial Reading Project. She made frequent trips to North Carolina to visit her aunt Pauline and, each time, she further resented the ordeal of traveling Jim Crow south of Washington, writing, "The bus was the quintessence of the segregation evil, because there the separation of the races was merely symbolic. The intimacy of the bus interior permitted the public humiliation of Black people to be carried out in the presence of privileged white spectators, who witnessed our shame in silence or indifference." She decided that she would help demolish Jim Crow and, believing that the testing ground of American democracy and Christianity was uniquely situated in the problems that faced Black folks and the disinherited whites of the South, she decided to apply for graduate school in the South. She was interested in intentionally shaking up the system. But because there were no graduate schools for Blacks in North Carolina, she also knew that she was gearing up for a fight when she decided to apply for graduate study at the University of North Carolina. She'd been impressed by the institution's work in race relations and was also eager to study under sociologists Guy Johnson and Howard W. Odum, both of whom were considered outstanding in the field of race relations. At it happened, her choice would prove eventful for reasons she could never have foretold.

On December 5, 1938, President Roosevelt visited the campus of the University of North Carolina to accept an honorary degree of Doctor of Laws. In his acceptance speech, Roosevelt told the audience, "I am happy and proud to become an alumnus of the University of North Carolina, typifying as it does American liberal thought and American tradition." Murray was incensed by the president, writing, "It seemed to me that he spoke as if the local Negro population did not exist. The 'liberal' university that he had embraced so warmly had never admitted a Negro student.... During the six years he had been in the White House, I had become increasingly dismayed over his apparent coziness with white supremacy in the South, his silence on civil rights, and his refusal to speak out for a federal antilynching bill, which the NAACP had modestly proposed." Murray voiced her concerns to the president in a letter and, because she thought he'd never read it, also sent a copy of it to his wife, Mrs. Eleanor Roosevelt.

To her surprise, Mrs. Roosevelt answered Murray's letter, writing, "Great changes come slowly. I think they are coming, however, and sometimes it is better to fight hard with conciliatory methods. The South is changing, but don't push too hard." Murray didn't appreciate being told not to "push too hard," but noted that at a protest against segregation at the Southern Conference on Human Welfare in Birmingham, Alabama, Mrs. Roosevelt moved her chair to the middle aisle, midway between the white and Black sections, a courageous move that even the *Afro-American*, a Negro weekly, took pause to comment: "If the people of the South do not grasp this gesture, we must. Sometimes actions speak louder than words." Murray was prepared to give the first lady the benefit of the doubt, and the two women struck up a friendship that lasted a lifetime. It was Eleanor Roosevelt who famously dubbed Murray "the Firebrand" on account of her fiery, stubborn nature and her inability to take "no" for an answer.

Despite this proximity to power, Murray still had not yet been admitted to the University of North Carolina. Other Black students were having the same problem: Lloyd Gaines, for example, had been rejected by the University of Missouri School of Law in 1935 on the grounds of race. With the help of the NAACP, he brought suit, charging denial of equal protection guaranteed by the Fourteenth Amendment. His lawyer was Charles Hamilton Houston, who brought the case before the Supreme Court and won, making it the first major breach in the wall of segregated education since *Plessy v. Ferguson*. Despite Gaines's win, Murray was still rejected by the University of North Carolina. She reached out to the NAACP for help; her case was taken over by none other than Thurgood Marshall, then assistant special counsel of the NAACP. The media soon caught wind of Murray's story and the situation quickly turned messy, with the *Daily Tar*, the university's student newspaper, running the headline Officials Faced by Negro Application... Administration Is Confronted with "Liberalism" Issue. On it went, with local papers as far-flung as the *New York Daily News* picking up the story. Worse was the fact that Murray's white great-grandfather had attended the university himself and much of the family's sizable estate had been donated to the school, and here Murray, his "illegitimate" Black granddaughter, an excellent student, couldn't gain entry.

Unfortunately, when Murray saw Marshall about the possibility of the NAACP picking up her case, he'd decided not to take her on, explaining that the association had to select those cases they knew for certain they could win. Murray's case was questionable in part because she still lived in New York City; North Carolina could argue that the state had no constitutional duty to provide nonresidents with graduate training. But, in arguing with Marshall, Murray struck upon the legal point regarding the "separate but equal" argument that she'd later hone and finesse, and he'd use to success himself. The University of North Carolina had granted attendance to a lone Chinese girl. If the state permitted nonresident white students to attend its educational institutions, didn't it also have an obligation under the Fourteenth Amendment to admit Blacks? Her personal experience led her to question the legality of the situation. She soon saw what no one else did. Instead of discussing the inequities of separate facilities, she formulated a frontal attack to *Plessy*, writing, "My approach was to enumerate the rights that affect the individual's personal status in the community, one of which is 'the right not to be set aside or marked with a badge of inferiority.'" The effect of *Plessy v. Ferguson* was, in her words, "to place the Negro in an inferior social and legal position" and "to do violence to the personality of the individual affected, whether he is white or Black."

Unfortunately, Murray couldn't use her own argument to help herself; the case was an uphill battle. She eventually accepted her defeat with the University of North Carolina, writing, "I was part of a tradition of continuous struggle, lasting nearly twenty years, to open the doors of the state university to Negroes, a struggle marked by modest beginnings and several bitter defeats... Each new attempt was linked with a previous effort, which, although unsuccessful, nevertheless had an impact on the forward movement.... Once begun, this debate would not be silenced until the system of enforced segregation was outlawed by everyone in the land." She enrolled at the historically Black Howard University instead and, in 1942, joined George Houser, James Farmer, and Bayard Rustin to form the nonviolence-focused Congress of Racial Equality (CORE). Graduating top of her law school class, she won the Rosenwald Fellowship, a scholarship that previous top graduates had used to attend Harvard University. Murray, however, couldn't go to Harvard because she was a woman. Murray had faced down Jim Crow only to turn around to confront the misogyny of what she called Jane Crow. Here again she set her mind to work, chiseling away at both, tirelessly publishing scholarly papers, articles, and books of every stripe—nonfiction, memoir, biography, and poetry—that tackled the racism and sexism that had defined so much of her life. Her life as a feminist, helping Betty Friedan and others to found the National Organization for Women (NOW) in 1966, was just as varied as her activist work in civil rights. Her very identity breached both worlds, and she was forever advocating for her place at the table, voicing her concerns that CORE wasn't doing enough to address the issues that women faced on the one hand and NOW wasn't doing enough to address the issues that Blacks faced on the other. The issues surrounding her sexuality and gender were largely private, and she, like Bayard Rustin, unfortunately wouldn't become involved in LGBTQIA rights. In a sense, she was too ahead of her time. Her private struggles only recently became our very public ones. Ever the pioneer, she became the first Black woman in the United States to become an Episcopal priest after the church changed its policy.

Within the scope of her life, Murray seemed to live multiple lives. She was a raconteur, a civil rights activist, a feminist, troublemaker, and poet, a woman whom her mother knew was extraordinary, and in possession of the thing most of us want but few of us have: true grit. In her incredibly moving poem *Dark Testament*, she writes about letting the dream linger. Because of her good work, it does.

The Radical:
Ernestine Eckstein

Ernestine Eckstein was a later contemporary of Murray. As one of the first lesbians of color to be publicly involved in the early gay rights movement in New York City, Eckstein worked in an area of activism that, for Murray, had remained a private affair. Born in South Bend, Indiana, in 1941, Eckstein first became involved in activism as a student at Indiana University, where she worked with the NAACP during the civil rights movement. Her experiences there later helped shape her activism with gay and lesbian rights. By 1963, Eckstein had moved to New York City, where she joined the more progressive CORE, an organization Murray had helped create. It wasn't until she'd visited a close male friend in the city, who had confided in her about his own homosexuality, that, in Eckstein's words, "things began to click."

In 1966, Eckstein was interviewed for *The Ladder*, a magazine published by Daughters of Bilitis, the first lesbian civil and political rights organization in the United States. She told editor Barbara Gittings that, before arriving in New York, she'd never known anyone who was homosexual. She said, "Never heard the word mentioned.... This was a kind of blank that had never been filled in by anything—reading, experience, anything.... I didn't know there were other people who felt the same way I did." Her history-making interview marked the first time a Black woman was featured on the cover of the magazine.

Having determined her own homosexuality, Eckstein tried to find a related activist organization. Because of her experience in the civil rights movement, she assumed that there would be like-minded groups for the gay and lesbian community. There wasn't much. She saw ads for the Mattachine Society—New York's first "homophile" (gay and lesbian) rights group—in the *Village Voice*, and joined. At twenty-four, it wasn't just her age, color, or gender that made Eckstein stand out in the older, all-white, all-male group. It was the fact that she was protesting at all. At the time, most gays and lesbians opposed public protest. Members of Mattachine were supposed to present as demonstrably straight an appearance as possible so as not to rile people's fear and hate. Remember that homosexuality was considered a mental disorder until the American Psychological Association declassified it as such in 1973. Eckstein didn't go for the group's reticence at all, rejecting the notion that homosexuality was a sickness, saying, "So far as I'm concerned, homosexuality per se is not a sickness. When our groups seek out the therapists and psychologists, to me this is admitting we are ill by the very nature of our preference. And this disturbs me very much." She continued, saying, "I think the best therapy for a homosexual is reinforcement of his way of life, by associating with people who are like him." It was hardly surprising, however, that in the 1960s, most members of the gay and lesbian community didn't want the attention. As the then-closeted *Washington Post* reporter Leroy Aarons later explained to former CNN reporter Edward Alwood, author of the 1996 book *Straight News*: "I thought they [protesters] must be totally reckless or weird—using their names and talking to reporters. My second thought was, what does this have to do with me? I had my job, I had my gay life, and I had my straight life. I had totally compartmentalized my life and I didn't like those elements of my life getting confused."

Eckstein went in the opposite direction, becoming one of forty-five people who, in 1965, participated in the third gay rights demonstration of the White House, the majority of whom were fighting for gays and lesbians to keep their government jobs. The idea of gay marriage was too radical a thought to entertain. As Eckstein said in *The Ladder*: "The homosexual has to call attention to the fact that he's been unjustly acted upon. This is what the Negro did. Demonstrations, as far as I'm concerned, are one of the very first steps toward changing society." She would later be elected vice president of the New York chapter of the Daughters of Bilitis before moving to California and joining San Francisco's Black Women Organized for Action. Though she didn't regard herself as radical, her very existence as a Black lesbian put her in the center of three struggles for liberation that were happening simultaneously. By the time she died in 1992, the country had experienced waves of LGBTQIA activism, much of it built on Eckstein's shoulders. A lasting photographic image is of Eckstein wearing shades on a picket line— the lone Black woman among white men—and carrying a sign that reads Denial of Opportunity Is Immoral. Radical? I'd say she was right.

ALL STRIPES AND COLORS

Because of sexism and misogyny—both within the Black community and within American culture at large—we've lost out. We've missed key contributions made by women, especially Black women, throughout our history, overlooking the work of Pauli Murray, Diane Nash, and Jo Ann Robinson, for example, who were just as influential in the early days of civil rights as John Lewis, Medgar Evers, or Thurgood Marshall were, and without whom many of the advancements made in the social justice movement wouldn't have been possible. I've always taken umbrage at Coretta Scott King's legacy being reduced to that of being Dr. King's wife. No doubt her role as his wife was significant, but what about the civil rights work she did before she'd met her husband and continued long after his death? She was an activist in her own right and, in fact, had encouraged King to get involved in the antiwar movement long before he finally did. She was a feminist before feminism was considered fashionable.

As a product myself of the traditional Black church that merged into the early civil rights movement, I can say that I've observed misogyny firsthand in both the ranks of the church and within the movement. For the Black community, this misogyny is partly rooted in the ugly history of racism: Black men have wanted to be treated as equals to white men. Psychologically, one way to accomplish this is to minimize women and "put them in their place." This desire to exert a distorted view of manhood is at best rooted in insecurity and at worst a vestige from slave-owning days. White supremacy is, by design, patriarchal, racist, and classist. When the Founding Fathers wrote "all men are created equal," they weren't talking about women, Blacks, or the poor. They were talking about themselves: landowning white men. There's also a predominant feeling among some Black men that, from the earliest days of slavery, Black women were treated better than Black men by white men. This is difficult to unpack. Who's to say one person's suffering is greater or less than another's? Rape may not be a lynching but it's still another form of emotional, mental, and physical death—and women were lynched, too. It's a perversion to punish Black women over something they couldn't control themselves, and it tears at the essence of who we are.

In 1989, academic Kimberlé Crenshaw coined the term *in-*

tersectionality to describe the specific oppression experienced by Black women, because they stand at the intersecting point where racism and misogyny converge. Today, the term has broadened to take into account the various ways power and oppression converge: Pauli Murray or Ernestine Eckstein didn't need an academic term to tell them how life as Black LGBTQIA women meant dealing with multiple fronts of oppression. For many, intersectionality is a way of life. It's also a hidden strength: people poised at the intersection of different types of oppression often more clearly understand how our differences can help inform and broaden the fight for justice so everyone gets a seat at the table. Reverend Jesse Jackson's original Rainbow Coalition was a maturation of this idea. While the term *rainbow coalition* first came from Fred Hampton, the head of Chicago's Black Panther political party, Jesse took it and ran with it. (Hampton's local arm of the Panthers was comprised of progressive whites, the Chicago Seven, hard-core Black panthers, among others, and he'd called his eclectic group the Rainbow Coalition.) Jesse gave it broader appeal, using it to describe his vision of America, this idea that everyone's a different color of the rainbow and, by virtue of our differences, can make unique contributions to the betterment of the American dream.

Through my early work with Shirley Chisholm and my interactions with Bayard Rustin and others, I learned how the struggle for civil rights, women's rights, and LGBTQIA rights are intimately entwined, and the more I've come to understand the struggles of other activist groups and movements, the more I see social justice today as a way of perceiving the entire landscape of activism. You cannot fight for one group without fighting for everyone: the poor, women, the gay community, the Asian community, immigrants, and anyone else who feels marginalized or whose civil rights are under attack. Otherwise, you're playing for the other team and falling victim to their tired tactic of divide and conquer.

How can we fight for fairness, justice, and equality for all without shining a light on the lives of extraordinary women, pioneers like Murray and Eckstein? We can't. Their legacy is part of the fabric of the American story. Their work paved a path forward for millions of girls when none before existed. If we are to confront the original sin of slavery, we must also face up to our country's misogynistic tendencies. It's not enough to simply acknowledge sexism and move on. We must course-correct by championing women's history, celebrating their voices and accomplishments, and partnering with them to help advance meaningful change.

6

A MORAL BEACON

"Moral courage is a rarer commodity than bravery in battle or great intelligence. Yet it is the one essential, vital quality for those who seek to change a world which yields most painfully to change."

—ROBERT F. KENNEDY

Much of American law itself, whether we're aware of it or not, is codified to protect the very system of white supremacy pioneers like Thurgood Marshall and Pauli Murray aimed to dismantle. They, along with other great legal minds before them, flipped the script, working to change the system from the inside, reinterpreting and applying legal arguments and language that, for decades, had been the purview of legalized racism itself. To change the system, they thought outside of it.

Thurgood created legal arguments that hadn't been attempted before; that was his genius. Murray possessed an exquisite mind, and was a fighter through and through, determined. I am forever in awe of such individuals for whom discipline of the mind is a defining strength. As a preacher and orator, I have much freer rein than that of a lawyer. If I see something that's outta line, I'm gonna say something. I can more freely express the rage of a community than a lawyer can. Not only can I speak directly to the people, but I can also speak to the politicians: truth to power. And yet, the social justice movement needs both types of players. The raw emotion and sense of passion that flares up whenever injustice rears its ugly head has to translate into sound, disciplined legislation. Otherwise, what's the point? Otherwise, I'm just a man on a soapbox. If I can think of one individual who not only flipped the script time and time again but who also occasionally went off script, forging his own path in the world of civil rights and applying the lessons learned to the social justice movement at large, all the while stirring up his own brand of controversy, it's James Meredith.

Several years ago, I spoke at Jackson State University in Jackson, Mississippi. Before Mayor Chokwe Lumumba introduced me, he pulled me aside and pointed out an elderly man sitting in the audience. What he didn't know is that I'd already recognized that shock of white hair and beard: James Meredith. A wave of excitement rushed over me as I realized that the man who'd first integrated the University of Mississippi was about to hear me speak. I decided to incorporate Meredith into my speech and mentioned that the civil rights icon had made a lasting impression on me as a child, which was true. I was in third grade when President Kennedy sent in federal troops to put down the Ole Miss Riot of 1962, but I still remember it like it was yesterday. For a while, it was all anyone could talk about. As an eight-year-old kid, I had an active imagination and could think only of Meredith hunkered down alone and hiding, while an angry white mob of segregationists dangerously roamed the campus. (It turned out my imagination was right-on.) I wondered if I would one day be as brave as he.

When I was eleven years old, Meredith staged the March Against Fear protest, in which he began a solitary walk on

June 6, 1966, intending to walk from Memphis, Tennessee, to Jackson, Mississippi, to call attention to racism and voter discrimination in the South. Shortly after he'd begun the march, he was shot by James Norvell, a white sniper. That didn't stop Meredith. He was sent to the hospital to recover while none other than Dr. King and about fifteen thousand supporters continued the march in his name. It was at this march that Stokeley Carmichael, leader of the Student Nonviolent Coordinating Committee (SNCC), first raised his fist and chanted, "Black Power," a call that would come to encapsulate his concept of militant Black nationalism. Meredith nonetheless returned to finish what he'd started, and one can only imagine that fear was indeed marched out of the South that day. Later on in his life, Meredith ran for Adam Clayton Powell Jr.'s seat in the House of Representatives. Powell had been one of my childhood heroes. The fact that anyone would dare to take on the larger-than-life, cigar-chomping New Yorker elevated themselves in my eyes.

"Though I've never met him personally, in a sense, I've known James Meredith one way or another all my life," I told the university audience. "His is a long shadow that falls across civil rights activists." I gave the audience a little background on the man and sensed Meredith wanted to say something himself, so I happily ceded the floor to him. Meredith spoke with the measured cadence of a man who knows himself deeply. Rather than speak about himself, however, he turned the lens back on me. He talked about how he knew me, that I was brought up under Wyatt Tee Walker, who was Dr. King's deputy director and on the first board of directors for NAN. Walker, it turned out, was connected to one of Meredith's attorneys, Constance Baker Motley. I knew of Motley but had never met her. Every story I'd heard of her revolved around her legal acumen and the fact that she was both dignified and hard as nails. She'd broken the proverbial glass ceiling for women years before Shirley Chisholm made her bid in politics and well before Kamala

Harris was studying for the bar. Meredith confirmed my suspicion. "She was the real deal," he said, nodding. Meredith and I kept chatting and I soon realized I'd yet to deliver the speech I'd been invited to give. Truth be told, I would have preferred to have kept our conversation going, but Meredith gamely gave the floor back to me. I'm not sure he'd anticipated being part of the evening's act. It was only later in my life that I gained a full appreciation of my interaction with Meredith and was able to contemplate the fascinating contradictions of his character.

The Rebel:
James Meredith

James Meredith may have been known as one of the early civil rights pioneers to break the color code, but his journey toward doing so started more than a decade earlier when he first donned air force blues. Born in Kosciusko, Mississippi, on June 25, 1933, Meredith was one of ten kids. Having heard that the air force had a reputation for treating Black troops as full American citizens, he joined up after high school. He spent his last three years in uniform, from 1957 to 1960, at Tachikawa Air Base near Tokyo, Japan.

One day during his travels near the base, Meredith came upon a young boy who was surprised to meet a Black man from the American South. The boy confessed to Meredith that he'd heard the South was a terrible place for Blacks. Meredith was surprised the boy knew the stories of the Little Rock Nine and Emmett Till, and was ashamed by the "stain and disgrace white supremacy" had made on both him and his country. He wrote, "I resolved to return to Mississippi to change things for the better.... I knew then that I had to leave the air force, come back to Mississippi, and go to war." And so he did.

Meredith returned to Mississippi where he studied at the all-Black Jackson State University. He longed to transfer to the University of Mississippi, nicknamed Ole Miss, largely because he knew that his enrollment there would help fracture the system of segregation in the South, that is, if he wasn't chased off or killed first. The conditions under which Black people lived under Jim Crow had already made Meredith a dead man walking. The way he saw it, he may as well help "drive a stake through the heart of the beast" or be killed doing it. Meredith strategically focused his ire on the University of Mississippi because it was considered the crowning gem of white endowment. At the time, the school proudly upheld its racist traditions— from its name ("ole miss" was what slaves called the plantation owner's wife) to its Confederate soldier mascot (plantation owner "Colonel Reb") to its open-armed embrace of the Confederate battle flag and its segregationist way of life. Meredith set his sights on tearing down its mantle of oppression and, with the legal help of the NAACP, sued the university. Thurgood Marshall assigned the case to Constance Baker Motley as lead attorney, asserting that she had a better chance of winning than he because in the Deep South, in Marshall's words, "all the white men had Black mammies." An all-white jury or judge, he figured, would be more amenable to a Black woman than to a Black man. In 1962, after roughly fourteen months of delaying litigation, Supreme Court Justice Hugo Black vacated an order of a lower court and issued the final order that Meredith be admitted to the University of Mississippi.

Meredith had won the battle, but as he'd soon discover, he'd just entered the war.

The same day that the order came down, September 13, Mississippi's governor, Ross Barnett, attempted to bar Meredith's entry by issuing a proclamation directing state education and university officials to defy the court orders, setting up what looked like a constitutional crisis between the state of Mississippi and the federal government. In his book *Three Years in Mississippi*, Meredith wrote, "Mississippi had declared itself in effect no longer subject to the laws of the United States. The United States now became officially a party to my case against the state of Mississippi." In a televised address to the people of Mississippi, Barnett declared, "We must either submit to the unlawful dictates of the federal government or stand up like men and tell them, 'Never!'" Barnett had the Mississippi Legislature pass a law banning the enrollment of anyone with a charge of "moral turpitude" in state or federal court and then had Meredith arrested for accidentally writing "1960" instead of "1961" while registering to vote. Meredith found himself caught between two legal systems: the federal government, which was trying to dispense justice, and the Mississippi system of justice, which was more interested in having Meredith jailed. As Meredith recounted, "This was my first and only time in jail of any kind. I was put into a big cell with a large number of other Negroes who were charged with crimes ranging from petty thievery to murder." He confessed, "Jail is not my idea of the best place from which to fight a war. As a matter of fact, one sure way to remove me from this world is to put me in a Mississippi jail without just cause." The Fifth Circuit ordered his immediate release and Attorney General Robert F. Kennedy and the

Department of Justice stepped into the fray, eventually charging Bennett with contempt. Once freed from jail, Meredith made multiple attempts to register at the university but was physically blocked each time by either Barnett or a rotating roster of other segregationists, including lieutenant governor Paul B. Johnson Jr., along with any number of state troopers. On September 28, the Fifth Circuit threatened to both imprison and fine Barnett if Meredith was not registered by October 2.

In a series of telephone calls, President Kennedy and Attorney General Robert Kennedy tried to convince Barnett to let Meredith onto campus to register for classes. The president vowed that, if he couldn't persuade Barnett with his words and political charm, he'd have no choice but to use the force of federal troops, a risky move, one he acknowledged could cost him Southern votes and, worse, lives. The Kennedy-Barnett standoff had a Civil War feel to it, with Barnett being an old-style Southern Democrat who believed that segregation laws trumped all else, including Congress and the Supreme Court. Kennedy, of course, was the face of the Democratic Party, a blue-blood Yankee, who understood integration was the hot-button topic of his presidency. He'd won the thirty-fifth office of the presidency by a sliver, and still needed to court Southern Democrats to his favor. Barnett likely knew the tides of change were rolling across the country— integration would soon be a done deal—but, according to author and historian Bill Doyle, the Mississippi governor needed to save face, writing, "Ross Barnett desperately wanted the Kennedys to flood Mississippi with combat troops because that's the only way Ross Barnett could tell his white segregationist backers, 'Hey,

I did everything I could, I fought them, but to prevent bloodshed, in the end, I made a deal.'"

On Saturday, September 29, hours after an Ole Miss football game at Jackson, Meredith was escorted to campus by members of the Mississippi Highway Patrol. If it was Meredith's wish to avoid large groups of angry students, it was short-lived once the school band returned from the game dressed in traditional Confederate uniforms and waving the Confederate battle flag, which featured the same fighting colors as the Ole Miss Rebels. Not exactly a warm welcome. Throughout the day and into the evening, chants and cheers followed Meredith around campus:

Two, four, six, eight,
We don't wanna integrate!
Two, four, one, three,
We hate Kennedy!

According to the *New York Times*, there were other cries and racial taunts, too, with mobs of students yelling, "Get a rope!" The following day, Meredith was escorted to his dorm room where he was greeted by five hundred federal marshals assigned for his protection.

By Sunday evening, former Army Major General Edwin Walker appeared on campus and further enflamed a group of students who'd gathered in front of the lyceum. (Walker, it should be noted, had been forced to retire from the army when he was ordered to stop giving out racist literature to his troops but had refused to do so.) Within an hour of Meredith's arrival, a riot broke out, with thousands of volunteers showing up on campus at Walker's urging. The rioting mob of about three thousand people consisted of high school and college students, known Ku Klux Klan members, residents of the town of Oxford, and a mix of those outside the area. The mob patrolled the campus, searching for Meredith and doing all the things violent rioters do. They smashed streetlights. They started fires. They burned down a mobile television unit. They raided classrooms and laboratories, searching for weapons and materials to make Molotov cocktails. President Kennedy deployed members of the Mississippi National Guard along with army troops from Memphis, Tennessee, during the middle of the night, led by Brigadier General Charles Billingslea.

Meredith remained hunkered down in his dorm, Baxter Hall, as the federal troops clashed with the mob. Rather than de-escalate the situation, Governor Barnett incited it further, declaring, "We will never surrender," in a radio address. The mob attacked the officers, lit General Billingslea's car on fire, and, in the end, killed two civilians: French journalist Paul Guihard and twenty-three-year-old Ray Gunter, a white jukebox repairman. More than three hundred people were injured. On October 1, 1962, the fifteen-hour riot was quelled. In the end, over thirty thousand troops were deployed, alerted, and committed during the Battle of Oxford—the largest for a single disturbance in American history until the insurrection of January 6, 2021. Speaking of the riot to interviewer Anthony Lewis and Burke Marshall, Robert Kennedy admitted, "The idea that we got through the evening without the marshals being killed and without Meredith being killed was a miracle." Some historians have argued that the integration of Ole Miss was the last battle of the Civil War.

The next day, Meredith, escorted by US Marshals, attended his first class, an American history course, never mind that he'd just changed the course of American history himself. During his tenure at University of Mississippi, Meredith was treated with derision by his classmates and was continuously harassed. Those few white students who were nice to him, sharing their lunch table, for example, found their lockers vandalized or worse. As for being the first Black to integrate the school, Meredith wouldn't have been out of line for wanting to feel a bit heroic. Instead, he later said that he felt as if he was "the most segregated Negro in America." His room was equipped with a switch to notify a sixteen-man patrol guard in case of trouble, its bright red light a warning and a comfort both. Because he'd already accumulated credits at another school, he didn't need to attend the school for very long in order to graduate. In fact, he was awarded a bachelor's degree after just two semesters. Meredith claimed, however, that it was never about getting the degree. Speaking to the National Visionary Leadership Project, he said, "It was about power. It was about citizenship. It was about enjoying everything any other man enjoys. It ain't never been about education." At a 2016 ceremony for Black History Month at Fort Hood, Meredith said bluntly, "What I did at Ole Miss had nothing to do with going to classes. My objective was to destroy the system of white supremacy." He acknowledged he'd had powerful allies who helped, most notably President Kennedy, who had sent in the best of the United States Army. Meredith would go on to receive a law degree from Columbia University.

In 2006, Ole Miss erected a statue in Meredith's honor. Over the years, Meredith has both argued for and against his own statue, initially saying it and the Confederate statue on the circle in front of the lyceum should be removed. The statue, like the man himself, has been a frequent point of controversy, with a former Ole Miss student getting a six-month prison sentence after he and two other Sigma Phi Epsilon fraternity members placed a noose and an old Georgia state flag, which contains the Confederate battle emblem, on the statue. Meredith never wanted his statue to be a "Black thing." His real focus has always been to destroy white supremacy, no matter the form it takes, saying in a 2008 interview with the *Jackson Free Press*, "There is absolutely no difference between segregation to maintain white supremacy and desegregation to maintain white supremacy, or integration to maintain white supremacy, or Black this, white that, and other state-funded things." He continued, "I am a citizen of the United States of America. That's the designation that I want everybody to reach."

It might be surprising to learn that the man who claimed he was on a mission from God to dismantle white supremacy and to uplift Black and brown people was then mired in controversy in the 1980s and 1990s for seemingly running counter to his own mission by running as a Republican for Congress, serving as an adviser to Senator Jesse Helms of North Carolina, a conservative who opposed the civil rights movement, and for supporting David Duke, a former member of the Ku Klux Klan, who ran for governor of Louisiana in 1991. In interviews since, Meredith claims those experiences were among his most important because he learned, in his words, "what politicians on the inside know about the opposition." If Marshall and Murray were trying to change the system from the inside, Meredith was trying to infiltrate it or at least understand it from the inside out. He's oftentimes been a vocal critic of the movement in teasing out some of its nuances, including the view that many poor whites in America haven't been given a fair shot at the American Dream, a truth Donald Trump capitalized on to drastic effect. Meredith challenges us to truly think about what we believe, and then to argue and test out those beliefs from every angle.

There are some who dismiss Meredith because of his controversial stances. In the march toward the fulfillment of social justice, are we looking for saints or are we looking for righteous troublemakers? The fact that Meredith may have embraced some questionable figures later in his life doesn't negate what he did on September 29, 1962, when he walked onto the campus of the University of Mississippi, the yoke of school integration hung across his shoulders. It doesn't lessen the effect of the sniper's bullet that he took when he marched for voting rights. It touches a nerve in me. Let's not get into purity politics because none among us are so holy. The balance lies in how we leave this world. Did we make it a better place for our sons and daughters? Our grandchildren? If the answer in our heart of hearts is yes, then I'm willing to overlook some of the mud splatter on my shoes.

Commenting on the worldwide movement for George Floyd, Meredith wrote, "Today, Black and brown people are inspiring the world with their strength, determination, and willingness to see the struggle through to total victory. I believe that this global uprising will never stop, and it will move into every heart, home, and community on Earth, until the day when all people are treated with dignity, respect, and love that God intends for us. I believe that on that day, white supremacy will finally be buried forever." Part of understanding the historic sweep of history is that movements, while made up of ordinary people, are bigger than any one individual. James Meredith is that rare example of someone who understands that progress means you oftentimes get a little dirty, especially when you're working out front of everyone else.

THE DISINHERITED AND THE MALADJUSTED

When I first started doing activism work, I didn't present as polished. I was no Sidney Poitier. I didn't come out of an Ivy League college nor was my father a preacher nor his father before him. I didn't have the pedigree. What I had was a lot of mud on my shoes. My ancestors were slaves. My mother dropped out of grade school and worked in the fields. My father had some financial success, but it was short-lived. After he left the family, my mother struggled to raise us, leaving for work before the sun came up. Nothing from my personal background undoes the work I've done. If anything, the mud on my shoes has only helped inform and shape my activism. It was only after I'd made my name in some battles, and this after decades of fighting, that the elites who'd once rejected me started welcoming me instead. One thing I've noticed is that the elites like to tell you that you've been given their stamp of approval. I guess it's so you remember that it can also be taken away. I don't let that get the best of me, though. Whenever someone from the establishment says something like, "Well, Sharpton, you've proven yourself to be this, that, or the other, someone we respect now," I always gently push back.

"Yeah," I say, "you accept me now. The question is if I'll ever accept y'all." It's just enough to keep everyone, including me, on their toes. Chances are, if you're doing something only to court the favor or approval of someone other than yourself, it's not worth doing in the first place.

W. E. B. Du Bois popularized the term "the Talented Tenth," this idea that emphasized the importance of developing leadership qualities among the most able 10 percent of Black Americans. He was talking about higher education but this concept—that the elite Black is somehow better than the average Black—shut the door on what I call the disinherited ninth, people like George Floyd and Eric Garner, those individuals who, for whatever reason, society has deemed "unfit" to reap the attention or rewards of their own triumphs and struggles. Dr. King had a term to describe us, too: "the maladjusted." In a speech at Western Michigan University in 1963, he said, "We all want the well-adjusted life…. But I say to you, my friends…there are certain things in our nation and in the world [about] which I am proud to be maladjusted and which I hope all men of goodwill will be maladjusted until the good societies realize. I say very honestly that I never intend to become adjusted to segregation and discrimination." He then listed other societal ills to which we should never become adjusted: religious bigotry, economic disparity, the madness of militarism, the self-defeating effects of physical violence.

On a Montgomery bus in 1955, one such maladjusted youth was a Black girl named Claudette Colvin. Dark-skinned, pregnant, and unwed at the age of fifteen, Colvin was the very definition of the disinherited, an unlikely hero. In defiance of both Jim Crow and the comfort level of Black leaders, she bucked the system and made a stand. Her pioneering bravery paved the way for Rosa Parks, the more polished of the two women, who later carried the mantle of the movement on her shoulders. It was Colvin, however, who truly proved Dr. King right: it's the maladjusted who make the rest of society readjust.

The Trailblazer:
Claudette Colvin

In 1955, fifteen-year-old Claudette Colvin boarded a city bus in Montgomery to go home from school. A white passenger boarded, and the bus driver told Colvin and her friends to stand at the back of the bus. Colvin's classmates moved; she did not. The police were called. Colvin was arrested and taken to an adult cell where she waited, nervous and afraid, for her mother and her pastor to post bail. Before you go on thinking that Colvin made some rash decision guided by her life as an outspoken teenager, think again. Colvin, though young, wasn't new to civil rights; her decision hadn't been impulsive. She'd been studying the Constitution at school and, prior to her arrest, had recently written a school paper on the problems of segregation in the South. She was also a member of the NAACP's Youth Council, a group that met every Sunday at Rosa Parks's apartment.

At the time, Parks was a respectable woman in her forties, married, church-going, and, as branch secretary for the local NAACP, already invested in the movement. (The story goes that she'd gotten the secretarial job because she'd been the only woman in the room at a meeting. The men asked her to take notes and, in her words, she was "too timid to say no.") The two women couldn't have been more opposite in background, appearance, and demeanor, and yet, if Parks needed an example of courage before she performed her own act of civil disobedience, she found it in Colvin. When Parks heard that the teenager had been arrested, she jumped into action, fund-raising money to help with her impending court case. Fortunately or not, two of the three charges against Colvin were dropped, including the charge of breaking Montgomery's segregation law, which meant Colvin couldn't challenge it. When Colvin was asked later about why she didn't move on the bus, she replied, "I say it felt as though Harriet Tubman's hands were pushing me down on one shoulder and Sojourner Truth's hands were pushing me down on the other."

Nine months after Colvin's stand, Parks decided that she, too, felt the weight of history on her and had had enough. Despite the fact that there were other incidents that predated both Parks and Colvin, including as far back as 1940, when Pauli Murray was also arrested and imprisoned for refusing to sit at the back of the bus in Richmond, Virginia, the civil rights movement had yet to gain real traction and couldn't capitalize on those earlier moments. By the time Parks made her stand, however, those moments, combined with the outrage that accompanied Emmett's murder, along with related issues of brutality and voter suppression, added up to a movement. Black leaders quickly rallied around Parks. Following her arrest, the Montgomery Improvement Association (MIA) was formed, and Dr. Martin Luther King Jr. was elected as its president. Its first order of business was a 382-day bus boycott, which Parks helped broadcast, even electing to be arrested when rumors spread that anyone involved in the boycott would be jailed.

Colvin would go on to be one of four plaintiffs, along with Aurelia Browder, Susie McDonald, and Mary Louise Smith, in *Aurelia S. Browder v. William A. Gayle*, which challenged the constitutionality of bus segregation laws in Montgomery. She was represented by none other than Charles D. Langford and Fred Gray in what was Gray's first civil rights case fresh out of law school. Langford and Gray filed the federal district court petition that became *Browder v. Gayle* on February 1, 1956, two days after segregationists bombed Dr. King's house. Despite winning, Colvin was largely abandoned by community leaders, who deemed Parks a more accessible spokesperson for the movement.

While I've never met Colvin, I did grow up knowing about her. Rumor was she didn't get the attention of the movement because she was an outspoken, dark-skinned, unwed, pregnant teenager. And she was poor. Parks was simply more palatable: older, married, quiet, and principled. Already in her forties, she was also more mature, and probably better able to withstand the stress, chaos, and media attention than the younger Colvin. Parks was simply more attractive as a public figure, and the movement needed a symbol. Today, we'd say Parks was more "mediagenic." It's unfortunate because Colvin wasn't any less courageous. In fact, you could argue that Colvin's bravery was greater because she had more to lose by taking a stand. We choose our heroes, and in 1955, the world picked Rosa Parks. While I've always understood the strategic decision made by the civil rights leaders to laud Parks, and have immense respect and admiration for Parks herself, so much so that I was honored to do her eulogies in 2005, I also have an equal amount of respect for Colvin. At the time, there was no celebration for Colvin. No groundswell of support behind her. She made a personal sacrifice and put herself on the line when no one else would lay themselves down for her. How many other Claudette Colvins has history overlooked? How many other Black men and women have taken a stand when no one else was watching? To do such a thing is a profound measure of who you are as a person and shows where your moral compass points. It's one thing to take a stand when you know there's going to be a reaction. It's another thing entirely when you do so in the darkness of the night.

At Parks's funeral, I asked everyone to make what I called a "Rosa Resolution." That is, a resolution to do something that'll make a difference in the world because she made a difference for us. It was a way to both honor her legacy and to carry it forward. Today, I'm encouraging you to make a commitment to being courageous in Colvin's name, to stand up for yourself and for others in the name of social justice: a "Colvin Commitment." It doesn't matter what your background is. It doesn't matter if you're not one of the so-called "power brokers" of the world. Take courage in Colvin's example. We need both acts of bravery—Colvin's raw courage and Parks's principled stance—in order to successfully build a movement. If we had one but not the other, it wouldn't work. There's room for different styles of activism and camps of thought so long as we're all generally headed in the same direction.

After her Supreme Court victory, Colvin moved to New York, where she worked as a nursing aide for more than thirty years. In 2017, the Montgomery Council passed a resolution saying that March 2 would be named Claudette Colvin Day in the city and, in 2019, four granite markers were unveiled in Montgomery to honor the plaintiffs in the suit *Browder v. Gayle*. These accolades, while moving, fail to convey our full debt to one of the women whose name—not Parks's—is on the Supreme Court ruling that dismantled bus segregation.

DON'T LOOK BACK

Movements happen because of the cause and effect of several smaller incidents, known and unknown, that build to a climate or consciousness of change. Then, when the right spark hits, the fire starts. One such spark was a young girl named Ruby Bridges.

Ruby, like James Meredith, came to symbolize the desegregation movement in education. Unlike Meredith, she was only six
years old when she was escorted by federal marshals past a mob
of hate-filled white protesters standing guard outside the William Frantz Elementary School in Louisiana. Most Americans
know the story of Ruby Bridges—she's frequently heralded as
an example of human resilience in the face of difficulty. Photographs from her first day of school are seared into our public
conscience: Ruby neatly dressed in a pretty dress with polished
shoes, a smart book satchel in her hand, and grown men in suits
flanking her every side. The image was so stirring that Norman
Rockwell chose it as the subject of his 1963 painting *The Problem
We All Live With,* his first assignment for *Look* magazine. (For
some time, Rockwell's painting hung outside the Oval Office
during Obama's first term.) And yet, while Ruby's story is certainly one of triumph, we tend to gloss over the personal history of the Bridges family and the hardships they jointly faced.

Ruby's mother, Lucille Commadore, was born in Tylertown,
Mississippi, the child of sharecropping parents. When she was
in the eighth grade, Lucille dropped out of school to help her
parents in the fields. She married Abon Bridges, a mechanic,
when she was just nineteen years old. Both were uneducated,
neither could read nor write. One year later in 1954—the same
year as the landmark ruling of *Brown v. Board of Education*—Ruby
was born. In search of a better life and education for their children, the family decided to move to Louisiana. Besides Ruby,
the Bridgeses had two other children. The youngest, Mary, was
just three months old when they relocated.

In 1960, Louisiana was ordered to desegregate. School dis-
tricts created academic entrance exams for Black children to take
to enroll in white schools. Much like the literacy tests used to
keep people of color away from the voting booths during Jim
Crow, the academic tests were designed to make it difficult for
Blacks to test into the all-white school system. Of the nearly

two hundred children who took the test, only six passed. One of those six was Ruby Bridges. When the Bridges family met with Superintendent Redman to find out how he planned to integrate Ruby at the local elementary school, he asked Lucille and Abon if they were praying people.

"We are," Lucille responded.

"Good," he said. "'Cause you're gonna need to pray."

Abon was a gentle man who didn't want any part of school integration. As a soldier in the Korean War, where he was awarded the Purple Heart, he'd experienced segregation on the front lines. His experiences there told him that things would never change. He knew the cruelty of white supremacy and feared for his daughter's safety. Lucille, however, saw only an incredible educational opportunity for her daughter that both she and her husband had been denied. She was convinced no harm would come to their daughter. After lengthy family discussions, Abon finally relented. Neither could have anticipated what lay in wait.

When Lucille and Ruby showed up for the first day of school, Lucille was overwhelmed by the show of armed forces. Then she saw the sea of angry white protesters. They carried signs with messages like All I Want for Christmas Is a Clean White School. High school boys gathered to sing a new chorus to the "Battle Hymn of the Republic": "Glory, glory, segregation, the South will rise again." The mob threw eggs and tomatoes at the mother-and-daughter duo, none of which hit them, thanks to the protection of the marshals. When they got to the front of the school, an armed policeman stood in their way.

"You cannot come in," he told them.

A field marshal responded, "The president of the United States says we can."

In an interview for the 2016 traveling exhibit "The Power of Children" at the Altharetta Yeargin Art Museum in Texas, Lucille said, "And then, a little later on, one of the city policemen was arrested because he pulled out his gun to shoot." It was only later that Lucille realized that he'd most likely meant to kill her—Ruby wouldn't have wanted to go to the school if her mother had died with her trying. Returning home from school that first day, Lucille was followed by a line of cars, from which passengers pitched bottles and other objects at her and her car. Neighbors of the Bridgeses had gathered at a bar at the end of the block and returned fire, throwing bottles themselves until the field marshals stepped in, armed with machine guns. "I didn't know how bad things would get," Lucille said. "I remember being afraid on the first day Ruby went to the school, when I came home and turned on the TV set and I realized that, at that moment, the whole world was watching my baby and talking about her. At that moment, I was most afraid."

Ruby and Lucille were escorted by four federal marshals to school every day, enduring the taunts together and holding their heads high. If that was life outside of the school, inside it was also difficult, but for another reason: Ruby was largely by herself. Once she'd successfully entered the school, she discovered that the white students had been withdrawn from it, because most of the parents had boycotted the integration. For the rest of the school year, Ruby spent most of her time with her teacher, a white Boston native woman named Barbara Henry. As a class of one, Ruby learned to read and write in a largely empty building, more abandoned than desegregated. Henry said, "There was never a hand offered the entire year to do a single thing for Ruby and me."

As an adult, Ruby admitted that the worst part of the whole experience for her was being lonely. She desperately wanted someone to play with. A few white families finally relented and brought their kids to school, but it wasn't until spring that Ruby was allowed to see or play with them. By her second year of school, about a hundred white students returned. One of the first children to return, a girl of six with curls of blond hair, approached Ruby to tell her that her mother said they couldn't play together. A few minutes later, their teacher found them jumping rope. As one white mother confessed, "Most of the mothers around here were more scared than bothered by Ruby. But the kids, they never seemed afraid, and they wouldn't let us get too afraid either." Despite this, angry crowds of adults still gathered outside every day for a whole year to protest. As an adult, Ruby said, "Mrs. Henry was an amazing teacher, and she did everything she could to keep my mind off of what was happening outside, because you could hear them screaming and shouting, but that went on all day." Amazingly, Ruby never missed a day of school.

The stress took a profound toll on the Bridges family—not only did Abon lose his job and grocery stores refused to sell to Lucille, but Abon's sharecropping parents, who lived in a small rural town, were constantly harassed, and feared lynching. They were eventually evicted from their land, where they'd lived and worked for a quarter-century. By the time Ruby had reached seventh grade, her parents had separated, unable to carry the burden of having to navigate years of hatred placed squarely on their shoulders. In her book *Through My Eyes*, Ruby wrote, "My parents had never really agreed about my going to William Frantz, and it put a wedge between them. Money problems and other family problems continued, too, which couldn't have helped. After my parents separated, my mother moved us children out of our house on France Street and into a housing project." Despite the next several years of familial hardship, including the death of her beloved father from a heart attack, Ruby grew up to become a success in her own right, today working as a civil rights activist and as chair of the Ruby Bridges Foundation, which she formed in 1999. In 2011, she was invited to the White House and, while viewing *The Problem We All Live With*, then-President Obama told her, "I think it's fair that if it hadn't been for you guys, I might not be here, and we wouldn't be looking at this together."

When asked in an interview what advice as an adult she'd have for the six-year-old Ruby, she didn't hesitate, saying, "It would be the same advice that the field marshals gave me. They said, 'Ruby, walk straight ahead and don't look back.' That's what they told me at six years old, and I've tried really, really hard to do that. I think that would be my advice to all of us who are on this path and want to see a better world for our children." In thinking more about Ruby's story, two individuals in particular stand out to me: Barbara Henry, her teacher, and Dr. Robert Coles, the Harvard child psychologist who began counseling Ruby in 1960, both of whom, in helping Ruby, also helped make the world a better place for all our children.

The Bravehearted:
Barbara Henry

As a young girl, Barbara Henry attended the Girls' Latin School (GLS) in Boston, where, for the duration of her six years there, she stared at a dictum posted on the wall in the Latin classroom: "Duty first, honor always, self last." That statement became a kind of moral beacon she'd come to depend on throughout her life, especially as Ruby's teacher. As the first public college prep school for girls in the United States, GLS put a premium on teaching its students to appreciate our shared commonalities—our sense of character and our ideals and goals—irrespective of class, community, or color. Henry said that this lesson, combined with the messaging of the Latin dictum, not only taught her the value of her own self-worth but also how to respect and see the self-worth in others no matter their background.

As an adult, Henry married a Louisiana native and moved to New Orleans, where she applied for a job in the city's school system. When the superintendent asked if she'd have a problem working in one of the desegregated schools, Henry thought it a strange question, posing one of her own in return: "Why would it make any difference?" Born and raised in the North and having spent some time overseas, Henry had already been part of a desegregated world for years. She was posted to William Frantz Elementary School.

The morning of November 14, 1960, Henry made her way to the school, her husband escorting her. When they saw the mob, her husband asked, "Whaddya think?" though he already knew Henry's likely answer. There was no way she was going to turn around. The first line of the moral dictum she'd learned at GLS came to mind: "Duty first." She'd already given the superintendent her word. She and her husband parked their car some distance away from the mob and then Henry, her husband walking with her as far as he could, made her way through the mob of protesters. Talking to the *Kiwanis Magazine*, she'd later report: "It was frightening, but perhaps one feeling of security was no one knew who I was, and I was the same color as the protesters." Not only did none of the protesters know her, but neither did anyone in the larger community: as a relative newcomer to the city, she was largely alone, a fact that may have helped insulate her, professionally and personally.

At first, the mob didn't notice her. It was only when she snaked her way through the barricades and approached the front door of the William Frantz Elementary School that she could feel the crowd shift its attention to her. At the door, she rang the bell once. She saw a man inside the building and tried to get his attention. He walked away. She rang the bell twice.

The same thing happened. Henry started to panic. It's in this next moment that history was made: Henry could have given up. She could have, in this moment of panic and disbelief, abandoned her sense of duty and honor and escaped. But she didn't. *Honor always.* In her words, "There was no other option but to be persistent." She rang the doorbell a third time. The door opened and the man apologized, having thought she was a journalist. The reception inside was bare, cold, and unwelcoming, the first-grade classroom cleared of its materials. It didn't matter. She'd crossed the threshold. She was inside. The following day she would meet Ruby for the first time.

The federal marshals had determined that the safest way to get Ruby into the school was through the basement and so Henry waited there the following morning. The doors opened and amid the towering presence of federal marshals stood a little girl wholly unaware of the mantle of change she wore on her shoulders. Recalling when she first saw Ruby, Henry told Scott Helman of the *Boston Globe*, "My first moments with Ruby are as clear today as they were then. This beautiful little Black girl, all dressed in pink. The only clue she was going to school and not to a party was she had her school bag and lunchbox. When kids are shy, they raise their heads a little bit. But enough for me to see her beautiful brown eyes and magnetic smile. I just fell in love with Ruby. How could your heart not be taken by a scene like that?" Ruby put her small hand in Henry's and together they walked into an empty school corridor, opening a new door in the civil rights movement and beginning a journey we're still talking about today. As of 2017, the student body of the charter school housed by the Frantz building was 98 percent

Black, the enrollment reflecting the changing demographic of the neighborhood it serves and the legacy it preserves.

The Ally:
Dr. Robert Coles

Having seen television footage of Ruby Bridges surrounded by the screaming mob outside of William Frantz Elementary School, Dr. Robert Coles, a child psychiatrist, thought to himself, *I would like to know that child. I would like to know what's happening to her.* Impressed by Ruby's courage and aware of her possible emotional distress, Coles reached out to Lucille and Abon, offering to talk to their daughter about her experiences. With their permission, he visited Ruby at her home for several weeks and wrote about her daily battles in an article for the March 1963 edition of the *Atlantic*.

After spending months with Ruby, Coles was, in his words, "rather puzzled by how normal and stoic and strong she was, going through this kind of living hell, with two hundred people waiting at 8:30 in the morning to tell her they were going to kill her. Two hundred people in the afternoon telling her they were going to kill her." Coles thought for certain that a child withstanding so much pressure would eventually start displaying psychological trouble. Coles said, "I waited and waited, and there weren't any symptoms.... Ruby just kept being the Ruby that she was, a normal six-year-old Black child."

One morning, Barbara Henry watched as Ruby made her way past the mob. Then she did something she'd never seen the child do before. She turned to face the angry protesters and said something to them, her lips moving slowly. Henry reported the incident to Dr. Coles, who spoke with Ruby about it at one of their sessions together.

"Ruby," he began, "your teacher told me today that she saw you talking with those people in the street."

"Doctor, I told her that I wasn't talking to the people."

"Well, who were you talking to, Ruby?"

"I was talking to God."

"Why were you talking to God?"

"I was praying for the people in the street."

"Ruby, why were you praying for those people?"

"Well, don't you think they need praying for?"

Cole admitted that the young girl's sense of compassion stopped him cold. Ruby went on to explain that her mama, daddy, and minister had told her to pray on them; they did as well. "I pray for them every morning," she said, "and I pray for them every afternoon when I go home." Her prayer, Coles would learn, was always the same: "Please, dear God, forgive them, for they know not what they do." Cole admitted, "I had no more questions." Cole would later remark that, while Ruby's parents were illiterate and the family was culturally and economically deprived, Lucille and Abon had instilled in their daughter lessons from the Book of Truth in a way that she was to live them out. Speaking to a reporter years later, Coles said, "I'd like to see some of us who have fancy educations bring up our children similarly.... It would be nice if some of us try to not only get an 'A' in Biblical literature or an 'A' in moral analysis or an 'A' in Southern history, but to get the kind of 'A' Ruby got."

Coles, a man who'd originally planned to become

a teacher only to be swayed into the medical field by the poet and physician William Carlos Williams, found his professional calling by listening to the smallest of voices—that of children. While Coles would go on to enjoy much professional acclaim, his time with Ruby was life- and career-defining. In 1995, he and Ruby released a children's book together called *The Story of Ruby Bridges*. In acknowledging Ruby's story, her dreams and fears—and those of countless other children over the years—he also ceded a larger voice to our humanity.

ON ALLIES

In both my personal and my professional life, I've encountered the support of allies like Barbara Henry and Dr. Coles in the most unsuspecting places and times. It took as much courage for them to do certain things as it did for us to do others. For example, when I was in high school, a white Jewish teacher named Eliot Salow took a chance on me when few people would. At the time, I was already working as the youth director for Dr. King's Operation Breadbasket. I'd also recently experienced the breakup of my family. It was an emotional time for me as I was struggling to live up to the promise of my role in Operation Breadbasket while privately tending to my familial wounds. And then, a ray of light: Mr. Salow.

With no prompting from me, Mr. Salow gave me booklets to study that explained different aspects of social activism: strategy, history, and biographies of popular figures. Like any good teacher, he saw that I needed guidance and, in his kindness, found a way to help. I've never forgotten his generosity. It was particularly meaningful to me that he reached out to me during a time in my life when things could have easily gone a different direction. I was angry and upset because of the deterioration of my family. But I was also angry and upset because when I looked around my Brooklyn neighborhood, all I saw was strife, pain, and poverty. My neighborhood was as broken as my family. Ambulances were slow to arrive, if they ever did. Mamas worked two, three jobs. Kids went hungry. Police were an occupying force. I'd gone from living in a middle-class, ethnically mixed neighborhood in Queens with my dad, mom, and sister, to living in the lower-class, predominantly Black neighborhood of Brownsville, Brooklyn, my mother a single parent. The inequality didn't sit right with me.

The booklets Mr. Salow gave me became my lifeline. I read them as much as I could. They soon became the substance of my budding activism. The funny thing is, Mr. Salow was just as sick of the living conditions in his school district as I was. It took me a while to get that. He saw in me a fellow activist and helped fan my inner flame. Today, we'd call him an ally. I just thought he was a good teacher. Since then, I've encountered other white allies in my life, including television executive Phil Griffin, who withstood criticism when he put me on MSNBC. To Phil's credit, he's championed many different American voices, and has helped clear the space for us to be heard. Allies come in all different colors, shapes, and sizes. In my line of work, it behooves me to watch out for them, and to help draw them out. After all, the passive compassion of a friend or colleague can often be channeled into righteous action, and that's what we're looking for here: less talk, more walk.

7

NO GREATER HONOR

"The right to vote is the most powerful instrument ever devised by man for breaking down injustice and destroying the terrible walls which imprison men because they are different from other men."

—PRESIDENT LYNDON B. JOHNSON

A few years ago, I had an enjoyable conversation with an elderly white man in Georgia. Our talk had naturally shifted to Black activism in the South when he mentioned the name Reverend Hosea Williams, an Atlanta native and an old friend of mine. We spoke briefly about Hosea Feed the Hungry and Homeless, Inc., the human services organization Hosea started in 1970 with his wife, Juanita. At first, the organization was named the Martin Luther King Jr. Poor People's Church of Love. It started as a soup line at Atlanta's Wheat Street Baptist Church where, every Sunday, Hosea fed the homeless. What began as a simple weekly service quickly grew into a massive organization, serving hot meals to five thousand people each Thanksgiving and Christmas by 2000. Over time, it has incorporated other services into its program and is known today as Hosea Helps, with a mission statement to investigate and raise public awareness about problems facing families in poverty and to mobilize financial resources, products, and volunteers to help stabilize those households. It's an impressive organization with a long reach, and an even longer history in Hosea himself, who'd been one of Dr. King's original field generals.

"I wonder why Hosea doesn't get the widespread recognition he deserves," I said aloud.

The white Southerner looked at me. "You don't understand," he said. I wasn't sure whether he meant it as a question or a statement.

"I don't?" I asked, curious where this conversation would lead.

The man answered me plainly, saying, "White America and the white media see Black leadership as either accommodating or confrontational. Even though Black leaders and white leaders may share the same goal, an accommodating Black leader makes white people feel comfortable. That way, we don't have to feel guilty or ashamed of the way Blacks have been treated. We don't get off the hook so easily with a confrontational Black leader."

It was a remarkably blunt assessment, refreshing in its honesty, and something I'd been aware of most of my life. I laughed, the man's words hitting close to home. For as long as I can remember, I've been told I'm too confrontational, too aggressive. He went on, saying, "President Obama—accommodating. Oprah Winfrey, Tiger Woods, John Lewis—accommodating. On the other side, I'd say Jesse Jackson, you, and—"

"Hosea Williams," I said.

"—confrontational." He nodded. "We don't know when y'all may go off on us. I'm just being brutally honest with you. The thing is, you don't care if you make us uncomfortable. I'd wager that much of what you do and how you do it is designed to make us feel discomfort."

"Well, the truth is often uncomfortable," I said, and this time he laughed.

He sighed. "You're right," he said.

We left it at that, but his words stayed with me long after we'd parted. The hard truth is that we need more people to step outside of their comfort zones to confront who we are as a nation. By "confrontation," I'm not advocating for violence of any sort. I'm not talking about taking up arms, storming the US Capitol, or engaging in hand-to-hand combat. By "confrontation," I mean taking a clear-eyed, sober, and compassionate assessment of our nation's ills, and then pushing for positive change through voting, legislative action, and social movements. It's only by taking a good hard look at our failures—both historic and present day—that we have any hope of course correction and making good on America's promise of freedom, liberty, and equality. Hosea Williams understood this. He wasn't afraid to take a stand and to show a mirror to white America. Dr. King knew this about Hosea, too, and strategically used his field general's strengths and personality to his advantage in negotiating for larger political and social change. Besides Hosea, other so-called field generals included men like Stoney Cooks, Bernard Lafayette, and James Orange.

While I didn't meet Hosea Williams until I was in my twenties, he was such a widely admired figure in Dr. King's circle that it seemed as if I'd known him my whole life. I'd grown up hearing tales of his adventures in the civil rights movement—from his involvement in Bloody Sunday, to his historic 1987 march against the Ku Klux Klan in the segregated all-white Forsyth County, Georgia, which, at the time, was the largest civil rights march in Georgia history, to his leadership in getting Savannah to be the first American city to ban "whites-only" lunch counters. The list of his accomplishments in the world of civil rights was far-reaching but so, too, were those in his professional life. Most people don't know it, but Hosea graduated with a master's degree in chemistry from Atlanta University (later Clark Atlanta University). He also worked as a chemist for the US Department of Agriculture and over the course of his life founded four chemical companies and a bonding company. After working closely with Dr. King, he'd go on to pursue a career in politics, unsuccessfully running for a host of different positions, even switching his party affiliation, before being elected to Georgia's state senate in 1974 as a Democrat, where he served until 1985 when he resigned to run against—and lose to—Wyche Fowler for the US Senate. He subsequently was elected to the DeKalb County Commission, a position his wife was later elected to herself, making her the first Black woman to run for public office in Georgia since Reconstruction, and the first Black woman to run for statewide office. Hosea's achievements—and his deep reservoir of personal courage—are all the more impressive when you consider that he was born a poor Black boy in segregated Georgia at a time when the most he could reasonably expect from life was hardship, violence, and white supremacy. As it turned out, his personal experiences in segregated Georgia are exactly what put him on the path toward activism and politics. As it says in Genesis 50:22: "You intended to harm me, but God intended it for good to accomplish what is now being done, the saving of many lives."

The Agitator:
Hosea Williams

Hosea Lorenzo Williams was born January 5, 1926, to unwed teenage parents, both of whom had been committed to a trade institute for the blind in Macon, Georgia. His mother ran away from the institute once she discovered she was pregnant. Hosea never knew his father. Unfortunately, Hosea's mother died during the birth of her second child and so Hosea was raised by his maternal grandparents, Lela and Turner Williams. When he was fourteen years old, Hosea escaped a near-lynching by an angry white mob for his having gone fishing with a poor white girl who lived near his grandparents. Fearing for himself and for the lives of his family, Hosea ran away from home. He soon enlisted in the US Army in an all-Black infantry unit under General George S. Patton Jr., becoming one of the more than 2.5 million Black men who joined the military during World War II. He was nineteen years old when, as an infantry gunner, a German shell exploded while he was in a foxhole in France along with thirteen other soldiers. Hosea was the only survivor. He hid out in that foxhole for two days with horrific injuries until an ambulance reached him. After spending the next year recuperating in a European hospital, he was discharged with a permanent limp and awarded a Purple Heart. Having witnessed the horrors of war abroad, Hosea returned home a decorated hero only to discover that the racism he'd felt as a kid was stronger than ever. America wasn't Nazi Germany, but it abetted a similar kind of deep-seated hatred. Different battlefield. Same battle.

Newly returned from World War II and still wearing his army uniform, including his Purple Heart, Hosea made the near-fatal mistake of drinking from a "whites-only" water fountain in Americus, Georgia. After taking a sip of water, Hosea was savagely attacked by a group of white men, and left so badly beaten his attackers thought him dead and called for the local Black funeral home to claim his body. It was only when Hosea was splayed out inside the hearse that the driver noticed that the dead man was, in fact, still alive. No hospitals in the area admitted Blacks even in the case of emergency. The driver raced to the nearest veterans' hospital more than one hundred miles away where Hosea spent more than a month in recovery. Speaking of the attack later in his life, Hosea said, "The very same people whose freedoms and liberties I had fought and suffered to secure in the horrors of war...they beat me like a dog.... So at that moment, I truly felt as if I had fought on the wrong side. Then, and not until then, did I realize why God, time after time, had taken me to death's door, then spared my life...to be a general in the war for human rights and personal dignity." He, like James Meredith and too many other Black men before and since, returned to America from fighting a war abroad only to find themselves called to a battle of a different sort, this one on their own home turf. Hosea threw himself into the fight for justice. His entry into the world of activism was nothing short of a spiritual calling. In what may have been the last interview of his life in 2002, he told Lance Robertson, "I never met God until I went to Montgomery, Alabama, and met Martin Luther King Jr. King was not my god but the true God revealed Himself to me through Martin Luther King Jr."

Inspired, Hosea attended meetings and marches with Dr. King in Montgomery. He saw that what Dr. King had started in Montgomery he could do in Savannah. One day, overcome with excitement, he grabbed the kids, jumped in his Cadillac, and took off driving, in his words, at "a hundred miles an hour." There was only one problem. He explained, saying, "And guess what I remembered? I forgot to introduce myself to that man." After sitting in the car for about thirty minutes and debating what he should do, he decided to continue to Savannah. It was there that he'd nurse the seeds of his activism, his dedication drawing the attention of Dr. King in due time.

Over the course of his life, he would be jailed more than one hundred times, once for sixty-five days—the longest continuous sentence served by any civil rights leader—and beaten countless times in his pursuit for equal rights. He never gave up, instead embracing the personal motto "unbought and unbossed" that Shirley Chisholm would also use in her successful 1968 campaign run for US Congress. He would go on to become one of the architects of the civil rights movement, but that doesn't mean he didn't anger or offend some people along the way, including the leadership of the local Savannah NAACP when he served as vice president under W. W. Law.

When Hosea wanted a place on the NAACP National Board of Directors, Medgar Evers, his friend, told him that he didn't have enough support from the organization nor from the state of Georgia itself. Roy Wilkins confirmed as much, telling Hosea that he was "too militant" and didn't "project the image that's compatible with the NAACP." Crushed, Hosea was wondering what to do next when he saw a sign for a meeting of the Southern Christian Leadership Conference (SCLC), where Dr. King warmly welcomed him into the fold, saying, "At least you had a chance to run. The NAACP kicked me out before I had the chance." At King's urging, Hosea became the executive director of the SCLC, the organization that organized the now-famous marches from Selma, Alabama, to the state's capital, Montgomery, to peacefully deliver a petition for Black voting rights to the known-segregationist Governor George C. Wallace. Hosea was severely beaten on the first of those marches, along with several other protesters, including John Lewis. A sad day for our country's character, March 7, 1965, would become known as Bloody Sunday.

Dr. King called Hosea a "bull in a china closet"; Hosea's self-described term was *thug* and he admitted that one of the hardest things he did in his life was to switch from a way of violence to one of nonviolence. Not one to back down from confrontation, he was an agitator in the classic sense of the word: heavyset and physically imposing, Hosea was that loyal friend everyone wants but few have. He was built like a bouncer, someone who didn't need to raise his fist to elevate the temperature in the room. People moved around *him*. They listened to him, too. Hosea was a man of the streets; he'd come up hard. So, he knew how to talk to the average Black man, and they knew they could trust him. If Hosea called for a march or a meeting, everyone showed up. He could mobilize the people so that by the time Dr. King arrived, there'd already be a mass of protesters and supporters ready to make good on King's messaging. Dr. King, in his measured and principled way, could get the church crowd going, for sure. But it was Hosea who mobilized the people on the streets. The movement needed both. It needed a man like Dr. King, who could lead the marches and interpret the movement to the media, but it also needed a general like Hosea, who could get the guy on the corner to march. Remember, Hosea was asking people to willingly put themselves in life-or-death situations in the march against oppression and white supremacy. He was asking them to risk their personal livelihoods, their jobs, and their reputations to take beatings and withstand firehoses, attacking dogs, and hateful language. Make no mistake: it was no cakewalk. Churchgoing, so-called "proper" Blacks may have thought twice before signing up for one of those marches but the average Black man from the street didn't; he had nothing to lose and everything to gain. Those were Hosea's people—the real lifeblood of the movement.

When I was first coming into my own as an activist, I'd met Hosea a few times here and there. It was only after I'd led one of my first marches against the white community of Howard Beach in Queens, New York, however, that we'd cemented our relationship. Hosea, like Jesse Jackson, was a mentor to me in the King tradition. He and I "got" one another; in a sense, we were cut from the same cloth. We'd both come up from disadvantaged backgrounds and were both fiery, unafraid to throw ourselves into the mix and be outspoken. Like Hosea, I'd made it my business to go directly to the people. It's interesting: I've found that white America gets nervous whenever a Black leader speaks directly to Black people, a holdover, perhaps, from the days when whites feared massive slave revolts. Hosea and I both understood the power in this dynamic, and used it to our advantage, forcing change on the ground and bringing people to the middle for negotiation. It was particularly meaningful, then, to have been awarded the Dr. Martin Luther King Medallion of Honor by Hosea. Hosea had these bronze medallions minted himself and gave them to activists he believed were working to uphold the King tradition. The day Hosea awarded me this medallion was also meaningful for another reason: it marked the first time I met Michael Hardy, who, back then, was working as a journalist but today is NAN's trusted lawyer and my longstanding right-hand man. Besides my mother's Bible, the medallion may be one of my most treasured personal belongings just as my relationship with Hardy is still one of my most trusted.

In 2000, when Hosea was terminally ill with cancer, I went to Atlanta to see him. I will never forget that meeting, one of our last. He looked weak, and I wondered if he'd have the strength to speak. At most, I thought I'd visit with him for about fifteen or twenty minutes before he'd want to sleep. I shouldn't have underestimated the man. As soon as he saw me, he pushed himself upright and lectured me over the next two hours, barely stopping to talk to take the occasional sip of water. Juanita kept checking in on us, but each time, Hosea would wave her away and refocus his attention on me. It was as if he knew his time was up and wanted to impart every last bit of knowledge to me. It was very touching. And so I listened. Our conversation went in many different directions. He spoke candidly about being with Dr. King on the balcony of the Lorraine Hotel, along with Jesse Jackson and Ralph Abernathy, when King was shot. He told me about the time he'd organized one of the first night marches in the history of the movement. He spoke about his personal struggles with alcoholism.

We spoke about the importance of voting rights and how, when he was coming up, there was a massive push to win the right to vote. Some fifty years later, we're facing a much more nuanced and, in some respects, more pressing battle, with Republicans attacking much of the Voting Rights Act. Despite all our progress, it seems we're reverting to a Jim Crow kind of political world, with many red states reasserting individual states' rights in elections, which, to me, is just a dog whistle for state-sanctioned racism that makes it more difficult for people of color to vote. At the time,

Hosea couldn't have possibly foreseen today's political climate and so he was speaking more broadly about how to get people to the ballot box. He explained to me that politicians don't matter at the voting booth. It's the people who matter, how we've got to vote for ourselves, and not for the cult-favorite politician. Our interests, our health care, our education, our kids' futures, our policing.

Hosea told me about the differences between those of us who came out of the SCLC tradition—direct action, nonviolent but proactive—and those who came from the NAACP and the National Urban League. Where the SCLC was rooted in the Black Christian church and favored having a centralized, charismatic leader as its base, the NAACP was created with a more decentralized chapter model in mind. As a social services organization, the National Urban League worked most closely with the private sector; they didn't call marches but would support other groups that did. He broke down each category of activism within the civil rights movement, and dissected the overarching strategies of each, telling me why this one worked better than that one when dealing with a particular issue, but how the reverse was true when a different situation presented itself. After an hour of this, my head was spinning. Two hours in, and I realized everything I thought I knew could fit inside one of Hosea's water bottles; his knowledge was a reservoir. We spoke about whether the lessons and tactics he'd learned could still be applied today.

"We're living in a different time than the one you came up in," I said.

"Yeah, you're right," he acknowledged. "Times do

change, but our core values don't. There's a difference: you can update the tradition, but you don't upend it."

I took his words to heart and have tried to model my activism since then on the core values that informed it in the first place. We spoke a bit longer and, as I was preparing to leave, he said he had one more thing he needed to tell me.

"Yeah?" I asked.

He said, "Don't you ever stop being from the streets. Keep pushing the envelope but never be violent. You and I are from the same tribe, but there aren't many of us."

"What tribe is that?" I asked.

"We stand in the middle. We can confront both the thugs *and* the suits. You and I are fluent in the language of both worlds." He continued, saying, "You came up under the SCLC tradition. Don't betray it." Here lay the old lion, readying his retreat, and lecturing to those he'd leave behind. It was as if he was saying, "Don't get it mixed up: you're no tiger and you're no sheep. You're a lion. Act like it."

He died the following year. His final homecoming march looked like any other he'd led in life with lines of people marching down Auburn Avenue and past Atlanta's state capitol and city hall. It was an open-casket funeral and Hosea wore in death the protest clothes he wore in life: denim bib overalls, a long-sleeved red shirt, and sneakers. It was an outfit that endeared him to the Southern Black farmer, several of whom sat quietly behind the local and national politicians in the last few pews of the church. "The sadness is that if Hosea can die, all of us must," Reverend Jesse Jackson said in his eulogy. "He exposes our mortality."

I thought of the Hosea I'd known when I was a young

man, how he'd knighted me with that medallion. I reflected on the Hosea I knew later in life, how he'd privately struggled with alcoholism yet never gave up his
public fight for social justice. And I thought about how,
without Hosea, the Summer Community Organization
and Political Education (SCOPE) Project of the SCLC
wouldn't have existed. That program was a vast and
far-reaching voter registration initiative over six Southern states and helped keep pressure on Congress to
pass the Voting Rights Act of 1965. There may not have
even been a Selma to Montgomery march, an event
that unquestionably changed the course of American
history and the trajectory of voting rights for Blacks.
But then, Selma may not have happened at all had it
not been for a man named Jimmie Lee Jackson. Jimmie Lee Jackson's courage gave rise to Hosea's fight
for justice just as Hosea's bravery later gave rise to
mine. The civil rights movement today is still made up
of lions, some more silver-haired than others but, like
Hosea, just as proud.

SOMETHING TO SAY

Like many other Blacks during the 1960s, Jimmie Lee Jackson
had tried to register to vote several times. Each time, he was
denied. On the night of February 18, 1965, the twenty-six-
year-old man, along with his grandfather, Cager Lee, and his
mother, Viola, joined a voters' rights protest after a meeting at
the Zion United Methodist Church in Marion, Alabama. The
FBI tipped off the local state troopers about the meeting. As the
troopers ambushed the protesters, Jackson and his family ran for
cover inside Mack's Café. The troopers followed and attacked
Viola. Jackson, attempting to rescue his mother, was shot two
times in the stomach by officer James Bonard Fowler, who later

claimed he'd acted in self-defense, believing Jackson was reaching for another officer's gun that had fallen to the floor. Jackson was taken to a Good Samaritan hospital in Selma where, several days later, he was served an arrest warrant for assault and battery with intent to murder a police officer. He later died from a second surgery under what today would be called questionable circumstances: a different doctor from a different hospital authorized the secondary surgery and then the operating surgeon increased Jackson's anesthesia rather than his oxygen supply.

Upon hearing of Jackson's death, the civil rights organizer James Bevel said, "We will march Jimmie's body to the state capitol in Montgomery and lie it on the steps so Governor George Wallace can see what he's done." While this didn't happen, four days after Jackson's funeral, about six hundred protesters took to the streets and, on Sunday, March 7, stood at the base of the Edmund Pettus Bridge, with Hosea Williams and John Lewis poised at the front of the line. The protesters were then beaten on the bridge by state troopers and by other white men who had been deputized that morning by the local sheriff. The day became widely known as Bloody Sunday, with television coverage of the attacks sparking national outrage. Lewis, his skull fractured from the beating he received on the bridge, nonetheless delivered an impassioned speech after he and Hosea led the wounded back to headquarters at Brown Chapel, saying, "I don't see how President Johnson can send troops to Vietnam—I don't see how he can send troops to the Congo—I don't see how he can send troops to Africa, and can't send troops to Selma." He continued, "Next time we march, we may have to keep going when we get to Montgomery. We may have to go on to Washington." At a meeting at the same church later that night, Hosea said, "I fought in World War II and I was once captured by the German army, and I want to tell you that the Germans were never as inhumane as the state troopers of Alabama."

Dr. King had originally planned to lead the march but had agreed not to once he'd heard that troopers would block it. When King heard that Hosea had been roughed up, however, he left Atlanta for Selma, and planned to retry the march two days later. Federal District Court Judge Frank M. Johnson threatened to issue a restraining order prohibiting the march until March 11, however, and President Johnson urged King to wait until a federal court order could provide them with protection. In the end, King and about two thousand supporters, several of whom were clergy, pushed ahead on March 9 anyway, stopping along the way to kneel and pray on the site of the Sunday attack. After prayers, they turned the march back to Selma. Following their demonstration, Johnson promised to introduce a voting rights bill to Congress.

While other civil rights leaders marched on Bloody Sunday, Hosea was the only one who was formally on Dr. King's staff payroll. John Lewis, for example, was the head of the Student Nonviolent Coordinating Committee (SNCC); he never worked directly for King. Because John's temperament was similar to that of Dr. King's, people often assume that the two men worked closely with one another. Their work naturally crossed over, but it was the unbought and unbossed Hosea Williams whom King came to see after he'd been attacked on the Edmund Pettus Bridge. Him and someone else, that is. This other individual was knocked unconscious on the bridge after being struck by an officer's billy club. Before passing out, she heard one officer say to another, "Well, if she's dead, just pull her to the side and let the buzzards eat her." When she next woke, she found herself in a hospital. At the time of the attack, Amelia Boynton Robinson was a well-respected, fifty-three-year-old community leader. She'd come to the march that day equipped with a plastic rain cap for protection against the dreary weather, and dressed in a light-colored coat, heels, and gloves, hopeful that no one would hit such a lady.

The Matriarch of a Movement:
Amelia Boynton Robinson

Amelia Isadora Platts was born August 18, 1911, in Savannah, Georgia, one of ten children. Her father, George, was a skilled construction worker and businessman who owned a wholesale woodlot. Her mother, Anna, was a seamstress. It was Anna who first planted the seed of an idea in Amelia, taking the ten-year-old girl traveling with her as she visited rural Black communities by horse and buggy, going door to door to get people to vote. It was an experience Amelia would never forget and one that later shaped her life as the matriarch of the Voting Rights Act of 1965.

As a young woman, Amelia graduated from Tuskegee Institute (now Tuskegee University) and soon became a home demonstration agent for the United States Department of Agriculture (USDA) in Selma, where she educated the rural communities about agriculture and homemaking. She met her future husband, Samuel William Boynton, another USDA agent, on the job. The duo worked together to help educate and empower rural Blacks, teaching them how to improve both their farming methods and their home economics as well as how to vote. They held meetings inside one-room country churches or in private homes and went over every step of the registration process, from showing them how to write their names and fill in the blanks of the registration document to advising them on how to speak and dress when they tried to register. In an interview with Washington University late in her life, Amelia noted that these lessons weren't easy. "It was terribly hard for those who were illiterate," she explained. "We had more illiteracy in this county than they had in most counties throughout the state, or in any other state." She continued, saying, "At that time, my husband was a registered voter and a voucher. Each person that came down to register had to have a voucher with him. But when he began to bring a number of people down there, three or four at one time...the registrar became very upset." Samuel also encouraged the rural Black man to buy land for himself, so the crops he planted would belong to him, his children would be free, and the decades' old system of sharecropping would be broken. Doing this wasn't enough, however, to help the rural Black overturn decades of oppression. Voting rights were key to changing the system. Amelia explained, saying, "It seems as though people didn't realize that they were not citizens until they became registered voters. Because they had no part in helping to elect the people who would be kind to us, who would do away with the discrimination, who would see that they got better jobs, would see that they were able to have the opportunity to do what anybody else is supposed to do as American citizens." Not surprisingly, the Boyntons made a lot of the local whites anxious. Looking for a reason to hang him, some white landowners suggested Samuel was working against the Hatch Act, the 1939 federal law that prohibits civil service employees from engaging in certain political activity.

In the 1930s, the husband-and-wife team joined the Dallas County Voters League to continue their work for voter registration. The couple ran three businesses—an insurance agency, a real estate office, and an employment agency—and inside her office on Franklin Street in Selma, Amelia hung a sign that read A Voteless People Is a Hopeless People. In the fall of 1962, SNCC's Bernard Lafayette and his wife, Colia Liddell, arrived in Selma to help get out the vote. Once he saw how well the Boyntons ran things, Lafayette assigned himself as their staff member rather than opening a brand-new SNCC office. The Boyntons had a long reach within the community. It's because of Amelia and Samuel's work that Selma became the foundation upon which SNCC could expand the fight for voting rights. Their work also happened to catch the attention of Dr. King. Unfortunately, Samuel died in 1963, and wouldn't see how much their good work would pay off. (Amelia would go on to marry two more times to Bob Billups and then James Robinson.)

After Samuel's death, Amelia doubled down and fought twice as hard, becoming a voting voucher herself and running for the House of Representatives, the first Black woman from Alabama to do so. The sign that once hung from her office window became her campaign motto as well. Despite losing the race, she nonetheless won 11 percent of the local vote, where only 5 percent of Blacks were registered. In the summer of 1964, Amelia reached out to the SCLC, inviting the organization and Dr. King to Selma to help invigorate the local voting movement, which had stalled because of a legal injunction that made it illegal for three or more people to meet and discuss civil rights or voter registration in the city. Her home at 1315 Lapsley Street quickly became the hub of a nationally geared campaign for voting rights, with Dr. King and his field officers using Selma as their main base of operations. Many of the ideas that later became the foundation for the 1965 Voting Rights Act were first discussed inside Amelia's home. King formally began his Selma campaign when about seven hundred Black folks showed up for a meeting at Brown Chapel in defiance of the injunction. About one year later, Amelia would be near the front line of marchers headed across the Edmund Pettus Bridge toward Montgomery.

Amelia felt it was especially important for her to show up. She explained, saying, "Having been a leader through the years, and having laid the foundation for the civil rights movement from 1930 to 1964, I felt as though all through that time it was my duty to lead. I felt that was because I came first from a family that was involved in politics. Then, too, I knew that I could not let the people down." Nothing could have prepared her, however, for what she faced at the bridge. "I saw in front of us a solid wall of state troopers, standing shoulder to shoulder," she reported. Besides billy clubs, the officers also wielded cattle prods, guns, and gas canisters. Gas masks concealed their faces. "Almost every white man who wanted to hurt a Black person was given a gun," Amelia said. When the marchers arrived at the first light across the bridge, they were told to stop. Amelia remembered, "Hosea Williams, who was at the head, said, 'May I have something to say?' And through the bullhorn, the answer was, 'No, you cannot have anything to say. Charge on them, men.' And the men came from the right side, from the left side, from in front of us, they came upon us and started beating us with their nightsticks, they started cattle prodding us, they started gassing us." As protesters fell to the ground from the beatings, some officers tried to make their horses trample them, but the horses refused.

Amelia would go on to participate in the second attempt made by the marchers and the final—and victorious—third march that left Brown Chapel on

March 21, under heavy guard provided by President Lyndon Johnson. By the time this third wave of marchers had reached their final destination at the Alabama state capitol, it was March 25 and had swelled to include over twenty-five thousand people. Later that same year, Amelia was a guest of honor at the White House when President Johnson signed the federal Voting Rights Act to law, an event seen as a direct consequence of the marches. In a 2015 interview with the *New York Post*, Amelia said about the day, "I wasn't looking for notoriety. But if that's what it took, I didn't care how many licks I got. It just made me even more determined to fight for our cause."

PRAYING ON SELMA

I first met Amelia at one of the commemoration events to celebrate the Selma to Montgomery marches. For these annual celebrations, John Lewis typically hosted a delegation mainly comprised of politicians—senators, congressmen and -women, and local council members—who'd set up shop in a nice Montgomery hotel, then drive over to Selma for Sunday morning service at Brown Chapel, which had been Dr. King's headquarters, and then march with everyone to or across the Edmund Pettus Bridge.

But there was another, less formal delegation in Selma and, as I soon discovered, it was informally presided over by none other than the matriarch of the voting movement herself: Amelia Boynton Robinson. The Selma get-together was more raucous and freewheeling, grass roots in origin, and with a more down-home kind of feeling. Originally called "The Annual Pilgrimage to Selma," it typically takes place over the first weekend in March. Over the years, it's gotten a little more formal, but still retains its identity as a lively jubilee, a celebration of voting rights for the people and won by the people of Selma, complete with entertainment, food, music, and art. Today it's called the Selma Bridge Crossing Jubilee or, more simply "the Jubilee," and includes a parade, a Miss Jubilee Pageant, a mock trial, and a commemorative march to the bridge. Every five years, the march goes all the way to Montgomery. It took me a while to know about it because, for whatever reason, I was typically invited to the political side of things. While the big-time politicians and power brokers were having congressional-type meetings in Montgomery, the people in Selma were more kicked back—or at least that's how it felt to me. It didn't take long for me to cross over: I was soon going to and participating in more events in Selma than I was in Montgomery. I found it to more closely reflect the true energy of the movement. Selma, after all, had been the heart of the voters' movement in Georgia. It was where Dr. King preached. It had been the starting point of the original march itself, and it was, metaphorically speaking, Amelia's backyard.

The first time I turned up in Selma, I got a little roasted. All the teasing was in good fun, but I gotta admit, it stung a little.

"Oh, look who decided to show up!"

"You sure you're in the right place, Rev?"

"See you're still wearing your suit!"

But if you think the attention stayed for very long on me, think again. Once everyone finished razzing me, all eyes were focused on the unofficial jubilee queen, Mrs. Boynton. By the time she and I met, she was already getting on in age. You wouldn't have known it, though. She was a bundle of energy.

The year 2015 marked the fiftieth anniversary of the Selma march. The guest speaker that year was President Obama. Along with the general audience, there was also a section roped off for special guests, which included Marc Morial, the head of the National Urban League, members of the NAACP, Martin Luther King III, Amelia Boynton Robinson, and myself, among others. Afterward, a select group was led to an outdoor tent for photo ops where we would then make our way to the bridge to march alongside the president. It was only after this first wave of marchers had crossed the bridge and the president and the first lady had been ushered away into cars guarded by the Secret Service that the mass of ten thousand or so other marchers could begin to cross the bridge.

While we were being directed by the photographers, Amelia and I huddled together and spoke. She was floored by the pomp and circumstance, the amount of security detail. I had endless questions I wanted to ask her: Did she think she'd make it off the bridge alive that day? What were dinners like in her home with Dr. King? Had she and Hosea been close? Then, in the middle of our small talk, she said something I've never forgotten.

"Rev," she said, "you gotta know something."

"Yeah, what's that?" I asked.

"I never left Selma."

I looked at her, waiting for her to elaborate. She repeated herself, this time her voice more defiant. "I was born here. I almost died on that bridge. And when it was over? The television crews left, the newspapermen went back to New York and Chicago. The politicians returned to Washington, DC. The out-of-town protestors returned to their hometowns. But where was I gonna go? I live here. I never left."

I thought about it: she took the risks and the pain when there wasn't anyone else standing shoulder to shoulder with her, both before the media showed up and long after it had left. There's strength in that kind of activism: it's a day-in, day-out kind of discipline, a quiet, solitary practice that you carry on no matter what, even when no one's looking—*especially* when no one's looking. I was reminded of Claudette Colvin. Their kind of activism is similar to having a religious calling. It's when you know in your heart of hearts that love and truth will find a way and, until they do, you're gonna keep praying...and marching.

And marching. And praying. Well, Amelia never stopped praying on Selma. She never stopped doing the work, and because she prayed for Selma, she prayed for us all.

Once the photo ops were finished, we made our way to the bridge. I stood diagonally to Amelia, who was in a wheelchair, and slightly behind President Obama. Amelia turned to me and said, "Little different than it was fifty years ago. We couldn't even vote back then and now we have a Black president."

As we marched across the bridge, President Obama reached out and held Amelia's hand and I took a handle of her wheelchair, and that's how we walked together. When we reached the other side of the bridge, I told Amelia, "This has been one of the greatest honors of my life: going over the bridge with you while standing behind the first Black president of America, and John Lewis to my left." She smiled and patted my hand. The next day, I was guest preacher at the mass for Sunday church. When I came down from the pulpit, Amelia pulled me close and said, "Now that was an honor for me: hearing you preach for the Golden Anniversary sermon. Yesterday was about politics. But today is about God. There's no greater honor."

Amelia never left Selma. She died in August of that same year. There's been talk about turning her home into a national landmark. I can't help but think that if Amelia were alive today, she'd be honored to receive such a distinction and yet she'd be the first to say that the true measure of her success and legacy is whether or not we can protect the Voting Rights Act. Its protection requires our constant vigilance, because make no mistake: it is under brutal assault, the consequences of which will be far-reaching and possibly devastating. As President Obama said in his 2015 commemoration speech: "If we want to honor the courage of those who marched that day, then all of us are called to possess their moral imagination. All of us will need to feel as they did the fierce urgency of now." Since then, our country has endured four years of the Trump presidency, a global pandemic, a widescale erosion of our voting rights, and a national uprising on issues of race and police brutality. The urgency has never been more fierce than it is right now.

About three years after Amelia's death, I found myself in Selma once again to celebrate another commemoration march. It was an especially popular year—all the Democratic primary candidates were in attendance, wooing the public and racking up sound bites. I was one of the featured speakers at Brown Chapel and, as I took my place at the pulpit, said, "I'm grateful to be here with the vice president." I turned around and looked at then–Vice President Joe Biden and said, "No, I'm not talking about you, Joe. I'm talking about Stacey Abrams." The church erupted in cheers and laughter.

Fast-forward to the march: as we approached the first hill, a car pulled up. The door opened and John Lewis, who was by then frail and weak from cancer, stepped out from the back seat of the car. Several of us rushed to help him climb to the top of a small stepstool, which he'd brought with him. It wasn't his only prop. He also had a megaphone.

"Fifty-five years ago, a few of our children attempted to march…across this bridge. We were beaten, we were tear-gassed. I thought I was going to die on this bridge. But somehow and some way, God Almighty helped me here."

Here's a man, I thought, *ravaged with pain and yet he's still traveled all this way to the same bridge where he was beaten over fifty years ago to continue fighting for our rights.* I may have been literally supporting him, helping to hold up his body weight, but it was he who first supported us, helping to lift us out of oppression. His last message to the American people was to vote, saying, "We must go out and vote like we never, ever voted before…. We must use the vote as a nonviolent instrument or tool to redeem the soul of America." We helped him step down. He thanked us and then returned to the back seat of his car. It was up to us to finish the march without him.

On the other side of the bridge, the crowds began to disperse. It was chaotic, as the ends of marches usually are, with groups of people heading off in different directions, people figuring out where to meet one another, calling and yelling to one another. In the pandemonium, I saw Stacey Abrams.

"Stacey!" I called out, and she came over to meet me. We were immediately swarmed by people wanting to take photographs with us. We took as many as we could before my SUV pulled up. I got in and, turning back, saw Stacey flanked by several well-meaning people but surrounded, nonetheless. I told her to get in the car and she did. Of course, I didn't know it then but that was the last time I'd see John Lewis. He died only a few months later. As fate would have it, the last time I saw Amelia Boynton Robinson alive had also been on that bridge, a place that had defined so much of their lives and the fate of our country.

Stacey and I drove away together that day, she, the modern-day equivalent of Amelia, and myself, an old lion, the Edmund Pettus Bridge looming behind us.

GENERATIONAL CHANGE

While my mother was originally from Alabama, the first election she voted in was in New York City, after she'd moved north. I remember she'd told me she couldn't vote in her hometown of Dothan because she'd failed to correctly answer the ridiculous questions the voting registrar had put to her—a common method to keep people of color away from the polls. My mother had been so proud when she was able to vote at long last. When I spoke at her funeral in 2012, I marveled at the fact that, within the span of her own life, she'd gone from not being able to vote in her own hometown to watching me run for president in 2004 to having President Obama send his condolences on her passing. To think she'd been denied the vote for most of her life! It was just as Amelia had said herself: we went from being denied the full benefits of citizenship to having a Black man at the helm and, today, a Black female vice president.

In the frustration of the day, it's easy to say there's been no change. You win the Chauvin verdict one day only to turn around for Daunte Wright's funeral the next. But my mother's life journey shows me that real change does happen. If you take a step back, you can see the generational shifts: it was only one generation from my mother not being able to vote to me running for president and only one more generation for the country to usher in its first Black president. Ordinary people did—and still do—change the course of this country. Change often doesn't come when you're pushing for it—the next generation feels the results. It takes time to catch up to the changemakers.

I often think of the now-iconic photograph of President Obama and five-year-old Jacob Philadelphia, which hung in a place of honor in the West Wing during Obama's tenure. The young Black boy was visiting the White House and, seeing the president, looked up and said, "I want to know if my hair is just like yours."

"Why don't you touch it for yourself and see?" President Obama lowered his head. Jacob patted his head and White House photographer Pete Souza took the photo. David Axelrod, Obama's longtime adviser, later commented on the photograph, saying, "Really, what he was saying is, 'Gee, you're just like me.' And it doesn't take a big leap to think that child could be thinking, 'Maybe I could be here someday.'" When I talk about change, I'm not only talking about the world of legislation or politics. I'm also talking about psychological change. I'm talking about the kind of change that compels a man's heart and mind.

My great-grandparents were slaves. Not even in their wildest imaginations could they have envisioned a Black man being president or their grandson, me, running for the presidency. But today, it's not impossible for my grandson to envision himself as president. Breaking the bonds of slavery is one thing. Changing the generational psyche of the slave mentality is another.

Substantive change takes more time, but symbolic change can be just as potent because it affects our psyches. Our role models inspire and uplift us. They pull back the ceiling of our diminished selves and ask us to dream bigger and follow our ambition so we can become someone greater than what our collective trauma tells us we should be. Just as Jacob saw himself in Barack Obama, so, too, can a young Black or Asian girl see herself in Kamala Harris today. That little girl can stop asking the question, "Will we ever have a female vice president?" and can start asking, "Why can't I be vice president?" Or, to take it a step further: president. A sense of empowerment can help change a person's heart and mind, their very life.

When a group of people have experienced the generational trauma of being told that they don't have power and that they don't matter, it's life-changing to affirm the opposite. Sometimes you host rallies and plan marches just to empower people and to help elevate their sense of self-worth. Because not to do so would be disempowering. The optics can often be enough to lift people's spirits and to enjoin the public to your cause. Imagine if, for example, George Floyd had been murdered and there had been no collective action, no call for justice from the masses, no rallies, no trial. A lack of response would have sent a message, too: Black lives really don't matter. Think of the young Black boys and girls living in Minneapolis who would then internalize that message. Of all the ways to die, snuffing out the human spirit may be the cruelest. So sometimes I call a march or a rally simply for no other reason than that it is life-affirming to do so. It sends the message that we're not expendable. That affirmation alone can often change the body politic because it influences the way people vote.

So, to change society, you must first change your mind. For

marginalized people—and by "marginalized," I mean everyone from members of the LGBTQIA community to Black and brown folk to women to the poor—you have to stop thinking that you're "less than," or that, for whatever made-up reason, you're undeserving. You are a person with integrity. You *are* deserving. You should be treated no less than the first-class citizen you are. Once you've empowered yourself, you have the power to change other people's minds, too. This is how we safeguard our rights. This is how we pay our respects to Hosea, Amelia, John, and all the other changemakers before and since. This is how movements are made: one heart, one mind, one person, one step at a time.

8

OUR LEGACY

"A democracy cannot thrive where power remains unchecked and justice is reserved for a select few. Ignoring these cries and failing to respond to this movement is simply not an option— for peace cannot exist where justice is not served."

—JOHN LEWIS, on the George Floyd Justice in Policing Act

I believe God put Hosea Williams and Amelia Boynton Robinson in my life for a reason. By their example, they both taught me to never become intoxicated with victory and to stay the course. It would have been easy to give in to the temptation of celebrating the legal victory of the Chauvin verdict, for example, but then I wouldn't have been emotionally present to help Daunte Wright's family. And if I had celebrated the short-term win of the verdict, I'd risk taking my eyes off the bigger prize: helping to secure lasting, federal legislation in George's name so other killings by police will stop.

There's a difference between sprinters and long-distance runners and, believe me, overturning the system of police brutality in America is like running a marathon. I couldn't afford to get caught up in the first hundred meters. I learned this from Hosea, who'd always warned me not to get blindsided by the media, nor politicians' games, nor by the comfort that came from a taste of victory. "Don't get too comfortable," he'd warn me time and time again. I knew what he meant: the minute you get comfortable, you forget why you were uncomfortable in the first place. Your moment in the sun doesn't shine on everyone. While you're resting comfortably, other people are in real pain. As a pastor, it's my moral imperative to help everyone rise.

Delivering justice on Derek Chauvin was, of course, meaningful but he's one drop in a much larger sea of inequity. And let's not forget: the fight against social injustice and oppression is multipronged. For example, it was on the heels of the Chauvin verdict that the Republicans ramped up their offensive against voting rights, effectively chipping away at the Voting Rights Act, and implementing restrictive voting laws. If our rights aren't being taken away by acts of police violence, they're being tamped down by voting restrictions, a corrosive prison system, redlining practices, or environmental injustice, you name it. Oppression is all-pervasive and erosive; no one escapes unscathed. This was on my mind as the days turned into the first calendar year of George's murder.

On the one-year anniversary of George's death, the Floyd family and Ben Crump were scheduled to appear in several meetings and press conferences on The Hill, and to meet in private with President Biden and Vice President Harris. To my way of thinking, the anniversary was an opportunity for Americans to come together and take stock of where we now stood. Had the ground shifted? If so, by how much? Movement on the George Floyd Justice in Policing Act had stalled or, to be more accurate, it had entered a heavy phase of negotiating, where each new concession had the possibility of derailing all we'd fought so hard to gain. We were in a determined yet fragile state and, while no one said it aloud, we were slightly apprehensive, cautious. When I say "we," I mean everyone from the senators who backed the bill, like Chuck Schumer and Cory Booker, among many others, to the civil rights leaders and lawyers—my colleagues—who helped shape the bill in the first place, to the Floyd family and the wave of protesters who showed up to Black Lives Matter marches or who rallied in George's name. We, the people. We steadied ourselves for the next storm, expending energy but not too much because we knew we'd be forced to call on our reserves later.

When he ran his presidential campaign, Biden kept saying he wanted to "turn down the temperature" in American politics. I understood he was employing the same strategy here regarding negotiations over the George Floyd Justice in Policing Act, and, at the time, I agreed with it. As someone who's accustomed to being in the fire, I can appreciate wanting to occasionally lower the heat. The risk, however, is that the momentum cools too much, and real change fades into rhetoric—all bark and no bite. I don't care how good a piece of legislation looks on paper. If it doesn't deliver anything of substance, it's useless.

The Monday before Philonise and Ben were due in Washington, DC, my cell phone rang: the president was on the line. Our conversation was gracious, with Biden announcing his deep concern for the passage of the George Floyd Justice in Policing Act. The best chance it had for survival was for him to keep negotiations low-profile and, most importantly, to not let the Republicans turn his support for it into a wedge issue.

"We'd rather have a hard bill with a soft deadline than a soft bill with a hard deadline," I said.

The fact that the bill sat languishing in the Senate's chambers, however, signaled a more entrenched fight than I'd anticipated. In the time that we'd been fighting for the passage of the George Floyd Justice in Policing Act, the House of Representatives had passed the COVID-19 Hate Crimes Act. With the former president referring to COVID in derogatory terms as the China virus, it's not surprising that Asian Americans and Pacific Islanders have been disproportionately targeted during the pandemic. That said, I often get the question, "How come politicians can pass a bill that protects Asian Americans and Pacific Islanders but can't pass the Policing Act, which largely addresses the disproportionate hostility against Blacks?" No one was opposed to the COVID-19 Hate Crimes Act—the House passed it 364–62 and the Senate 94–1. With the Policing Act, however, we're up against police unions and associations as well as the Fraternal Order of Police, which has a long and entrenched history in our country. It's a much more complicated and nuanced fight. Police unions finance some of the campaigns of the top politicians in our country. They, along with the gun lobby, form a well-oiled machine. We could pass a blanket Anti-Hate Bill, but what good would that do?

I frequently and patiently remind myself that change doesn't happen overnight. Privately, though, I was concerned: despite it being the one-year anniversary of his murder, George Floyd was no longer dominating our social and political attention. From my experience, the lack of attention on an issue at this stage in a movement either means that real, steadfast work is being done quietly behind the scenes or, conversely, nothing is being done at all. I decided to put my trust in Biden's words and give the senators the time, space, and support they needed to work it out. Biden reiterated that he wanted to meet with me along with other civil rights leaders to discuss this bill, the John Lewis Voting Rights Advancement Act, and his bipartisan infrastructure plan in more detail. We agreed, however, to table everything for the moment. For now, the world's eyes were, once again, on the Floyd family.

Before Philonise left for Washington, he and I spoke to go over the message he wanted to deliver to President Biden. He felt ready, and I could tell that he was in a good headspace. He was calm and, as always, openhearted, and ready to engage in meaningful conversation. We knew there was a possibility that issues would come up when talking about negotiating points for the bill, things like qualified immunity, the creation of a national registry, and the amendment of 18 U.S.C. Section 242, which would change the language of police misconduct from its current "willfulness" to a "recklessness" standard. This word change, while seemingly minor, is important, because while we couldn't prove that Chauvin intended to kill George—he didn't wake up that morning and say, "I'm gonna kill George Floyd today"—it could be argued that, with his knee on George's neck for nine minutes and twenty-nine seconds, Chauvin was reckless in his behavior and had intentionally created harm if not death. Changing the language from "willfulness" to "recklessness" holds police officers accountable for their on-the-ground actions. Court cases often rest on the interpretation of one word.

While Ben and Philonise met with the power brokers in Washington, DC, I hosted a separate event at the House of Justice in Harlem, with Mayor de Blasio, Congressman Hakeem Jeffries, and several other politicians in attendance. At one point during my opening speech, I asked everyone to kneel for nine minutes and twenty-nine seconds to honor the final moments of George's life. I've done this several times and in various settings around the country. I do it for two reasons: first, it's a way to collectively reclaim the final, painful minutes of George's life and offer them back to his family in a gesture of support and healing and, second, it helps people grasp what Chauvin did. Mayor de Blasio approached me afterward and said, "As much as we've been talking about George's death for the past year, I didn't really get it until today." He paused and looked at me. "You don't realize how long it is until you're down there on your own knee."

"I know," I said. "And you're doing it without anyone's neck beneath your knee. It takes real intent, some would say venom, to override the natural desire to stand." We stood quietly next to one another. I couldn't help but think of something Philonise had said to me earlier that morning: "Congress protects the bald eagle," he'd said. "Why can't it protect people of color?"

By the time Philonise gave his remarks at the press conference later that same day, he'd honed this question into a statement, saying, "This is the thing, if you can make federal laws to protect the bald eagle, you can make federal laws to protect people of color." I realized then that Philonise truly was his brother's keeper—not just of George but also of his fellow man. Philonise, the man who questioned everything, had become someone who now demanded more than simple answers. He wanted action.

Marchers gathered in cities around the country to pay homage to George's memory. Officials planned a citywide prayer vigil in Philadelphia and protestors came together in Chicago to call for police reform. Atlanta hosted a rally called My Daddy Changed the World, and invited Gianna, George's daughter, to be a featured guest. Rallies went off in Brooklyn, Los Angeles, and Dallas. While the day was obviously one of healing, it was also one of reflection, an opportunity to take stock of the collective momentum. After the morning service at the House of Justice, I headed to Minneapolis to be with some of the Floyd family, including several of George's cousins and his sister Bridgett, who'd organized a memorial march. Gwen Carr, Lesley McSpadden, and Sybrina Fulton were there as were a few distant relatives of Emmett Till. All told, there were about fifteen other victims' families who showed up to lend their support, their shared trauma a unifying bond.

At the time of this writing, more than thirty states and dozens of cities have adopted new rules limiting police tactics, including banning neck restraints and requiring police officers to intervene when a fellow officer uses extreme force. As the negotiations for the George Floyd Justice in Policing Act and the John Lewis Voting Rights Advancement Act have moved up the political ranks, however, I'm worried that we, the people, are no longer seated at the table. And once the voice of the people is removed from the negotiating table, you're left with a bunch of disconnected politicians bickering with one another about on-the-ground realities most of them have never known nor personally experienced themselves. It's why Philonise's voice is so critically important. It's why Gwen Carr's voice carries weight. It's why Sybrina Fulton's voice matters, and Lesley McSpadden's, too. It's why Mamie Till's voice started a movement. It's why Amelia Boynton Robinson's did, too. It's why demonstrations and marches and rallies matter: the people's voice gives politicians leverage. That is, if a politician is savvy enough to hear it and embrace it as such.

Speaking about her brother George at the one-year memorial rally, Bridgett said, "I will stand and be the voice for him. I will stand and be the change for him, be the legacy for him." A politician has got to be able to leverage Bridgett's voice for change and walk out of the negotiating room with a deal he or she can sell to the average American Black family. Otherwise, what have we gained? And how much have we lost? That's what we're talking about here. In the balance of those gains and losses, where does the Black family stand? What's our national legacy, and who's writing it?

THIS HALLOWED GROUND

About a week after George Floyd's one-year anniversary memorial, I found myself in Oklahoma to commemorate another anniversary: the centennial of the Tulsa Race Massacre. The centennial anniversary happened to fall on Memorial Day. Ironically, Memorial Day had fallen on May 25 the previous year, the day George Floyd died. As I made my way to Tulsa, I couldn't help but think of the countless Black servicemen and -women who had fought to secure our freedoms and liberties abroad, as

James Meredith had done or Hosea Williams had done, only to face a life-or-death battle in their own backyards.

The Tulsa Race Massacre was an especially violent chapter in American history. It started when Dick Rowland, a young Black teenage shoeshiner, was falsely accused of assaulting Sarah Page, a white elevator operator, who worked at the Drexel Building in Tulsa, Oklahoma. The boy was arrested. An angry white mob soon arrived at the courthouse, however, hoping to hang Rowland. There, the mob was met by twenty-five armed Black men, many of them war veterans themselves and dressed in their World War I uniforms, who'd come to help prevent a lynching. From there, the situation spun out of control, with mobs of white residents, some of whom were deputized and given weapons by city officials, attacking the Black residents of Tulsa, destroying more than thirty-five square blocks of homes, churches, schools, and businesses of the Greenwood District, effectively killing what had been known as Black Wall Street. As many as three hundred Tulsans died during the eighteen-hour siege that raged from May 31 to June 1, 1921. The city was reduced to ash. Ten thousand people were left destitute and homeless and placed in internment camps. No arrests of the mob were made, none. It's hard to say which was worse: the events of those two days or the campaign of censure that immediately followed.

Victims were buried in unmarked graves. Official documents detailing the massacre disappeared. Accounts were cleaned from newspaper archives. The offices of Tulsa's two Black-owned newspapers, the Tulsa *Star* and the *Oklahoma Sun* were destroyed; the *Star* never resumed publishing. Think about it: when Timothy McVeigh bombed the Alfred P. Murrah Federal Building in Oklahoma City in 1995, killing 168 people, people said it was the first terrorist attack in the history of the state as if the Tulsa Race Massacre had never happened. At 106 years old, Lessie Benningfield Randle is one of the oldest known witnesses to the massacre and she spoke about her experience before a congressional committee for the first time one hundred years *after* the massacre had happened. One hundred years! In all that time, President Biden was the first sitting president to come to Tulsa to bear witness to its tragedy.

We likely wouldn't have a full accounting of the massacre if it hadn't been for two Black women, decades separating them, who chronicled its horrific events. An eyewitness to the massacre, Mary E. Parrish recorded her firsthand account along with that of twenty survivors in a slim book called *Events of the Tulsa Disaster*. Decades later, Eddie Faye Gates, who was appointed to the Tulsa Race Riot Commission in the late 1990s, picked up where Parrish had left off, spending years tracking and interviewing dozens of survivors. Gates has also tirelessly advocated for reparations for massacre victims, appealing to both the state of Oklahoma and to the Supreme Court as recently as 2005. Their work has illuminated a dark corner of history, bringing attention to the lives of the forgotten, and on Parrish and Gates themselves.

The Journalist:
Mary E. Parrish

Born in 1892 in Yazoo City, Mississippi, Mary E. Parrish first visited her brother in Tulsa in 1918. The city made an impression on her. At the time, she was living in Rochester, New York, and studying shorthand at the Rochester Business Institute. Parrish was amazed by the differences between Rochester and Tulsa—not only were there more Blacks in Tulsa, but their businesses were varied and booming. In Rochester, Blacks were largely confined to service jobs, working in restaurants, hotels, rooming houses, barbershops, and beauty salons. But in Tulsa, Blacks owned and ran everything

from the post office to the local school and transportation systems, to the pool halls, restaurants, and night-
clubs. Even the Dreamland Theatre was in service to
the community, showing Black silent films and Black
vaudeville acts. It didn't take much to persuade Parrish
to pack her bags and move to Tulsa one year later. She
wrote, "But I came not to Tulsa as many came, lured by
the dream of making money and bettering myself in the
financial world, but because of the wonderful coopera-
tion I observed among our people, and especially the
harmony of spirit and action that existed between the
businessmen and -women." As Parrish noted, Greenwood Avenue, the "Negro's Wall Street" was like a city
within a city. "Some malicious newspapers take pride
in referring to it as 'Little Africa,'" she wrote.

A trained journalist, Parrish got a job teaching typing
and shorthand at the local branch of the YMCA. On
May 31, 1921, she'd wrapped up her class and headed
home as she'd done any other day. As she was settling into her evening book, her daughter Florence said,
"Mother, I see men with guns." Parrish went to the window and saw a group of armed Black men gathering
in front of their apartment. She went outside to get
the scoop and learned that the men were planning on
marching to the courthouse to protect Dick Rowland,
the teenage Black boy who'd already been arrested
for assaulting Sarah Page, who was white. (Rowland
had, most likely, accidentally stepped on Page's foot
as he'd exited her elevator.)

At the courthouse, five hundred armed white men
were waiting, a number that soon swelled to a thousand. Parrish wrote, "Someone fired a stray shot and,
to use the expression of General Grant, 'All hell broke
loose.'" By evening, the Frisco Street tracks and station

had formed the first battle line, dividing the business sections between white Tulsa and Black Tulsa. The city quickly turned into a war zone, with shots being fired and whites ransacking the homes of the Black residents. The fighting, looting, and terrorizing continued throughout the night and by three o'clock in the morning the city had begun to burn. As the flames tore through the city streets and the Black men ran out of ammunition, Parrish admitted, "The truth dawned upon us that our men were fighting in vain to hold their dear Greenwood." Unbelievably, planes then began to advance across the sky, with men firing down from them with rifles.

Parrish and her daughter, along with other refugees, traveled many miles into the countryside. When there was talk that the Red Cross would send trucks of food for the dispossessed hiding in the countryside, Parrish didn't believe it. "After spending such a dreadful night and day witnessing so much destruction, how could we trust a race that would bring it about?" she asked. "At that hour we mistrusted every person having a white face and blue eyes." At ten o'clock in the evening, after walking thirteen miles, she could make out distant smoke rising from the ruins. The bloodshed supposedly over, the Red Cross returned Parrish and her daughter to Tulsa, driving them through the white section of town and to Exposition Park where hundreds of Black folks stood huddled in lines, waiting for clothing, food, and an army cot on which to sleep. Parrish wrote, "There were to be seen people who formerly had owned beautiful homes and buildings, and people who had always worked and made a comfortable, honest living, all standing in a row waiting to be handed a change of clothing and feeling grateful to be able to get a sandwich and a glass of water." As the town was put under martial law, Parrish took stock of what little remained. The telegraph office was still standing, and she found telegrams from family and friends trying to locate her. "Am safe but cannot leave now," she wrote. Imagine if Parrish had left. She had every reason to: the businesses were gone, her neighbors were dead, homes were looted. Tulsa was an ember. To her credit, however, Parrish stayed and spent the next several weeks documenting the pain of a city and a people laid to ruin.

It was Henry T. S. Johnson, a Black pastor, who first asked Parrish to interview survivors on behalf of a statewide interracial commission. In speaking with survivors, Parrish learned that the enemy appeared to have been well-prepared, both with weaponry and with ambulances and trucks that picked up injured white folks. While the individual details of the firsthand accounts she gathered vary greatly, their underlying heartbreak doesn't—from the remembrances of ninety-two-year-old Jack Thomas, who, due to his age, escaped with his life but conceded that the massacre was "the worst scene that I have ever witnessed," to Richard J. Hill, who reported seeing white men shoot Black commuters as they made their way to work, to an anonymous witness, who watched groups of white men loot neighbors' homes, carrying out everything from the silverware to the living room furniture. Not all whites looted and killed. Some offered up their homes as safe houses. Others warned Black folks of dangerous areas and vouched for them so an angry mob would let them free—poor consolations in the face of so much misery.

Parrish's *Events of the Tulsa Disaster* was published

in 1923, and garnered little attention except among local historians and the survivors themselves. The two white-owned newspapers, the Tulsa *World* and the Tulsa *Tribune*, reframed the massacre as an aberration caused by the Black residents themselves. By the time Tulsa had burned, more than three dozen cities across the United States had experienced a similar kind of fate at the hands of white supremacists and known Ku Klux Klan members, prompting civil rights activist James Weldon Johnson to call the period from late winter to early autumn of 1919 the "Red Summer." In some cities, like Chicago and Washington, DC, Black folks fought back. Until Tulsa happened, Elaine, Arkansas, had suffered the worst causalities from such upheaval, with estimates of over one hundred Black residents murdered. Yet most of these stories were buried by the country's leading white newspapers or were given a small mention, with many journalists turning a blind eye to the larger pattern of white supremacy sweeping the nation.

Besides fearlessly chronicling the events of the Tulsa Race Massacre, Parrish also made recommendations for the federal passage of an anti-lynching measure, citing the Dyer Anti-Lynch Bill in her writing. That bill was first introduced in 1918 by Republican Representative Leonidas C. Dyer and was meant to establish lynching as a federal crime. As of this writing and despite the fact that lynching is considered illegal under federal law, no anti-lynching bill has been passed by both houses: in 2018, the Senate passed the Justice for Victims of Lynching Act, but the House of Representatives failed to, and in 2020, the House passed a revised version, the Emmett Till Antilynching Act. Senator Rand Paul has blocked the bipartisan bill from moving forward, saying it's too broad in scope.

For decades, the massacre was commonly called the Tulsa Race Riot. At the centennial anniversary, President Biden cleared up that nonsense, saying, "My fellow Americans, this was not a riot. This was a massacre, among the worst in our history, but not the only one." He went on to say, "I come here today to help fill the silence, because in silence, wounds deepen. As painful as this is, only in remembrance do wounds heal. We have to choose to remember. We memorialize what happened here in Tulsa so it can't be erased. We know here, this hallowed place, we simply can't bury pain and trauma forever. At some point, there will be a reckoning, an inflection point like we're facing right now as a nation." His words help us remember so we don't forget, but some of us—like Tulsa survivors Lessie Benningfield Randle and Viola Fletcher—remember not because we want to, but because the trauma has been too great to forget.

HISTORY NOT HEADLINES

A few weeks after the centennial of the Tulsa Race Massacre, I returned to Minneapolis to be with the Floyd family for Chauvin's sentencing. It was a little surreal to return to the same hotel ballroom where we'd first watched the conviction. This time around, there were fewer people. Some family members were at the courthouse but the majority of them were huddled together in front of the hotel's large-screen television, watching the indictment unfold in real time.

After explaining that he would let his written legal analysis of the case do most of the talking, Judge Cahill went on to say, "What the case is or what the case is not based on is emotion or sympathy but at the same time I want to acknowledge the deep and tremendous pain all the families are feeling, especially the Floyd family." He continued, "I'm also not basing my sentence on public opinion. I'm not basing it on any attempt to send messages." I raised my eyebrows a little at this, afraid that, in singling out the issue of public opinion, Cahill was suggesting that the movement or public outcry surrounding George's murder had been meaningless. I girded myself and looked at Bridgett. The atmosphere was less tense than it had been when we'd waited to first hear the verdict, but not by much.

"That doesn't sound good," she said.

I was beginning to think of what I would say if the sentencing was too light, too heavy, or if it was in the middle. I wasn't sure what to think. But then Cahill pivoted, and hit Chauvin with twenty-two and a half years in prison. It wasn't what the state wanted but it was a lot more than I thought we were gonna get. It was the first time in the history of Minnesota that a white cop was sentenced to that kind of time for killing a Black civilian. It was also a long time coming for our country to witness the delivery of justice in a case dealing with police accountability. As I've said before, I don't take joy in the sentencing of a man to prison but, in this case, justice was served and I felt a sense of vindication, that all the work had paid off. It was one of the first times I could look at a family and say, "We got justice." I've never been able to say that to Gwen Carr, and it still tears me up inside. Judge Cahill said he didn't take public opinion into account with his sentencing and yet I felt that we'd won in the court of public opinion, too, with or without Cahill's blessing or acknowledgment. The marches and rallies weren't for nothing; they helped turn the tide. They *were* the tide.

Philonise and I caught up after the day's press conference, with Philonise asking, "Reverend Al, that was historic, wasn't it?"

"Yes, it was," I said, nodding.

Ben Crump and I held back from everyone and took a few moments to ourselves.

"You realize that this will have been the biggest thing in your career," I told him. "Ben, we've come to the stage in both of our journeys where we're no longer working for tomorrow's headline. We're at the point where we can ask ourselves, 'How is history going to judge us?'"

Traveling home after Chauvin's sentencing, I had an extraordinary run-in with a stranger at the Minneapolis–Saint Paul International Airport. Strangers often ask to take photos with me, something I'm almost always happy to do. So, when a white man cautiously approached me at the airport, I assumed he wanted a photo.

"Reverend Al, I don't mean to disturb you," he said.

I walked over to him, and he quickly explained that he didn't want a photo. "I just wanted to tell you something," he said.

"Yes?" I asked.

He introduced himself and then said, "My great-great-great grandfather was Mississippi Confederate Colonel James Zacharia George, one of the early architects of Jim Crow." As he spoke, he kept his eyes trained on mine. I got the feeling he was watching for my reaction to his words. My security team tensed up a little and moved closer. I waved them away, which did little to calm them. My publicist, Rachel Noerdlinger, is a seasoned pro and knows how to handle most situations better than anyone in the media world, but even she approached us cautiously.

"Go on," I said.

"As a senator, he passed the disenfranchisement provisions in Mississippi's constitution that became much of the framework for Jim Crow. I told my family that I wanted to come to Minneapolis when Derek Chauvin was sentenced because our family owed it to America because of the damage my ancestor had done."

I was absolutely dumbstruck. "Let me ask you a question, would *you* mind taking a photo with *me*?"

He laughed. "Sure," he said.

We took the photo together and spoke a bit longer. I learned that he'd been in the military most of his life and wanted to define the future legacy of his family by correcting its past. This man is as great a changemaker as any I've written about in this book. He could have betrayed his better nature and followed a similar trajectory as that of his great-great-great-grandfather, but he didn't. Instead, he chose to rise up, stand tall, and change the course of his family's future and, ultimately, that of his country. He rejected the path of division, hatred, and suffering and, instead, chose the path of righteousness, love, and equality. He was making history, not headlines. Rachel later said that in all her twenty years of working with me, she'd never seen me so surprised. Moments like this give me hope; it's always good to meet a fellow traveler.

A few weeks later, history came knocking when I got a call from Ben, who told me that an unarmed seventeen-year-old boy named Hunter Brittain was shot and killed by a Lonoke County deputy sheriff in Arkansas. The boy's car had been acting up and, after being pulled over by Sergeant Michael Davis, he'd reached for a bottle of antifreeze in the truck bed to put behind the vehicle so it wouldn't roll into the squad car. According to Jordan King, Brittain's friend and an eyewitness, Officer Davis drew his weapon and fatally shot Brittain three times with no warning. The officer didn't have his body camera turned on, so no footage exists of the shooting. The Brittain family reached out to Ben and, through him, asked if I would be willing to do the funeral and help with some of the local protests.

"Of course," I said.

"Rev, there's something you gotta know," Ben said. "Hunter's a white boy."

"This isn't about Black or white; it's about what's right and wrong," I said, not missing a beat.

My team was concerned, however. The eulogy was to take place at an auditorium at the local high school in Beebe, Arkansas, the heart of Trump land, twenty minutes or so out of Little Rock and in Lonoke County, a rural county of seventy-three thousand, 90 percent white—not exactly my kind of crowd. Hunter, like George Floyd, did nothing wrong—but if we segregate how we react to the state's violence, then we're in the wrong. I told my team, "I'm doing it," because the issue couldn't be clearer to me: we don't just rise up for one race. We stand for what's right, period. This was an opportunity to drive that message home. The reason the Brittain family called us was because they needed our support and knew that the only chance they'd have of finding justice for Hunter was to speak out about his death.

Before the eulogy, Ben and I spoke in some detail with Brittain's grandma Ms. Becky and his uncle Jesse, both of whom voiced their support for the George Floyd Justice in Policing Act. When I stepped up to the podium in the auditorium, I was greeted by a majority-white crowd of about five hundred people or so. I could have counted the number of Black people in attendance on my hands, most of them from my own office. It was the one time in my life when I wished I could have swapped my suit for Hosea's uniform of denim overalls to better blend in with my audience, most of whom were wearing trucker hats, jeans, and work boots. It didn't matter, though: once I started speaking, our differences disappeared.

I went off, talking about how this boy shouldn't have been killed. If the cop had had enough time to decide to shoot, he'd also had enough time to turn on his body camera. "We need to condemn wrong no matter who is wrong," I said. The auditorium erupted in cheers and shouts. "It's wrong for those policemen to shoot first and ask questions later." I made a point of saying that perhaps Hunter's message to us was that we needed to unfreeze our hearts and minds in order to come together to find justice. It got so I had to keep stopping and starting, because half the audience couldn't hear me over the shouting. We may have been in an all-white high school auditorium, but to me it felt like church.

I relayed the tragic story of Hunter Brittain to President Biden and Vice President Harris when I met with them in June, along with the leadership of other civil rights organizations, to discuss the George Floyd Justice in Policing Act and the John Lewis Voting Rights Advancement Act. I brought Hunter to the White House same as I did George Floyd, and that's because both deaths speak to the urgency of passing the George Floyd Justice in Policing Act. The bill is designed to protect *every* citizen under the law no matter their race, background, gender, or age. It's the very definition of equal justice under the law.

All too often, our tragedies and triumphs feel isolated, and we forget their historical significance. We gloss over the fact that our lives are history in the making, and that we can be agents of positive change. The George Floyd movement showed me that the work is worth it. At the same time, I know there's serious work yet to be done. Our collective future rests on our ability to live up to the promise of our own hearts and minds so that the good work of people like Pauli Murray, Hosea Williams, and Amelia Boynton Robinson can be carried forward and the lives of those we've lost—Hunter Brittain, Eric Garner, Emmett Till, and too many others—have not been in vain.

9

THE STATE OF THE DREAM

"Spread the word, have you heard, all across the nation, we are going to be a great generation."

—YOLANDA RENEE KING

Sometime in the summer of 2021, I got a call from Martin Luther King III and his wife, Arndrea. Arndrea is president of the Drum Major Institute for Public Policy (DMI); Martin is its chairman. The organization was founded by Dr. King and his lawyer Harry H. Wachtel in 1961 and took its name from "The Drum Major Instinct," a sermon King preached from the pulpit of Ebenezer Baptist Church in 1968. Arndrea wanted to coordinate a national event around the issue of women's rights and voting for August 28. She asked if NAN wanted to be involved. Because we'd already mobilized a march the previous year, I hadn't anticipated doing another one for 2021. These events take a massive amount of work, and require significant manpower, outreach, and communication, not to mention money and resources. As Arndrea spoke, however, I knew I couldn't sit this one out. At the time, Texas had yet to pass its restrictive abortion law, but it was clear, even then, that women's rights were under attack. And then there was the matter of voting restrictions. Since January 2021, forty-eight states have introduced 389 bills that amount to voter suppression. Whenever laws are passed that suppress the voting methods that enrich our democracy, it behooves you to look at who's being restricted from the voting booths. Time and time again, it's people of color, a population that commonly votes as Democrats and, in 2021, flipped the US census: for the first time in the history of our nation, the white population has declined. Trump may have trumpeted the glory days of yesteryear with his MAGA slogan but the 2021 census captured a portrait of the future of our country in all its beautiful diversity and strength.

As I listened to Arndrea, I realized that the stakes were too high for us not to say or do something. The DMI had already begun partnering with March ON, a nonprofit organization of women-led and grassroots political activist groups that grew out of the massive women's marches of 2017. Arndrea was going to piece this thing together one way or another. I could either sit on the sidelines or buck up. By the end of our phone call, I had committed myself and NAN to the cause. If everyone worked together, we believed we could organize a large national march in Washington, DC, and smaller ones spread across other cities. We had about three months to plan. It would be a substantial undertaking, but if there's one thing I've learned as an activist it's that sometimes the causes come to you. If you don't move quickly, you lose momentum. If you lose momentum, you also lose the moment—your collateral is gone. It's best to roll up your sleeves, put your head down, and get to work. No whining. No bellyaching. Everyone went into overdrive. Martin, Arndrea, and I did as many interviews and calls as we could, drumming up publicity and coordinating our efforts with other organizations. It's a beautiful thing to watch everyone come together in this fashion; you realize that you're not alone in the march toward progress. There are like-minded peaceful warriors throughout this country.

As we were planning the march, the Republican-controlled Texas Legislature passed a major bill that overhauled election laws in the state, one in a series of bills designed to restrict voting rules state by state. I called a meeting of the civil rights leadership: the NAACP, the National Urban League, the National Council of Negro Women, Black Women's Roundtable, the Lawyers' Committee for Civil Rights Under Law, the Leadership Conference on Civil and Human Rights, and NAN. We agreed: it was time to take the matter to the president.

We met with President Biden and Vice President Harris for about two hours—it was at this meeting that I first mentioned Hunter Brittain to Biden and Harris. We spoke candidly and went over several issues with them in detail, including, among other things, the importance of dismantling the filibuster. This arcane and out-of-date Senate rule, which creates a de facto sixty-vote threshold for major legislation, stands in the way of just about every major initiative of the Biden administration. The filibuster was consistently used to block civil rights bills in the House in the 1920s; by the era of Jim Crow, it was a generally accepted tool used to effectively stamp out civil rights. Supporters of the filibuster argue that it protects minority rights, preventing the Senate majority from running over its opponents. But that argument misconstrues what kind of minorities need protection in a democracy, and from whom. It fails to take into account that the minorities who need protection are the same as those whose rights the filibuster was designed to block. The filibuster lets the people who already have power stay in power, and effectively prevents any meaningful change to federal voting legislation. It's not in the Constitution; it's not in any law anywhere. It's a Senate tradition that's deeply tied to the past when today, more than ever before, we need to look to the future.

In a 1963 news conference, Dr. King denounced the filibuster, saying, "Senators...will use the filibuster to keep the majority of people from even voting—and certainly they would not want the majority of people to vote because they know they do not represent the majority of the American people." That pretty much sums it up. It should be revoked. And if not revoked, then carved out. If the Republicans can do a carve-out for a Supreme Court nominee, why can't Biden do a carve-out to help protect the fundamental right to vote? That said, the bully pulpit of the presidency can, at times, be a more effective tool than the filibuster. A president's words can help shift the national discourse. We asked Biden to come out and make an unwavering statement about the importance of voting rights. We finished the meeting and stepped outside where a throng of reporters were gathered. I told them, "This will be a summer of activism."

THE BULLY PULPIT AND THE THORN

The next day, I received a call from Cedric Richmond, senior adviser to President Biden, who informed me that Biden was planning a major speech on the issue of voting rights at the National Constitution Center in Philadelphia the following week. The choice of venue was strategic as it was a stone's throw from the Liberty Bell and Independence Hall, where the Constitution and the Declaration of Independence were signed when someone like me wouldn't have been allowed in the building. The White House extended invitations to all eight of the major civil rights leadership. I ended up attending for all of us and was seated up front, next to the president's sister. My colleagues missed a show. President Biden's speech that day was incredibly moving—not only did he frame voting rights as a moral reckoning, but he did so with force, eloquence, and clarity. He didn't stop there. He also addressed white supremacy and called Trump out—not by name per se—but by saying that "bullies and merchants of fear" were a threat to democracy. It was truly a great speech. In many respects, it reminded me of President Lyndon B. Johnson's "And We Shall Overcome" speech, which he delivered to Congress in 1965, weeks after the Selma to Montgomery marches. I remember sitting with my mother in our living room, both of us glued to the black-and-white television, listening to Johnson urge his fellow Americans to, in his words, "open your polling places to all your people." He spoke bluntly about what he called the "American problem"—the issue of unequal rights for Blacks—and outlined a sweeping plan of action, signing the Voting Rights Act five months later. Biden's speech carried much of the same rhetorical grace as Johnson's did and yet, something was missing.

After receiving several standing ovations, President Biden came to the front row to greet his supporters. He hugged his sister, then turned to me and asked, "What did you think?"

"Mr. President, great speech. I almost thought Lyndon Johnson was speaking. But," I ventured, "one word was missing."

"What's that?"

"Filibuster," I said. If he'd addressed the issue of the filibuster, it would have been a slam dunk in my book. I knew he'd handle the matter his own way, but I'd hoped to have the issue out in the open. We can talk in circles about Jim Crow and white supremacy and the big lie, but the filibuster goes to the heart of the matter. Look, President Biden needs to navigate the politics of the Senate and I get that. At the same time, I'm going to keep raising the issue until it gets addressed. The filibuster is the thorn in America's side, and I'm going to keep pulling at it.

INTERPOSITION AND NULLIFICATION

A few weeks later, Martin Luther King III, his wife, Arndrea, and I decided to visit The Hill to meet with some of the senators and congressmen and -women on their own turf to talk in more depth about the filibuster, the George Floyd Justice in Policing Act, S. 1 of the For the People Act, and other hot-button topics. Senator Lindsey Graham greeted us with his trademark Southern charm, and started the conversation by talking about James Brown, who'd been like a father to me. Most people don't know it, but James had been a lifelong conservative and had supported Graham early on in his political career. I told Graham that James and I had frequently gotten into political arguments with one another, and as soon as I'd said it, I realized that I was likely walking into one with Graham that very moment. After some small talk, we quickly got down to business. Graham was adamant that he wouldn't support Senate Bill 1 nor the John Lewis Voting Rights Advancement Act. I can't say I was surprised. We argued our points, going back and forth. After a while, I respected the fact that he was candid; it was clear he wasn't going to budge. As we were wrapping up, he said, "If I were y'all, I'd be doing exactly what you're doing: marching and raising hell, 'cause if you can turn public opinion, that's what matters. But right now, you don't have me on voting. We can talk about the George Floyd Justice in Policing Act, though." We proceeded to discuss various points regarding the George Floyd bill. Graham's standing—"no" on voting; a possible "yes" on the George Floyd Justice in Policing Act—was indicative of the Republican stance nearly down the line.

In one of the last meetings of the day, we sat with Congressman Clyburn of South Carolina, who stressed the importance of the word *nullification* when dealing with the issue of voting rights. It reminded Martin of something his father had said in his famous "I Have a Dream" speech when he alluded to the Alabama governor's lips dripping with words of interposition and nullification. This notion of nullification hit home for me a few days later when Secretary of State Brad Raffensperger suggested that Georgia's Fulton County election director and board members needed to be suspended and replaced by the state election board, a move that certainly dripped of voter nullification. A state-run committee or board empowered with the authority to overturn elections results essentially nullifies Article 1, Section 4 of the United States Constitution. Alexander Hamilton's fifty-ninth essay of *The Federalist Papers* explains why states can't be given that kind of authority. In short, nullification cuts democracy off at the knees. It's one of the reasons why the insurrection of January 6, 2021, was so dangerous. Plain and simple: when you nullify the voice of the people, we're no longer a democracy. Martin, Arndrea, and I left Washington, DC, that day feeling determined. We knew that the march on Washington was our chance to make a collective statement not only about the state of Dr. King's dream, but also about the integrity of democracy itself.

HOW YOU SHOW UP

We decided to go a different route this time. Rather than marching to the Lincoln Memorial, which was Dr. King's original route and what most anniversary marches have followed since, we took the march to the US Capitol. Now, you gotta remember that the reason Dr. King went to the Lincoln Memorial in 1963 was because in 1863 President Lincoln signed the Emancipation Proclamation. One hundred years later Dr. King brought his case to Lincoln to symbolically illustrate the fact that Lincoln's promise to America's Black citizens had yet to be fulfilled—they were still being treated as second-class citizens. We wanted the march of 2021 to represent everyone, because the constitutional right of voting affects our entire body politic. Voting is the beating heart of democracy itself. We wanted to lay today's issues squarely on the president, his administration, on every senator and member of Congress, and on every local official across this land. Voter suppression and nullification is *the* clear and present danger to our democracy today, no question about it. So, why not change the optics to focus on the US Capitol?

We started at McPherson Square Park, marched past the Black Lives Matter Plaza, the White House, and the Washington Monument. The day itself was sweltering, but it didn't seem to matter. Everyone was in good spirits, cheering each other on. As I marched toward the Capitol, I took stock of the people around me. It seemed everyone had showed up: Philonise Floyd, Ben Crump, Gwen Carr, several senators, congressmen and -women, the head leadership of the NAACP, the Urban League, the Congressional Black Caucus, and just about every other civil rights group and women's rights group you can imagine. It was an incredibly diverse crowd, comprised of people of every background, age, and gender. It was, as Jesse Jackson would have said, "a rainbow coalition." After the debasement that was the insurrection of January 6, I thought, *This is how you show up to the US Capitol: non-violently, organized, and with respect.* As I said then: "You saw an insurrection against people's right to vote. Today, you saw that twenty thousand walked through the streets to the Capitol to represent Dr. King's resurrection of the right to vote. No windows broken, nobody harmed. No disorder. This is how you come to the Capitol." I didn't know it then, but the crowd ended up being closer to fifty thousand strong. As I stood in front of the Capitol and marveled at the scene—democracy in action—I couldn't help but remember the very first march of my life.

THE ORIGINAL TROUBLEMAKER

The earliest memory I have of marching was when I was about nine years old. A new hospital called Downstate Medical Center was being built in Brooklyn. There were no Black construction workers on the job. Bishop Washington, who ordinarily wasn't very political, nonetheless recognized the importance of standing up on this issue and so he, along with Reverend William Jones and Reverend Gardner Taylor, organized several rallies and a march. It was the first time I'd seen my church, Washington Temple, transform itself into an agent of change, with the congregants joining the rallies after Saturday's morning service. Dr. King's church had done the same thing, organizing marches after morning service. It was an activist tradition I later incorporated into the House of Justice, too.

Bishop Washington was arrested along with everyone else. I remember feeling a kind of pride in the arrests because I knew the pastors were standing up for all of us. Some of the kids in my neighborhood had fathers who were construction workers—

good, hardworking people—and why didn't they deserve to work on a project that was literally in their backyard? And wasn't a hospital supposed to serve the whole community? Being a kid, I wasn't arrested. I did, however, attend the rallies with the rest of my church after the first waves of arrests. Well, guess what happened? We won. Black constructions workers were put on the job.

About three years later, I joined Operation Breadbasket, a division of the SCLC, as head of the youth division. It wasn't long after I joined that we marched on the A&P grocery chain and Robert Hall stores because they didn't have Blacks on their board of directors nor in upper management. Our demonstrations gained traction once Huntington Hartford, whose family was the original owner of A&P before the company went public, endorsed our boycotting efforts. His involvement helped tip the scales in our favor. The A&P in New York ended up giving shelf space to Black-owned companies, which later became a national policy with the company. These early experiences were important in my development as an activist. I saw firsthand how nonviolent, faith-based movements can force change. Hartford's involvement wasn't lost on me either: allies are essential, especially when they can apply pressure from the inside of an organization or political establishment.

The A&P boycott was especially memorable because it was the first time I saw Jesse Jackson get arrested for protesting. His example taught me that some fights are worth putting yourself on the line. Because I'd seen my mentors Jesse Jackson and Bishop Washington—men I considered to be good churchgoing leaders—get arrested for protest work, I never feared getting arrested myself so long as I was standing up for something I believed in. In activism, you often *want* to be jailed because arrests help draw attention to the issue at hand. It's like a badge of honor; there's nothing criminal about it. What's criminal is having a political, economic, and cultural system that profits from the disenfranchisement of its people.

Activism work has long been integrated into the Black church, the church being one of the few places slaves and newly freed Blacks could first openly congregate. In between the gospel and the verse, you'd better believe there was some talk about the state of the union, Toussaint Louverture and the Haitian Revolution, and the Emancipation Proclamation. Outside of this, though, is the Bible itself: the path to social justice is clearly outlined in the pages of the Good Book. Starting with the second book in the Old Testament, Exodus, the Bible contains some of the earliest examples of social justice uprisings, including the liberation of the Hebrew slave. The notion of liberating a people from unpaid servitude and outright oppression, and of whom the pharoah had commanded the death of all newborn children—that is a social justice movement. The Bible begins as early as this second book with opposing the genocide of these young children based on their race. The rest of the Old Testament is about what happens to these free people, the children of Israel—from Moses to Joshua and the Promised Land, setting up the state of Israel, and leading all the way up to Jesus's coming. I've never understood ministers who say that social justice has nothing to do with religion. My activism is not only rooted in my faith but is also guided and nurtured by it.

Listen, Moses didn't lead a revival meeting. He led a fight against slavery. Joshua led people into forming a new state. When Jesus was crucified, one of the charges levied against him was that he had stirred up the people. He had healed a man who was lying by the pool of Bethesda on the Sabbath day, and for this he was branded a disturbance, a criminal who disobeyed the law. His act of healing someone who the rest of society, including the churches and the synagogues, had ignored was one of the earliest forms of civil disobedience, making Jesus the original righteous troublemaker. When you're called an agitator, a radical, a dissident, or worse for standing up to advance the fight for equal rights and protections under the law, know that you are walking on hallowed ground and in the footsteps of righteousness.

COMING FULL CIRCLE

One year from when I began this book, I found myself exactly where I'd started: marching in Washington, DC, in the middle of, this time, a Delta variant–fueled pandemic. While some of the events of both marches were similar, a lot had changed. First, I was happy to see that the interracial, intergenerational momentum that we'd seen come out of the George Floyd movement of 2020 had sustained itself. That's big; it's foundational. The other important takeaway was that the march of 2021 didn't depend on location nor nostalgia for its success. A lot of people come to the marches on Washington because they want to rekindle that moment in history when Dr. King was alive and preaching from our beacon on the hill. The march of 2021 wasn't a memorial march yet people still showed up—not to march to the Lincoln Monument, not to relive the words of Dr. King as resurrected in the form of several modern-day speakers, but to make it be known that today—not yesterday, not one hundred years ago—we are a country in need of real reform. Unfortunately, much of the problems that need to be reformed are the same ones that have plagued this country since its early days.

We're still talking about police reform. We're still talking about voting. Disenfranchisement. Women's rights. We're still raising our voices and speaking out about white supremacy and hate crimes. If I didn't know any better, I'd get frustrated or, like some of my peers, depressed. But remember: when Dr. King spoke in 1963, he was talking about the repercussions of something that had happened one hundred years prior, and Jesus was advocating on behalf of the powerless long before Dr. King made his speeches. Here's what gives me hope: the righteous troublemakers of the world don't allow the frustration of the day to impede their work. They understand that you continue fighting, marching, preaching, and praying until you win. Period. And then you wake up the next day and you do it again.

I guarantee that everything we're going through today has already been experienced by previous generations of troublemakers. They had much of our same doubts, insecurities, and fears. They were haunted by the same question that drives us today: Can I make a difference? Despite their doubts, insecurities, and fears, they still did the work. That's what made them righteous. They worked on blind faith. Even when they couldn't see the end of the road, they kept marching. Why? Because righteousness itself is a worthy cause, and if you're going to be on any one road, you may as well be on the long, winding one that leads toward social justice. That decision alone gives your life meaning. That decision alone will sustain you; it has me.

The troublemakers profiled in this book tackled issues and situations particular to their historical time. They worked in different fields from one another. Some worked in the legal world. Others were already active in the civil rights movement. Some were simply in the right place at the right time to begin their activism. Others weren't so lucky, their activism borne from trauma. It doesn't matter. They each took a stand. None were perfect individuals, but listen, activism is risky work with high stakes often charged by raw emotions. Everyone has personal flaws. We each struggle with our own demons, yet our very human failures don't negate moments of profound grit and bravery. On the contrary, they often better illuminate our greatest feats.

When I first began writing *Righteous Troublemakers*, I wanted to shine a light on the unsung changemakers of the social justice movement, those individuals who forged a path forward when none seemed possible. What I didn't realize then but know now is that I also wrote this book for you, a future changemaker. We may not know one another, but I'm counting on you to grab the baton from the past generations of troublemakers—people like Pauli Murray, Ernestine Eckstein, and Moses Wright—and start running. The long road to social justice isn't just a marathon, it's also a relay race, with each generation building on the previous generations' successes. As I said in my speech at our country's Capitol, "It's time for all Americans to come together and join this non-violent, non-partisan movement in the spirit of Dr. King and the values he pushed this nation to uphold." It's up to us—we, the people—to make Dr. King's dream a reality. He gave us a vision; it's up to us to do the work.

Today, more than ever before, we need a coalition of righteous troublemakers, individuals unafraid and undaunted by the hard work set before them to heal a nation. It's my hope that you're up to the task. As Hosea would say, "You're no sheep. You're a lion." Bravehearted and strong.

I'll see you at the next march.

★ ★ ★ ★ ★

ACKNOWLEDGMENTS

As I have written this book, *Righteous Troublemakers*, I have been mindful that those who are given this label—both known and unknown—have had the support of family, staff, and friends on their journeys. I, too, have been blessed with many people who have helped me become who I am today. That is why I am able to contribute to social justice in this country.

Let me thank my daughters, Dominique and Ashley, who have been able to grow into their own level of engagement and activism. They have understood that my absence during many of their childhood years was to give them a solid foundation on which they can firmly stand. They have made me proud, and have taken the values of their church and mother and weaved them into the activism they learned from me to create their own unique brands of leadership.

Also, my first and only grandchild, Marcus Al Bright. He's my heart. I work every day to see him have a better world.

Let me thank and acknowledge Aisha McShaw, my girlfriend, adviser, and constant source of strength and encouragement in my life. As she pursues her own entrepreneurial ambitions as a fashion designer, she never hesitates to support me in my ministry and social activism. She has been a real strength and encouragement to me through writing this book.

I would also like to thank my girlfriend's daughter, Laila, who finds a way to be a pleasant source of strength to her mother and me as we pursue our goals.

To my best friend throughout this whole journey, the one who has talked me off the cliff more times than I would like to acknowledge, and who has helped me understand that there isn't a movement without righteous troublemakers. He is the personification of this—Dwight McKee from Chicago, Illinois.

I must acknowledge Rev. W. Franklyn Richardson—one of the most outstanding and preeminent faith leaders and pastors of social activism in this country—who not only chairs National Action Network's board but has founded and chaired with great diligence throughout this pandemic the Conference of National Black Churches, which has done immeasurable work.

To our NAN board member Tanya Lombard, who has grown in the corporate world while keeping the sensitivity of a righteous troublemaker who get things done.

Jennifer Jones-Austin, who—aside from being a policy expert—has become a major go-to person on policy about race, health care, and social justice. She is an invaluable part of our NAN board, as well as the fabric of the American social justice movement. She is the daughter of my pastor and mentor Dr. William Augustus Jones, who taught me the Martin Luther King tradition.

I would like to acknowledge all of the over thirty board members of the National Action Network, who give me their full support and provide me with so much latitude and tangible support to continue my work at NAN, on television, on radio, and now, writing books.

I must thank Rashida Jones, the president of MSNBC, who has taken over in an aggressive and effective way, and who has allowed me to continue to serve as the host of *PoliticsNation*, going now into my eleventh year, and has done so with her gentle but firm encouragement, as she has guided the ship.

And Cesar Conde—Chairman of the NBCUniversal News Group—is one of the most engaging, creative, and committed people I have met in media.

To my dear friends, the other hosts at MSNBC: my little sister Joy-Ann Reid, who is peerless in her journalism, and her commitment and courage to go forward, and Joe Scarborough, Mika Brzezinski, and Nicolle Wallace. We have all become personal friends, and we understand each other's sensitivities and concerns. We communicate as much off the air as we do on the air, and I consider these four very instrumental in my growth and understanding of the broader world.

I must also acknowledge the staff and senior producers of *PoliticsNation*—led by executive producer Moshe Arenstein—who have put this show together with such skill that it makes me look good, but they are the ones who are making everything work behind the scenes.

Certainly, I must thank again Cathy Hughes and Alfred Liggins, the founder and CEO respectfully, of Urban One, for giving me a voice on syndicated radio and around this country for the past fifteen years. There is no one like Cathy Hughes, and no one has executed this task better than Alfred Liggins, who has become the face of Black communications.

I would also like to thank my *Keepin' It Real with Al Sharpton* staff, headed by Fatiyn Muhammad, a man who has been around me for thirty years, and who has come into his own as a host while continuing to produce my show.

Let me also thank my colleagues in the civil rights movement who have worked and supported me throughout the years from the Obama to the Trump administration, and now the Biden administration: Marc Morial, president of the National Urban League; Derrick Johnson, president of the NAACP; Sherrilyn Ifill, president and director-counsel of the NAACP Legal Defense and Education Fund; Melanie Campbell, CEO of the National Coalition of Black Civic Participation and convener of the Black Women's Roundtable Public Policy Network; Damon Hewitt, president and executive director of the Lawyers' Committee for Civil Rights Under Law; and Wade Henderson, who has returned to be president and CEO of the Leadership Conference on Civil and Human Rights.

Let me thank Signe Bergstrom for her invaluable help in shaping this manuscript, and her understanding and sensitivity, which I have never seen in my years of working.

A special thank-you to Peter Joseph at HarperCollins, and my agent, Josh Getzler, who has pushed and made work happen that would not otherwise have happened. Thank you, too, to Farris Blount III, for his assistance with research.

Last but not least, let me thank the members, staff, chapter leaders, and rally attendees of National Action Network. We're now in 120 cities, under the direction of my younger brother, the best field director in civil rights, Rev. DeVes Toon, who takes my wrath and turns it into a lifesaver for so many who are struggling for freedom. I could not have made it without the efforts of Rev. Toon.

To the over fifty people on staff at National Action Network, who get up and work hard every day without recognition to make our six regional offices function in service of others. Without them, there would be no National Action Network, and there would be no Al Sharpton, and you would not be reading this book.

I thank all of you who, like some in this book, have been righteous troublemakers, because what has been trouble for some has brought peace to others. Even if you never get recognition, know that you will get satisfaction.

One of my mentors once told me that those who need recognition for good work don't deserve it; those who deserve it don't need it.

BIBLIOGRAPHY

Adgate, Brad. "Nielsen: How the Pandemic Changed At Home Media Consumption." *Forbes*. August 21, 2020. https://www.forbes.com/sites/bradadgate/2020/08/21/nielsen-how-the-pandemic-changed-at-home-media-consumption/?sh=2a4c47435a28.

Alexander, Elizabeth. "The Trayvon Generation." *The New Yorker*. June 22, 2020. https://www.newyorker.com/magazine/2020/06/22/the-trayvon-generation.

"Amelia Boynton Robinson." *National Park Service*. https://www.nps.gov/people/amelia-boynton-robinson.htm.

"American Experience; The Murder of Emmett Till; Interview with Moses Newson, journalist." 2003. GBH Archives. Web. August 6, 2021. http://openvault.wgbh.org/catalog/V_72E139A5CAC6475D984C9C E93F483DBA.

Arango, Tim. "'Gentle Steering of the Ship': How Keith Ellison Led the Prosecution of Chauvin." *New York Times.* April 21, 2021. https://www.nytimes.com/2021/04/21/us/keith-ellison-chauvin-trial.html.

Arradondo, Medaria. "Minneapolis Police Chief Medaria Arradondo on George Floyd's Killing, Policies During Protests and Reform for His Department." Interview by Lesley Stahl. *60 Minutes.* June 21, 2020. https://www.cbsnews.com/news/minneapolis-police-chief-medaria-arradondo-geroge-floyd-killing-60-minutes-2020-06-21/.

Asmelash, Leah. "60 years ago today, 6-year-old Ruby Bridges walked to school and showed how even first graders can be trailblazers." CNN. November 14, 2020. https://www.cnn.com/2020/11/14/us/ruby-bridges-desegregation-60-years-trnd/index.html.

Ball, Howard. *A Defiant Life: Thurgood Marshall and the Persistence of Racism in America.* New York City: Crown, 2001.

Barbaro, Michael, host. "Why Is the Pandemic Killing So Many Black Americans?" *The Daily—New York Times*, Published May 20, 2020. Updated February 3, 2021. *New York Times*, https://www.nytimes.com/2020/05/20/podcasts/the-daily/black-death-rate-coronavirus.html?showTranscript=1.

Bedwell, Michael. "Black lesbian Ernestine Eckstein was protesting when most gays thought protests were crazy." *LGBTQ Nation.* October 14, 2019. https://www.lgbtqnation.com/2019/10/black-lesbian-ernestine-eckstein-protesting-gays-thought-protests-crazy/.

Beito, David T., and Linda Royster Beito. *Black Maverick: T.R.M. Howard's Fight for Civil Rights and Economic Power.* Chicago: University of Illinois Press, 2009.

Bellware, Kim. "'It's been nights I stayed up apologizing' to George Floyd, says teen who documented his death for the world." *The Washington Post.* March 30, 2021. https://www.washingtonpost.com/nation/2021/03/30/darnella-frazier-george-floyd-chauvin-trial/.

Bendery, Jennifer. "Obama Takes Over White House Press Briefing to Speak on Trayvon Martin." *HuffPost*. Published July 19, 2013. Updated July 24, 2013. https://www.huffpost.com/entry/obama-trayvon-martin_n_3624483.

Bierschbach, Briana. "Families, civil rights leaders reflect on one year since George Floyd's killing." *Star Tribune*. May 23, 2021. https://www.startribune.com/families-civil-rights-leaders-reflect-on-one-year-since-george-floyd-s-killing/600060500/.

Blakemore, Erin. "How Thurgood Marshall became the first Black U.S. Supreme Court justice." *National Geographic*. October 2, 2020. https://www.nationalgeographic.com/history/article/thurgood-marshall-first-black-supreme-court-justice-history.

Bond, Julian. "The Media and the Movement: Looking Back from the Southern Front," in Brian Ward, ed., *Media, Culture and the Modern African American Freedom Struggle*. Gainsville: University Press of Florida, 2001.

Boroff, David. "'Not Problematic' Was Dylann Roof given a Burger King meal after his arrest for the Charleston shooting?" *The Sun*. December 11, 2020. https://www.thesun.co.uk/news/13454100/dylann-roof-burger-king-meal-mass-murder-church/.

Brathwaite, Lester Fabian. "The Importance of Being Ernestine Eckstein, Pioneer in the Early Gay Rights Movement." *NewNowNext*. February 27, 2019. http://www.newnownext.com/ernestine-eckstein-gay-civil-rights-pioneer/02/2019/.

Bridges, Lucille. "My Story: Mrs. Lucille Bridges (The Power of Children)." Spring Branch ISD. January 28, 2016. YouTube video, 3:38. https://www.youtube.com/watch?v=CoJ1NXclO4w.

Bridges, Ruby. *Through My Eyes*. New York City: Scholastic Press, 1999.

Brodsky, Megan. "Ole Miss Riot (1962)." *BlackPast*. March 25, 2018. https://www.blackpast.org/african-american-history/ole-miss-riot-1962/.

Buchanan, Larry, Quoctrung Bui, and Jugal K. Patel. "Black Lives Matter May Be the Largest Movement in U.S. History." *New York Times*. July 3, 2020. https://www.nytimes.com/interactive/2020/07/03/us/george-floyd-protests-crowd-size.html.

Campbell, Amy Leigh, "Raising the Bar: Ruth Bader Ginsburg and the ACLU Women's Rights Project." *Texas Journal of Women and the Law*, vol. 11, 2000. https://www.aclu.org/files/FilesPDFs/campbell.pdf.

Carr, Gwen, with Dave Smitherman. *This Stops Today: Eric Garner's Mother Seeks Justice After Losing Her Son*. Lanham, Maryland: Rowman & Littlefield, 2018.

Carroll, Nicole. "Ruby Bridges was 6 when she walked into a segregated school. Now she teaches children to get past racial differences." *USA TODAY*. Published August 12, 2020. Updated August 27, 2020. https://www.usatoday.com/in-depth/life/women-of-the-century/2020/08/12/19th-amendment-ruby-bridges-now-teaches-kids-racism-and-peace/5555100002/.

Cheney-Rice, Zak. "Darnella Frazier's Nightmare Year." *Intelligencer—New York Magazine*. July 9, 2021. https://nymag.com/intelligencer/2021/07/darnella-fraziers-nightmare-year.html.

Chin, Denny, and Kathy Hirata Chin. "Constance Baker Motley, James Meredith, and the University of Mississippi." *Columbia Law Review*, vol. 117, no. 7. https://columbialawreview.org/content/constance-baker-motley-james-meredith-and-the-university-of-mississippi/.

Clinton, Hillary Rodham, and Chelsea Clinton. *The Book of Gutsy Women: Favorite Stories of Courage and Resilience*. New York: Simon & Schuster, 2019.

Cobb, Jelani. "George Floyd, the Tulsa Massacre, and Memorial Days." *The New Yorker*. May 25, 2021. https://www.newyorker.com/news/daily-comment/george-floyd-the-tulsa-massacre-and-memorial-days.

Cole, Devan. "John Lewis Urges Attendee of Selma's 'Bloody Sunday' Commemorative March to 'Redeem the Soul of America' by Voting." CNN. March 2, 2020. https://www.cnn.com/2020/03/01/politics/ john-lewis-bloody-sunday-march-selma/index.html.

Coles, Robert. "In the South These Children Prophesy." *The Atlantic.* March 1963.

———. "Robert Coles Speaks on Ruby Bridges." May 5, 2013. YouTube video, 5:23. https://www.youtube.com/watch?v=XPK3zQM2dHU.

Crump, Ben. *Open Season: Legalized Genocide of Colored People.* New York City: HarperCollins Publishers, 2019.

Dewan, Shaila. "What we know about the judge in the Derek Chauvin trial." *New York Times.* March 29, 2021. https://www.nytimes. com/2021/03/29/us/judge-cahill-chauvin-trial.html.

Donald, David Herbert. "Protest at Selma: Martin Luther King, Jr. & the Voting Rights Act of 1965." *The New Republic.* November 3, 1978. https://newrepublic.com/article/72530/protest-selma-martin-luther-king-jr-the-voting-rights-act-1965-0.

Doyle, William. *An American Insurrection: James Meredith and the Battle of Oxford, Mississippi, 1962.* New York City: Anchor Books, 2003.

Duster, Chandelis. "Waters calls for protestors to 'get more confrontational' if no guilty verdict is reached in Derek Chauvin trial." CNN. April 19, 2021. https://www.cnn.com/2021/04/19/politics/maxine-waters-derek-chauvin-trial/index.html.

Ellis, Nicquel Terry, N'dea Yancey-Bragg, Rachel Aretakis, Joshua Bote, Claire Thornton, Ryan W. Miller, and Grace Hauck. "'This dream is still alive': Thousands rally for racial justice at March on Washington." *USA TODAY.* Published August 28, 2020. Updated August 30, 2020. https:// www.usatoday.com/story/news/nation/2020/08/28/march-washington-2020-thousands-gather-sharpton-nan-rally/3442726001/.

"Emmett Till's Death Inspired a Movement." *Smithsonian National Museum of African American History & Culture.* https://nmaahc.si.edu/blog-post/emmett-tills-death-inspired-movement.

Fazio, Marie. "Sharpton and Crump warn that the 'world is watching' as witnesses begin to testify." *New York Times.* March 29, 2021. https://www.nytimes.com/2021/03/29/us/al-sharpton-ben-crump-george-floyd.html?searchResultPosition=1.

————. "What we know about Medaria Arradondo, the Minneapolis chief." *New York Times.* April 5, 2021. https://www.nytimes.com/2021/04/05/us/medaria-arradondo-minneapolis-police-chief.html.

Featherston, James. "Slain Boy's Uncle Points Finger at Bryant, Milam, but Admits Light Was Dim." *Jackson Daily News.* September 21, 1955.

Fernandez, Manny. "In Houston, Thousands Wait in the Heat to Pay Respects to George Floyd." *New York Times.* June 8, 2020. https://www.nytimes.com/2020/06/08/us/george-floyd-viewing-funeral-houston-unrest.html.

Film at Lincoln Center [@FilmLinc]. "'I think it is very important that films make people look at what they've forgotten.'—Spike Lee." *Twitter.* February 11, 2021. https://twitter.com/filmlinc/status/1360011883445694465?lang=en.

Firestone, David. "Speakers Stress Racial Healing at Service for Dragging Victim." *New York Times.* June 14, 1998. https://www.nytimes.com/1998/06/14/us/speakers-stress-racial-healing-at-service-for-dragging-victim.html.

Forliti, Amy. "The 12 jurors deliberating in the trial of Derek Chauvin." *Associated Press.* April 19, 2021. https://www.fox21news.com/news/national/the-12-jurors-deliberating-in-the-trial-of-derek-chauvin/.

Forliti, Amy, Stephen Groves, and Tammy Webber. "Key moments in closing arguments of Chauvin trial." *AP News.* April 24, 2021. https://

apnews.com/article/us-news-george-floyd-trials-death-of-george-floyd-646ff1f6eee0e38e1552cd9c6b85e48f.

Fox, Margalit. "Amelia Boynton Robinson, a Pivotal Figure at the Selma March, Dies at 104." *New York Times*. August 26, 2015. https://www.ny-times.com/2015/08/27/us/amelia-boynton-robinson-a-pivotal-figure-at-the-selma-march-dies-at-104.html.

IE Staff. "Who is Darnella Frazier, the 17-Year-Old Who Filmed George Floyd's Fatal Arrest?" *Inside Edition*. June 12, 2020. https://www.insideedition.com/who-is-darnella-frazier-the-17-year-old-who-filmed-george-floyds-fatal-arrest-60134.

Golshan, Tara. "This is one of the most iconic photos of Barack Obama's presidency." *Vox*. July 25, 2016. https://www.vox.com/2016/7/25/12282926/dnc-michelle-obama-little-boy-hair-photo.

Graham, David A. "The Election in Which Eric Garner's Death Didn't Matter." *The Atlantic*. May 6, 2015. https://www.theatlantic.com/.politics/archive/2015/05/the-election-in-which-eric-garners-death-didnt-matter/392525/.

Grant, Jonathan. "Martin Luther King Day in Georgia 1987: Hosea Williams marches on Forsyth County." *Brambleman*. January 18, 2020. https://brambleman.com/martin-luther-king-day-in-georgia-1987-hosea-williams-marches-on-forsyth-county/.

Greenhouse, Linda. "Thurgood Marshall, Civil Rights Hero, Dies at 84." *New York Times*. January 25, 1993. https://www.nytimes.com/1993/01/25/us/thurgood-marshall-civil-rights-hero-dies-at-84.html.

Harmon, Rick. "Timeline: The Selma-to-Montgomery Marches." *USA TODAY*. March 5, 2015.

Hass, Trevor. "President Donald Trump called George Floyd's death 'a grave tragedy.'" *Boston.com*. May 30, 2020. https://www.boston.com/news/national-news-2/2020/05/30/george-floyd-death-donald-trump/.

Heller, Karen. "Ben Crump has become the go-to attorney for racial justice: 'I feel like I'm running out of time.'" *The Washington Post.* June 19, 2020. https://www.washingtonpost.com/lifestyle/style/ben-crump-attorney-floyd/2020/06/18/3e1007ba-af09-11ea-856d-5054296735e5_story.html.

Henry, Barbara. "Barbara Henry, a civil rights crusader." Kiwanis International. December 18, 2018. YouTube video, 13:30. https://www.youtube.com/watch?v=Hfc9i9gfsd8.

Henry, Barbara, and Scott Helman. "Teaching Ruby Bridges." *The Boston Globe.* July 11, 2014. https://www.bostonglobe.com/magazine/2014/06/27/teaching-ruby-bridges-reflecting-classroom-that-made-civil-rights-history/r0ozyM4GQWzD25g5mzhtqN/story.html.

Houck, Davis W., and David E. Dixon, editors. *Women and the Civil Rights Movement, 1954-1965.* Jackson: University Press of Mississippi, 2009.

Interview with Amelia Boynton Robinson, conducted by Blackside, Inc., on December 5, 1985, for *Eyes on the Prize: America's Civil Rights Years (1954–1965).* Washington University Libraries. http://repository.wustl.edu/concern/videos/x059c891p.

Interview with Rosa Parks, conducted by Blackside, Inc., on November 14, 1985, for *Eyes on the Prize: America's Civil Rights Years (1954–1965).* Washington University Libraries, Film and Media Archive, Henry Hampton Collection. http://digital.wustl.edu/cgi/t/text/text-idx?c=eop;cc=eop;rgn=main;view=%20text;idno=par0015.0895.080.

"James Meredith and the March Against Fear." National Archives. Reviewed May 27, 2020. https://www.archives.gov/research/african-americans/black-power/sncc/march-against-fear.

"Joe Biden Tulsa Race Massacre Anniversary Speech Transcript." *Rev.* June 1, 2021. https://www.rev.com/blog/transcripts/joe-biden-tulsa-race-massacre-anniversary-speech-transcript.

Johnson, Sam. "Two White Men Go on Trial Monday for Slaying of Negro." *Jackson Daily News.* September 18, 1955.

Jones, Ryan M. "Who Mourns for Jimmie Lee Jackson?" National Civil Rights Museum. https://www.civilrightsmuseum.org/news/posts/who-mourns-for-jimmie-lee-jackson.

Kempton, Murray. "Heart of Darkness." *New York Post.* September 21, 1955, in Christopher Metress, ed., *The Lynching of Emmett Till.*

Kennedy, Robert F. *Robert Kennedy: In His Own Words.* New York City: Bantam Books, 1989.

King, Ledyard, and William Cummings. "'Make it stop': George Floyd's brother Philonise urges Congress to 'do the right thing.'" *USA TODAY.* June 10, 2020. https://www.usatoday.com/story/news/politics/2020/06/10/george-floyds-brother-philonise-testify-before-congress-police/5327191002/.

King, Wayne. "James Meredith and Ole Miss: Decade After a Bloody Insurrection." *New York Times.* October 1, 1972. https://www.nytimes.com/1972/10/01/archives/james-meredith-and-ole-miss-decade-after-a-bloody-insurrection.html.

King, Jr., Martin Luther. *I Have a Dream: Writings and Speeches That Changed the World.* San Francisco: HarperOne, 2003.

Kirkland, W. Michael. "Hosea Williams (1926-2000)." *New Georgia Encyclopedia.* Published March 24, 2006. Edited August 14, 2020. https://www.georgiaencyclopedia.org/articles/history-archaeology/hosea-williams-1926-2000.

Klein, Betsy. "Trump declares victory as US unemployment drops to 13.3%." CNN. June 5, 2020. https://www.cnn.com/2020/06/05/politics/trump-unemployment-numbers-protests/index.html.

Ladd, Donna, and Adam Lynch. "A Soldier's Story: The JFP Interview with James Meredith." *Jackson Free Press.* September 24, 2008. https://www.jacksonfreepress.com/news/2008/sep/24/a-soldiers-story-the-jfp-interview-with-james/.

"Landmark Designation Report, Emmett Till and Mamie Till-Mobley House." City of Chicago Department of Planning and Development. November 5, 2020. https://www.chicago.gov/content/dam/city/depts/zlup/Historic_Preservation/Publications/Emmett_Till_and_Mamie_Till-Mobley_House_report.pdf.

Langer, Emily. "Lucille Bridges, who stood by daughter Ruby through school desegregation, dies at 86." *The Washington Post.* November 11, 2020. https://www.washingtonpost.com/local/obituaries/lucille-bridges-who-stood-by-daughter-ruby-through-school-desegregation-dies-at-86/2020/11/11/ab37a36e-241d-11eb-952e-0c475972cfc0_story.html.

Lee, Spike. "Spike Lee on a Pivotal Moment in the Civil Rights | Oprah's Next Chapter | Oprah Winfrey Network." OWN Network. November 12, 2013. YouTube video, 5:48. https://www.youtube.com/watch?v=26umVgTsm-o.

Leitch, Will. "Spike Lee Talks Obama, the End of Mookie's Brooklyn, and the Hollywood Color Line." *Vulture.* July 8, 2012. https://www.vulture.com/2012/07/spike-lee-on-reality-tv-minstrelsy-and-hollywood.html.

Leone, Beret. "Rev. Al Sharpton hosts Minneapolis vigil, demands action." KTTC-TV. May 28, 2020. https://kttc.com/2020/05/28/rev-al-sharpton-hosts-minneapolis-vigil-demands-action/.

Leonhardt, David, and Ian Prasad Philbrick. "One Year Later." *New York Times.* May 25, 2021. https://www.nytimes.com/2021/05/25/briefing/george-floyd-legacy-anniversary.html.

Lozano, Juan A., Nomaan Merchant, and Adam Geller. "'He is going to change the world': Moving funeral held for George Floyd, a man who galvanized a nation." *Click 2 Houston*. Published June 9, 2020. Updated June 10, 2020. https://www.click2houston.com/news/local/2020/06/09/live-blog-houston-prepares-to-say-goodbye-to-george-floyd/.

Luckerson, Victor. "The Women Who Preserved the Story of the Tulsa Race Massacre." *The New Yorker*. May 28, 2021. https://www.newyorker.com/news/us-journal/the-women-who-preserved-the-story-of-the-tulsa-race-massacre.

"Martin Luther King: I am proud to be maladjusted." Ronnie Stangler, MD. http://ronniestanglermd.com/martin-luther-king-i-am-proud-to-be-maladjusted/.

Meredith, James. *A Mission from God: A Memoir and Challenge for America*. New York: Atria Books, 2012.

————. *Three Years in Mississippi*. Bloomington: Indiana University Press, 1966.

Meredith, James, and William Doyle. "James Meredith: I am George Floyd." CNN. December 19, 2020. https://www.cnn.com/2020/06/18/opinions/i-am-george-floyd-meredith-doyle/index.html.

Meyer, Zlati. "The COVID Hate Crimes Act becomes law today: Here's what it does." *Fast Company*. May 20, 2021. https://www.fastcompany.com/90638856/the-covid-hate-crimes-act-becomes-law-today-heres-what-it-does.

Morrison, Aaron, and Kat Stafford. "Thousands Gather at March on Washington Commemorations." *The Associated Press*. Updated August 28, 2020. https://www.wbur.org/news/2020/08/28/march-on-washington-commemorations.

Murray, Pauli. *Song in a Weary Throat: An American Pilgrimage*. New York City: HarperCollins Publishers, 1987.

"NCNW, Ben Crump file suit against Johnson & Johnson." *The Louisiana Weekly.* August 16, 2021. http://www.louisianaweekly.com/ncnw-ben-crump-file-suit-against-johnson-johnson/.

Nickeas, Peter. "Why a North Carolina district attorney is not prosecuting the Andrew Brown Jr. killing." CNN. May 18, 2021. https://www.cnn.com/2021/05/18/us/district-attorney-andrew-brown-jr-decision/index.html.

Olson, Rochelle. "Hennepin County Courthouse locked down days before Chauvin trial set to begin." *Star Tribune.* March 3, 2021. https://www.startribune.com/hennepin-county-courthouse-locked-down-days-before-chauvin-trial-set-to-begin/600029784/.

Omega Institute. "Galvanizing for Change: An Interview with Gwen Carr." *HuffPost.* September 28, 2017. https://www.huffpost.com/entry/galvanizing-for-change-an-interview-with-gwen-carr_b_59cd5d7ee4b0f58902e5caa4.

Oppel Jr., Richard A., Robert Gebeloff, K.K. Rebecca Lai, Will Wright, and Mitch Smith. "The Fullest Look Yet at the Racial Inequity of Coronavirus." *New York Times.* July 5, 2020. https://www.nytimes.com/interactive/2020/07/05/us/coronavirus-latinos-african-americans-cdc-data.html.

"Oral history interview with Hosea Williams." Digital Library of Georgia. May 15, 1998. https://ohms.libs.uga.edu/viewer.php?cachefile=dlg/phc/williams19980515.xml.

"Ottawa W. Gurley: The Visionary of a Generation." *Black Wall Street.* http://blackwallstreet.org/owgurley.

Pagones, Stephanie. "Activists allegedly refusing to leave George Floyd Square after Chauvin verdict, call for demands to be met." *Fox News.* April 22, 2021. https://www.foxnews.com/us/activists-leave-george-floyd-square-chauvin-verdict-demands.

Parrish, Mary E. Jones. *Events of the Tulsa Disaster.* 1922. https://archive. org/details/events-of-the-tulsa-disaster/page/n1/mode/2up.

Paybarah, Azi. "How a teenager's video upended the police department's initial tale." *New York Times.* April 20, 2021. https://www.nytimes. com/2021/04/20/us/darnella-frazier-floyd-video.html.

Pinn, Anthony B., ed. *Pauli Murray: Selected Sermons and Writings.* Mary- knoll: Orbis Books, 2006.

Reed, Roy. "Alabama Police Used Gas and Clubs to Rout Negroes." *New York Times.* March 7, 1965. https://archive.nytimes.com/www.nytimes. com/learning/general/onthisday/big/0307.html.

"Rev. Hosea L. Williams." Hosea Helps. https://4hosea.org/on-hosea- williams/.

Robinson, Amelia, B. *Bridge Across Jordan.* Schiller Institute, Revised Edition, 1991.

Rollins, Chandler. "PepsiCo Meets with Al Sharpton, Emmett Till Fam- ily." *Jet.* May 9, 2013. https://www.jetmag.com/news/pepsico-meets- with-al-sharpton-and-emmett-till-family/.

Sack, Kevin. "A Final March for Hosea Williams, and Many Trib- utes." *New York Times.* November 22, 2000. https://www.nytimes. com/2000/11/22/us/a-final-march-for-hosea-williams-and-many- tributes.html.

Samuels, Alex. "How Views on Black Lives Matter Have Changed—And Why That Makes Police Reform So Hard." *FiveThirtyEight.* April 13, 2021. https://fivethirtyeight.com/features/how-views-on-black-lives- matter-have-changed-and-why-that-makes-police-reform-so-hard/.

Sanburn, Josh. "One year after filming Eric Garner's fatal confrontation with police, Ramsey Orta's life has been upended." *Time.* https://time. com/ramsey-orta-eric-garner-video/.

Schudel, Matt. "Amelia Boynton Robinson, activist beaten on Selma bridge, dies at 104." *The Washington Post*. August 26, 2015. https://www.washingtonpost.com/national/amelia-boynton-robinson-activist-beaten-on-selma-bridge-dies-at-104/2015/08/26/9478d25e-4c11-11e5-bfb9-9736d04fc8e4_story.html.

Schulz, Kathryn. "The Many Lives of Pauli Murray." *The New Yorker*. April 10, 2017. https://www.newyorker.com/magazine/2017/04/17/the-many-lives-of-pauli-murray.

Sharpton, Al. "Rev. Al Sharpton on the Derek Chauvin guilty verdict." CNBC Television. April 20, 2021. YouTube video, 7:33. https://www.youtube.com/watch?v=1VtTb69t81M.

"Simeon Wright Oral History Interview." C-SPAN. First aired May 29, 2014. C-SPAN video, 1:29:01. https://www.c-span.org/video/?317933-1/simeon-wright-oral-history-interview.

Smith, Suzanne E. "Black Wall Street, Collective Memory, and Reparations." *AAIHS*. June 4, 2021. https://www.aaihs.org/black-wall-street-collective-memory-and-reparations/.

"Spike Lee Quotes." *BrainyQuote*. https://www.brainyquote.com/quotes/spike_lee_263499.

Stolberg, Sheryl Gay. "'Pandemic Within a Pandemic': Coronavirus and Police Brutality Roil Black Communities." *New York Times*. Published June 7, 2020. Updated July 27, 2021. https://www.nytimes.com/2020/06/07/us/politics/blacks-coronavirus-police-brutality.html.

Tkacik, Christina. "Thurgood Marshall's roots in Old West Baltimore." *The Baltimore Sun*. September 5, 2017. http://darkroom.baltimoresun.com/2017/09/thurgood-marshalls-roots-in-old-west-baltimore/#1.

Tyson, Timothy B. *The Blood of Emmett Till*. New York City: Simon & Schuster, 2017.

"Viola Liuzzo." *Learning for Justice*. https://www.learningforjustice.org/classroom-resources/texts/viola-liuzzo.

Wakefield, Dan. "Justice in Sumner," in Christopher Metress, ed., *The Lynching of Emmett Till: A Documentary Narrative*. Charlottesville: University of Virginia Press, 2002.

Wang, Vivian. "Erica Garner, Activist and Daughter of Eric Garner, Dies at 27." *New York Times*. December 30, 2017. https://www.nytimes.com/2017/12/30/nyregion/erica-garner-dead.html.

Waters, TaMaryn. "George Floyd family attorney Ben Crump hopes Chauvin verdict sets 'precedent' for future justice." *USA TODAY*. April 21, 2021. https://www.usatoday.com/story/news/nation/2021/04/21/lawyer-ben-crump-shifts-legal-fight-george-floyd-pamela-turner/7316785002/.

Weber, Bruce. "2 Fiery Personas, but No Sparks, in Courtroom." *New York Times*. January 24, 1992. https://www.nytimes.com/1992/01/24/nyregion/2-fiery-personas-but-no-sparks-in-courtroom.html.

Weerts, Christine. "Hosea Williams Led Civil Rights Marchers 56 Years Ago at Edmund Pettus Bridge." *The Federalist*. March 5, 2021. https://thefederalist.com/2021/03/05/hosea-williams-stood-next-to-mlk-and-john-lewis-56-years-ago-at-edmund-pettus-bridge/.

Weiner, Jeff. "Travyon Martin: Controversy, racial strife familiar for attorney Benjamin Crump." *Orlando Sentinel*. April 6, 2012. https://www.orlandosentinel.com/news/trayvon-martin-george-zimmerman/os-trayvon-martin-benjamin-crump-20120406-story.html.

"What happened to the key figures in the Emmett Till case?" *Mississippi Clarion Ledger*. September 13, 2018. https://www.clarionledger.com/story/news/2018/09/13/what-happened-key-figures-emmett-till-case/1275626002/.

Whitten, Ellen. "Injustice Unearthed: Revisiting the Murder of Emmett Till." William Winter Institute for Racial Reconciliation. https://www.winterinstitute.org/wwi-archive/archive-ellen-whittens-revisiting-the-murder-of-emmett-till/.

"Who is Pauli Murray?" Pauli Murray Center for History and Social Justice. https://www.paulimurraycenter.com/who-is-pauli.

"Who's testified in the Derek Chauvin trial." *KSTP Eyewitness News*. Published April 7, 2021. Updated April 15, 2021. https://kstp.com/news/who-has-testified-in-the-trial-of-former-minneapolis-police-officer-derek-chauvin-george-floyd/6066971/.

Wines, Michael. "'Looting' Comment from Trump Dates Back to Racial Unrest of the 1960s." *New York Times*. May 29, 2020. https://www.nytimes.com/2020/05/29/us/looting-starts-shooting-starts.html.

Wines, Michael, and Aishvarya Kavi. "March on Washington 2020: Protestors Hope to Rekindle Spirit of 1963." *New York Times*. Published August 28, 2020. Updated November 4, 2020. https://www.nytimes.com/2020/08/28/us/march-on-washington-2020.html.

Winter, Deena, Nicholas Bogel-Burroughs, and Jenny Gross. "Minneapolis Removes Memorial Barricades from 'George Floyd Square.'" *New York Times*. June 3, 2021. https://www.nytimes.com/2021/06/03/us/george-floyd-memorial-minneapolis.html?searchResultPosition=1.

"Wisdom from a Trailblazer: Ruby Bridges Talks Racism in Education." NPR. December 1, 2010. https://www.npr.org/2010/12/01/131727013/Wisdom-From-A-Trailblazer-Ruby-Bridges-Talks-Racism-In-Education.

Wright, Moses. "How I Escaped from Mississippi." *Jet*. October 13, 1955.

"50 Years After the Murder of Emmett Till, the Investigation Continues." *Democracy Now!* August 26, 2005. https://www.democracynow.org/2005/8/26/50_years_after_the_murder_of.